International Socialism 117

Winter 2008

Contributors

Ian Birchall is the author of *Sartre Against Stalinism*.

Paul Blackledge teaches in Leeds and is the author of *Reflections on the Marxist Theory of History*.

Claire Ceruti edits the South African magazine *Socialism from Below*.

Neil Davidson is the author of *The Origins of Scottish Nationhood* and *Discovering the Scottish Revolution*, and has recently edited and introduced (with Paul Blackledge) *Alasdair MacIntyre's Engagement with Marxism*, set to be published in 2008.

Andy Durgan is the author of *The Spanish Civil War* and a member of En Lucha in Spain.

Chris Ealham is a historian and the author of *Class, Culture and Conflict in Barcelona, 1898-1937*.

Iain Ferguson lectures in social work at Stirling University and is the author of a new book, *Reclaiming Social Work: Challenging Neoliberalism and Promoting Social Justice*.

Keith Flett is the author of *Chartism After 1848: The Working Class and the Politics of Radical Education*.

Donny Gluckstein is the author of *The Nazis, Capitalism and the Working Class* and *The Paris Commune: A Revolution in Democracy*.

Joe Hartney is a computer systems analyst who works in Edinburgh.

Mike Haynes is the author of *Russia: Class and Power, 1917-2000* and co-editor of *History and Revolution: Refuting Revisionism*.

Costas Lapavitsas is the author of *Social Foundations of Markets, Money and Credit* and is currently working on a special issue of *Historical Materialism* dealing with the ongoing financial crisis.

Joe Lineham works as a translator and teacher in the Basque Country and is a regular contributor to the Basque press.

Ken Olende is a journalist on *Socialist Worker*.

Matt Perry is a history lecturer at Newcastle University and the author of *Marxism and History*, *Jarrow Crusade* and *Prisoners of Want*.

John Rose is the author of *The Myths of Zionism*.

Dan Swain is an activist in Liverpool.

Leo Zeilig is the author of *Revolt and Protest: Student Politics and Activism in Sub-Saharan Africa* and a researcher at the Centre for Sociological Research in Johannesburg.

The misery of New Labour

The Brown bounce has become the Brown belly flop—and one into an ever stormier ocean. The immediate source of New Labour's misery is obvious. Those who live by the image die by the image. Nothing distinguishes Labour's post-Thatcherite programme for making capital happy from that of David Cameron's Tories. A couple of poor speeches and misjudged donations from a property developer were all it required to turn an 8 percent opinion poll lead into a 10 percent lag. But New Labour has more to fear than a spell of unpopularity in the polls.

The turmoil in the financial markets looks ever more serious by the day (see the interview with Costas Lapavitsas in this issue). Most mainstream economic forecasters expect it to spill over into at least a slowdown in US economic growth and, more likely, an all-out recession. Much of the discussion has moved from whether the economic downturn will occur. It now centres on the degree to which the other sections of world capitalism will be able to "decouple" themselves from America's problems.

The Northern Rock affair has certainly shown how little ten and a half years of New Labour government have done to repair the long-term fortunes of capital operating in Britain. There is suddenly a suspicion that the replacement of a million and half jobs in manufacturing by a similar number in finance amounts to a facelift, not a heart transplant. The *Financial Times* fears a property crash like that of the early 1990s.

This leaves the Brown government with very little room for manoeuvre. Its policy of holding public sector pay rises below the rate of inflation began before the financial crisis erupted. Now it will be keener than ever to placate big business and the City by enforcing the policy. Yet no government since the Second World War has succeeded in holding down pay for three years in the way Gordon Brown intends without eventually provoking wide-scale industrial action.

Last year union leaders did Labour a considerable favour. The health and local government unions managed to avoid any action. Postal union leaders persuaded their members to call off their highly effective series of strikes for an offer that conceded very little. This left civil service workers isolated for the moment—although 80,000 were on strike as we went to press. But, it has to be repeated, the battle over public sector pay is due to continue for more than another two years, with teachers balloting for action early this year. And strikes of some sort or other are no longer a rarity, even if we are still a long way from the high strike figures of the 1980s, let alone the early 1970s.

Any industrial action raises political questions about New Labour—especially about why union leaders fund New Labour. This question came up again and again on picket lines in last year's strikes on London Underground and in Royal Mail. The thirst for a left wing political alternative to New Labour will grow stronger if Brown's reaction to the political donations furore further weakens the union leaders' supposed influence within the party.

Meanwhile, the other major cause of disillusion with Brown—the "war against terror"—is not going away. The failure of the US to crush resistance in Iraq and Afghanistan is causing it problems in an ever widening area, as is shown by the tensions on the Turkish border with Iraq, the inability of the Ethiopian army to subdue Somalia, the spill-over of the Afghan war into Pakistan, the recurrent political instability in Lebanon and the continued threats against Iran.

Brown sought to remove the focus for anti-war feeling, while demonstrating his continued commitment to Bush's wars, by moving most British troops from Iraq to Afghanistan. But such gestures have not been enough to blot out people's memories of what has been done to Iraq, or the suspicions these memories raise about any sort of imperialist intervention. This is shown most clearly by the angry reaction every time threats are made against Iran.

The liberal media columnists periodically claim the anti-war movement no longer exists. But its demonstrations and rallies are big by historic standards, even if they are not on the same gigantic scale as in 2002-3. Any attack against Iran would produce a similar response to the Israeli attack on Lebanon 18 months ago, but almost certainly much bigger. The 15 March international day of demonstrations, marking the fifth anniversary of the Iraq war, provides an opportunity once again to prove the liberal media wrong—and to increase New Labour's misery. We can increase it even more if we tie the arguments over the war to the arguments over public sector pay and protests over deteriorating public services.

Pakistan: over the edge?

The title of an article we ran on Pakistan 18 months ago was "On the Edge of Instability". Now the country is well inside the arc of instability created by the "war on terror", adding to the multitude of problems besetting US and British imperialism all the way from the Horn of Africa to the Indus.

The crisis in Pakistan has not just been of the Musharraf regime. It is also part of the crisis of US power in the region—witness the suggestion by Robert Kagan, co-founder of the Project for the New American Century, that it should prepare to send troops into the capital, Islamabad, if the situation gets out of control.

Pakistan was born 60 years ago as the stepchild of British imperialism, a by-product of the divide and rule policies used to rule the whole subcontinent for more than a century and half. It was then succoured through most of its life by US imperialism as a useful Cold War client state.

But increasingly it became a politically unstable client state. Partition of the subcontinent corralled into a single state half a dozen linguistic groups, supposedly bound to each other by a single Muslim identity. In fact there were bitter divisions over religious beliefs and practices, while the pattern of capitalist development exacerbated national, class and religious divisions as economic growth was accompanied by increasing rather than diminishing poverty, and in recent years by counter-reforms in public provision.

Politics came to be centred on the struggles of particular ethnic or religious groupings within the middle class to secure for themselves well paid posts that were not available for all. The use of right wing Islamist groups such as Jamaat-i-Islami by US imperialism, Saudi Arabia and successive Pakistani governments (the civilian governments of Nawaz Sharif and Benazir Bhutto as well as the military government of Zia ul-Haq) to intervene against the USSR in Afghanistan provided them with arms, money and influence well beyond their popular support (only about 10 percent in elections) and gave a violent edge to political clashes between different groups.

Every government since the 1970s has relied on backing from the state's generals and bureaucrats on the one hand, and alliances with pick and mix selections of the ethnic and politico-religious groupings on the other. Principles have never played a role in this. Allies can suddenly turn on each other and sworn enemies suddenly work together. The sheer scale of corruption under the Bhutto and Sharif governments of the 1990s meant that liberal minded sections of the middle class actually welcomed the military coup which brought Musharraf to power in 1999. They believed that the armed forces, as the embodiment of the national identity, could never be as bad as the politicians. They also saw him as a barrier to the right wing politico-religious parties. Over the past year they have discovered how wrong they were.

From the outset Musharraf used the same corrupt political methods as his predecessors. He consciously promoted the influence of the MMA coalition of religious parties in order to ensure a safe outcome in stage managed elections. (His own party formed a coalition government with them in the province of Baluchistan.) Then last year he let loose one of the politico-ethnic thug parties, the MQM, to attack and kill scores of those demonstrating in Karachi in support of the lawyers' movement that sprang up around sacked chief justice Iftikhar Chaudhry.

But the liberal section of the middle class has not suffered the most under Musharraf. Workers and peasants have been hit hardest by the increasing poverty. Military control of the national railway network and the use of naval ratings in Karachi docks have been used to keep down potentially very powerful workforces. Temporary contracts deny union rights to tens of thousands of workers in Karachi's textile mills. Musharraf has pushed through a succession of privatisations. The military tried to seize the land of thousands of peasants in the "canal colonies" of Okara in the Punjab and shot down some of those who resisted.

Musharraf also faced two other forms of resistance which dealt him serious blows. There is an armed movement for national rights in the huge, but not very heavily populated, province of Baluchistan. Then there is the armed resistance of what is known as the "Pakistani Taliban" in the north west of the country. This began as a spill-over of the war in Afghanistan into "tribal areas" of Pakistan, particularly Waziristan. Peasants were drawn into the Taliban-led struggles of fellow Pushtuns on the other side of a border, which they have rejected ever since it was drawn by the British in the 19th century.

The ideas of those leading the resistance are, as Riaz Ahmed, of the International Socialists of Pakistan, writes from Karachi, "obscurantist". But the repression they are fighting is real enough. On 30 October 2006 the US forces bombed a madrassa (religious school) in Bajur, killing over 80 students. Riaz writes that 757 people were killed in north Waziristan by Pakistani military aerial bombings between July and October 2007. In response a full-scale rising has developed: "Since July 2007, 278 soldiers and 72 policemen have been killed and over 361 soldiers captured, including 240 captured without resistance on 2 September. There appears to be a mutiny in the Pakistani military, which is fighting a lost war against the tribes and Taliban in Waziristan and huge parts of North West Province."

The politics behind the lawyers' movement and those of the war in north west Pakistan are very different. But the combination undermined the standing not only of Musharraf but of the military as a whole. Hence Musharraf's desperate attempt to bolster his position by declaring a state of emergency and ordering mass arrests on 2 November. But this exposed his weakness rather than his strength, leading him finally to take off his uniform and promise to lift the state of emergency before elections in the hope that this would restore stability.

Pakistan's ruling class and US imperialism may have been losing some of their faith in Musharraf, but not in the central role of the military in Pakistan's politics. Their ideal solution would be for one of the former prime ministers, Benazir or Sharif, or perhaps both, to strike a deal with the military to stabilise the situation. But they are terrified that things have already gone too far for such an agreement to work.

Certainly, it cannot be an answer for the mass of people. Benazir and Sharif were both integral to the alignment with imperialism, the corruption of Pakistan politics, the growth of poverty and the encouragement of ethnic and religious strife. With or without Musharraf, neither has a political project that corresponds in any way to the popular mood that provoked the upsurge against military rule.

Hope lies with the potential shown by the upsurge in the great cities. Riaz writes how the movement among the lawyers sparked off the first struggles for decades among students: "Two days after the declaration of emergency, on 6 November, the privileged students of an elite management science university, LUMS, rose in their hundreds against dictatorial rule. The day after, over a thousand of them marched inside the campus, with a couple of hundred daring to protest outside the campus too. That inspired other local colleges and universities and by 9 November the state-run Quaid-e-Azam University in Islamabad and its neighbouring military controlled science and technology university, FAST, had daily demonstrations of students.

"Over 5,000 students of Punjab University demonstrated against the right wing Islami Jamiat-e-Talba and the military dictatorship on Friday 17 November. This was the second big demo in two days. On Thursday over 3,000 students came out of their classes to protest against the collaboration of Jamiat with the police in the kidnapping, beating and handing over of the somewhat popular leader Imran Khan as he tried to bring out a rally of students against the emergency. The way in which Jamiat collaborated angered millions across the country and spontaneous demonstrations erupted the next day, forcing an apparent end to an age-old campus hegemony by the right wingers… A huge number of female students are in the forefront of the demonstrations."

It is impossible to tell at the time of writing where these movements will go next. Reports suggest that the collaboration of university authorities with right wing Islamists has pushed back the student protests in Punjab University. But that does not detract from the importance of what occurred. Were the movement, having spread from lawyers to students, to impact upon workers—among whom there has been a small upturn in struggle over the past two years—the explosive potential would be enormous. The weakness, as in many other parts of the world, is that the old left has been very weak, very demoralised and in no condition to provide leadership to mass movements that suddenly emerge, apparently from nowhere. But sometimes new leaderships crystallise out of mass movements.

Lessons from Venezuela's referendum

There are two sorts of defeats the left can suffer. There are devastating defeats that set it back years or even decades. And there are small defeats from which it can learn.

The defeat for Hugo Chavez's referendum on a new constitution in December was of the second sort. But if the lessons are not learnt quickly, the ground will be laid for a defeat of the first sort. This would put at stake not just the constitutional changes, but all the gains that Venezuela's workers, peasants and urban poor have made over the past eight years.

The referendum was important. It was the method by which the dominant wing of Chavismo intended to build upon victory in the presidential election a year earlier. They have always seen the "Bolivarian Revolution" as something carried out from the top down. Their vision has been that Chavez will do good things for those below, with talk of "popular power" as a cover for uncritical, adulatory support for *el comandante*.

Hence the two central planks of the constitutional changes: allowing Chavez to stand again for president in five years time and every seven years after that; and increasing his power to rule by decree, without being subject to any other body, be it the Chavista parliament or bodies of "popular power". Most of the other proposed changes—such as the shorter working day or the extension of social security rights to the informal sector—were already within the power of Chavez and parliament under the existing constitution.

It was the top-down approach which came to grief. The main cause of the failure was not the campaign of the right, backed by private TV channels and big national newspapers. The opposition vote was only 200,000 higher than that received by their defeated candidate in the presidential election 12 months earlier. What mattered was that three million people who voted for Chavez then abstained in the referendum. Among those who did not vote for the constitution were 1.2 million of the 5.5 million who have signed up for membership of the new United Socialist Party of Venezuela (PSUV) launched by the Chavistas.

There was widespread agreement about the reasons for abstention in the many commentaries on the left wing website *Aporrea*—the indispensable source of real information about Venezuela for anyone who can read

Spanish. Again and again there have been complaints about the corruption and lack of democratic control of many of those who are supposed to introduce socialism from above—ministers, mayors and deputies.

Speaking to the Argentinian paper *Pagina 12*, one of the best known Chavista activists, Lina Ron, said, "We were betrayed by a great many elements, people who have had different posts in the government, mayors, governors, ministers, members of the supreme court, who have turned their back on the commandante."

Heinz Dieterich, by no means on the far left, writes of the "domination of a new political class whose tentacles reach from control of Caracas airport via influences in the intelligence services, in the foreign ministry and over nomination of generals in the armed forces to powerful economic activities". Chavez, he writes, is able to "stand at a certain distance from the cases of corruption, the ineptitude of his ministers and the lack of serious debate in the cabinet" but "pays the price for this through lack of information over what is really happening, and the way his entourage in the presidential palace, full of opportunists who are too inept for the positions they hold, guarantee the bureaucratic control of the process but not its closeness to the people".

Much further to the left, Stalin Perez Borges and the other revolutionary socialists of the *Marea Clasista y Socialista* (Socialist and Class Tide) tell how "there is a bureaucratic and corrupt structure in governorships, mayors, ministries". One result has been the incapacity to confront the hardships which the still-capitalist economy is producing: "The government speaks of socialism and equality as a project, but does not solve crucial social problems like insecurity, housing, the wages problems facing wide sections of people, while other sections continue to enrich themselves through big business and their economic and political power."

There is a strong danger that this disillusion will grow worse over the coming months. Rising inflation is already eating into the living standards of the masses, and there are shortages of certain basic goods because of the refusal of farmers and foodstuff processors (including those in the new co-operatives created by the government) to accept price controls. This is not mainly a result of sabotage by big capitalists, as it was in Chile in 1973, but rather the logic of capitalist market mechanisms that have been left intact. The danger is that such conditions will further demoralise layers of people and enable the right to go beyond celebrations over Chavez's referendum defeat to push forward for real victories for themselves.

The Venezuelan upper middle class have a rabid hatred of Chavez and the Bolivarian process. But they have not achieved anything like a decisive victory yet. The public stance of some of their leading figures after the referendum was one of reaching out to the "moderate", more conservative elements of Chavismo. Teodoro Petkoff, economics minister in the mid-1990s and one would-be leader of the opposition, issued a call to this effect, saying the no vote could not have won "without an important part of those who support Chavez".

One small social democratic party, Podemos, broke with Chavez to urge a no vote. It is no secret that there are others still in the governmental apparatus who want to compromise with the opposition. At least one minister has said, "Venezuelans are not ready for socialism." That sort of retreat would be disastrous for the mass of people who, since they defeated the coup against Chavez in April 2002, have pushed forward the process from below. It would leave the capitalist economy completely intact—and with it the impact of inflation on the living standards of the mass of the population. It would give new confidence to the rich to demand economic concessions at the expense of the poor. It would leave the giant corporations that dominate most of the media free to propagate their message of hate against the remnants of the progressive reforms.

It would also provide a cover for the many army officers who sympathise with the right to organise themselves in a way they have not dared to since the failed coup attempt. One of the most dangerous myths surrounding Venezuela is the one spread in books and articles by Marta Harnecker, Diane Raby and others that its military officers are different to those elsewhere in Latin America. It is even claimed that it was the army, not the mass movement, that saved Chavez in 2002. That myth received a serious blow weeks before the referendum when the officer who had been portrayed by official Chavismo as the "hero" of 2002 , Raúl Baduel, turned against Chavez only weeks after resigning as minister of defence. There will be many others still on active service who share the upper middle class's hatred of Chavez. No doubt the Venezuelan rich and their allies in the CIA will seize any opportunity to begin organising them.

It is not good enough when the revolutionary process has suffered a defeat, albeit not a fatal one, to say things can simply continue as before. The defeat was the outcome of relying on a top-down approach which introduced some reforms but left intact the capitalist economy and the main parts of the machinery of the state. More defeats will follow unless the movement from below develops structures of its own capable of acting independently of the presidential palace.

We have insisted before that the PSUV is not such a structure. Established by presidential edict from the top down, it includes, alongside hundreds of thousands of dedicated activists, a good number of corrupt bureaucrats, refugees from the pre-Chavista parties who still exist at every level of the state apparatus, people who dream of an authoritarian Cuban model, and even some capitalists who profit from their Chavista connections. If it failed to motivate nearly a fifth of its members to vote in the referendum, it is certainly not a tool for carrying through a real revolution or even combating counter-revolution. At best it can provide a debating forum out of which can emerge a real revolutionary current—and then only if the leadership allows freer debate than hitherto.

The prime task of the left outside Venezuela is, of course, to show solidarity against any attempt by the Bush White House to seize upon Chavez's new weakness as an excuse to impose its own bloody solutions on the country. But the prime task inside Venezuela is to hammer home the lessons of 2 December and to draw together the many, many activists who are beginning to see that the reformist road of socialism from above is not a viable option.

The credit crunch

Costas Lapavitsas, a leading Marxist economist, spoke to International Socialism about the unfolding financial crisis and its lessons

Can you explain how the current crisis, centred on subprime mortgages, developed in the US economy?
As with all credit and financial crises, this has roots that go some way back. After the 9/11 attack in New York instability and fear pervaded financial markets. In order to steer the US and world economy out of a tight corner there was a reduction in interest rates and loosening of credit, encouraging people to borrow to sustain demand.

Banks took advantage of this and started to push mortgages. The subprime problem developed gradually. This is typical of credit crises. First, banks lend on fairly good terms but then competition sets in. At first, things look OK because the banks get away with it. Then they begin to engage in increasingly risky lending, such as lending on subprime mortgages.

Risky lending was made easier by the recent transformation of the way banks assess lending. In the past getting a mortgage, or most other loans, was a fairly relational process. The borrower would go to the banker and seek a personal relationship, trying to persuade the banker of his or her creditworthiness. Some of the small and medium borrowers in the US and the UK would even go for meals with the bankers, join the same local clubs, and so on. But in the past two decades, peaking in the past seven or eight years, this has fallen by the wayside, and now assessment of credit has become a pseudo-scientific quantitative process. This is called credit scoring. Bank employees tick a few boxes in an assessment form, assign some points per answer and, if the applicant is above a certain threshold, give them the loan.

When mortgage applications are judged on this basis, all that banks need is a number rather than a long-term relationship. As long as lending appears to be going well, they have an incentive to lower the threshold. And they continue lowering it in the face of intensified competition from other banks. This greatly helped to create the subprime crisis.

Riccardo Bellofiore refers to the creation of consumer debt as a sort of "privatised Keynesianism".
There is certainly an element of that. There are even voices calling for more of this, should the unfolding crisis turn into a recession. This kind of Keynesian-inspired response has never gone away. That is also what the Federal Reserve did in the US after 2001. They know how to take such action as a short term response to crisis, but the longer term reaction of the economy to the current crisis has every chance of being very severe.

What was the role of the increasing complexity of finances in exacerbating the subprime crisis?
The subprime market is not very large. Nobody knows exactly how big it is, but it is not more than 15 to 25 percent of the total volume of mortgages currently outstanding in the US. That's bad enough, of course, but what makes it into a potentially major crisis is what has happened to finance more generally over the past 15 to 20 years. Once banks made the mortgage loans—based on "scientific" credit scoring—they proceeded to sell them. In other words, they treated loans as assets that would guarantee payment of a stream of interest to whoever owned them. That is what "securitisation" is about—selling bits of paper that give rights to interest payments accruing on separate loans.

A whole host of new institutions emerged that began specialising in that. They would obtain cheap credit in the environment of low interest rates after 2001, use it to make loans, and then securitise them. Other financial institutions would also use cheap credit to buy the new securities. Still other financial institutions would combine several of these securities to create even more complex, "synthetic" Collateralised Debt Obligations, which give their holders the right to interest accruing on the earlier securities, and so on. In this baroque and opaque world, fuelled by cheap credit, it did not take long before just about all the major financial institutions across the world found themselves holding securities that contained bits of subprime mortgages.

What was originally a small sickness within the US economy grew enormously because of the way capitalist credit works. Since it has spread so widely—assets being created on the back of other assets that ultimately go back to the subprime market—the valuation of bank assets, and ultimately bank solvency, has also become deeply problematic.

The rating agencies, which assessed the risks associated with these assets, have also played a role.
That is all part and parcel of securitisation. For the buyer to purchase securitised assets with any kind of confidence, somebody independent of the seller has to appear and say, "Yes, these represent good flows of interest in the future." That's the role of the rating agencies. They are approached by the seller of the securities, and there is a lot of pressure on them to approve what the seller is doing. After all, it is not easy if you are Moody's to tell Citigroup, "What you are trying to securitise is a load of rubbish." If the rating agencies did that, they would risk losing business. It appears they were giving "triple A" ratings without doing any serious investigation of the underlying loans.

More broadly, though, the crisis is not the result of malfunctioning rating agencies but of the failure of markets. The financial market, which is supposed to assess everything that is put up for sale and then price it appropriately, has obviously failed, and failed dramatically. Yes, the various agents must take their share of the blame, but the system as a whole is really to blame. After all, one of the key functions of banks in the capitalist economy, presumably, is to check borrowers before they advance them money that ultimately belongs to depositors. On what grounds did the banks pass this function on to someone else who obviously did not do the job well? And is there anyone in contemporary financial markets who properly checks the creditworthiness of those who borrow other people's savings?

Marx makes the distinction between two sorts of financial crises. Some are just small problems at the top that create a panic; others indicate much more deep-seated problems. It is very easy to confuse one with the other. So the 1987 stock exchange crash created absolute panic for about a month and then, a year later, it seemed to have gone. How serious is this one?
This is the most difficult question to answer. I am not going to make a prediction because you can end up looking like a fool six months later. I prefer to discuss the broad determinants of crises and draw conclusions in that way. Marx's point is a very important guideline in understanding and discussing financial crises today. Financial crises are a permanent feature of contemporary capitalism. Every few years there is a financial crisis of one type or another and, as you say, some of them blow away, while others

have long-lasting and terrible effects like the one that started in Japan 15 years ago. Even today Japan has not returned to what it used to be.

So the real question is whether what we are witnessing now is a passing storm or a Japanese-type crisis. And the further question is, why does contemporary capitalism keep throwing out these crises?

In answer to the first question, my sense from what has gone on so far is that this may prove a deep and long-lasting crisis. Most of the world's major financial institutions hold some problematic securities or have advanced problematic loans. Until that bad credit works its way out and is dealt with, all these institutions will be hampered in advancing fresh credit. And if fresh credit is not easily available, the capitalist economy does not work well.

Before they can deal with the bad debt problem, however, they have to know how big it is. And no one knows how big it is, for the reasons that I have already mentioned. But the longer it takes them to deal with it, the longer the malaise will last.

It is interesting too that the reaction of those in power has so far been similar to the reaction of the Japanese authorities back in the early 1990s. At the time the Japanese were blamed for being incompetent. At first they did not realise that banks held so much bad debt, and then tried to keep the lid on it, pretending that it was nothing really. Then they imposed a freeze on the housing market. Only gradually did they admit how extensive the problem was. Well, it has taken over three months for the US authorities to begin to comprehend the extent of the problem. And they are now talking about freezing interest rates in the subprime market.

But I do not see any obvious way of dealing with these problems, even after fully realising how big they are. The big US banks, for instance, at the behest of Ben Bernanke, chairman of the Federal Reserve, have been trying to create a "super-fund" that would acquire bad debts and help clean the portfolios of banks. That is a classic response of banks to such problems—we saw a similar thing in Britain with the secondary banking crisis in the early 1970s. And in similar fashion, the healthier banks in the US are now refusing to contribute money to such a fund, asking, "Why should I take your problems on my balance sheet?" This is truly a brotherhood of wolves.

When you spoke at the recent political economy school hosted by this journal you pointed out that there have been recent stockmarket crises and currency crises, but this is a banking crisis. Can you spell out a bit more what that means?
That is why I keep going back to what happened in Japan in the 1990s. For ten years various Western commentators argued, "The Japanese crisis

occurred because the Japanese were inept." But the Japanese crisis was a true banking crisis, and there has not been a true banking crisis in the Western economies for a long time.

A banking crisis is different to a stockmarket crisis. The stockmarket is basically a market in loanable capital through which companies buy other companies. Prices are based on expectations and they have a strongly fictitious element. The actual traded volumes of loanable capital, moreover, are relatively small. A stockmarket slump certainly has the potential to do some damage to companies and banks, but its effects can also be limited.

Banks, especially large commercial banks, are different—they are the foundation of the capitalist financial system because they create most of the fresh credit and they create money. They are not like other financial institutions of similar size such as pension funds. If banks carry bad debt and cannot deal with it, the financial system as a whole cannot work well.

That is what we are witnessing now. The epicentre of the crisis lies in the money market, which has been unable to function properly since last August. The money market is where the banks lend to each other, something that is fundamental to capitalist finance. Money market lending gives flexibility to banks and is a reliable way of pricing what they sell. If the money market does not work well, then banks cannot work well. Since August the money market has gone from a complete freeze to just about chugging along. The reason is obviously that banks do not trust each other, since all of them carry assets that are contaminated by subprime loans. Deep uncertainty in the money market has meant that the financial system has had increasing difficulty in creating fresh credit.

How can this crisis in the credit system feed back into the wider system of productive capital?
The crises of recent years have been quite different from the crises of the 19th century that Marx analysed, as well as from the crises of the 1970s that a lot of us experienced at first hand. Traditionally, banks lent to productive enterprises and their profits were a share of the surplus value generated in production and paid to them as interest. Today big businesses at the core of real accumulation rely less and less on the banks for borrowing, and less and less on external finance in general. Investment seems to be financed increasingly through retained profits. As a result, in the past two to three decades financial institutions have had to seek other sources of profit. And that has meant moving increasingly into areas that are not directly connected with the generation of value and surplus value.

In doing so, finance has become relatively autonomous from productive enterprises as well as growing rapidly. The process of real accumulation and value generation has not grown to anything like the same extent.

So what happens is that banks engage avidly in expanding consumer credit and housing credit. They have also become far more involved in facilitating participation in financial markets by corporations and others. Rather than directly lending to big business, banks charge fees to big business for help with floating shares, bonds and other securities on the open market. Consumer credit, mortgage lending and fee incomes are the fastest growing sources of bank profits.

In that context banks have an almost inbuilt incentive to create bubbles, particularly when they lend for consumption and housing. If banks expect to get their profits increasingly out of interest drawn from wages and salaries, rather than surplus value, they have a problem. There is no guarantee that wages and salaries will grow systematically in future. Indeed, in the past 20 years real wages in the US have been stagnant.

Another way of putting this is that the options for banks are inherently limited if they focus on lending to private individuals. They can increase their profits by appropriating a larger part of wage income, but obviously this has its limits, especially if real incomes are not rising. Banks can also manufacture asset price bubbles. If financial asset prices rise, banks can make additional profits by drawing fresh groups of individuals into the market under the pretext of capital gains and secure lending. If banks create a housing bubble, for example, people appear to become richer even though real incomes are not necessarily rising. Fresh groups of borrowers are attracted into the markets, or existing ones become more heavily indebted, and banks make extra profits by transforming an increasing part of aggregate personal income into loanable money capital.

When these bubbles burst, the first to feel the pinch are workers and others who have borrowed excessively. Millions of people in the US have already lost, or are due to lose their homes this year and next. It is shocking that at the moment not a word is said officially about their plight. But as workers and others are hurt by the burst of the bubble, consumption suffers and this has knock-on effects on real accumulation too.

It is clear that this is not the same mechanism as described in classical Marxist analysis where the capitalist firm would borrow, over-expand production, be unable to sell its products and therefore find it impossible to honour its debts to banks and others. Then the firm would be forced to curtail its output, and possibly even go bankrupt. The current crisis has followed a different mechanism. There will be an impact on the real economy, but the paths will be unusual.

You seem to be talking about a system in which wages are held down and in order to consume all the goods produced by capitalist enterprises it is necessary for consumers to spend beyond their means, backed up by rising house prices. When this system goes into crisis it can no longer consume everything produced. That then impacts on the real economy.

A better way of looking at it is that banks are lending to consumers because that is the easiest way of making profits at present. Real wages are stagnant, lending creates rising asset prices, and the bubbles that result are the way of sustaining lending and giving an appearance of profitability. Ultimately, though, banks increase their profits out of wages and salaries. The figures for the share of individual disposable income appropriated by banks in the US in recent years are telling. According the Federal Reserve, the average share of disposable personal income used to meet debt service payments has risen steadily from 15.6 percent in early 1983 to 19.3 percent in June 2007.

And the reason is that there are fewer profitable outlets for financial capital in production?

I would be careful in phrasing it like that. It is not so much that real accumulation does not generate enough profitable avenues for banks to lend. Rather productive capitals can increasingly meet their financing requirement either by retaining profits or by borrowing directly in open markets for bonds and other instruments. This is very clear with Japanese companies that have historically relied on big banks for finance. If they want external finance for their investments now they are more likely to issue bonds in international markets. Banks have been edged out of this business, and have to seek other avenues of profitability for themselves.

It should also be mentioned in this context that banks make substantial profits out of individuals by managing bank accounts, transferring money, making payments, keeping money safe, and so on. These are simple money-dealing activities.

In short, over the past ten to 12 years banks have been very profitable. They have appropriated large parts of the wage and salary income of ordinary people, either by lending to them or by managing payments and deposits. It is natural to ask, "Have the banks at least been efficient in their banking activities while doing this?" And the answer is that there is no evidence at all of such efficiency. Indeed, mainstream empirical studies of banks in the US and the UK show consistently that banks are inefficient and very expensive. Anyone who has tried to send money abroad from the UK through a bank will know what I mean.

Martin Wolff and various other writers in the Financial Times have been quoting figures from an IMF study from two years ago about global balances. Essentially they see the root of the crisis as being in the transfer of funds from East Asia across the Pacific to the US—and now a transfer of funds from US firms who put money into financial markets—which creates a mass of cash looking for outlets.

That is a very important part of the total picture. We know that on a global scale certain key countries have been generating enormous surpluses—China mainly, India on a much smaller scale and increasingly in the past two to three years the oil exporters, Russia and the Gulf countries. The oil exporters collectively have now possibly overtaken China. These financial surpluses are generated from balance of trade surpluses. This, again, as far as developing countries are concerned, is a novel and pathological phenomenon, with the exception of the oil exporters. Developing countries should not chalk up balance of payments surpluses at early stages of their development because such surpluses mean they are accumulating savings in excess of investment. That is not how capitalist development should be taking place. That is certainly not the way to expand demand and create jobs in countries that contain vast poverty.

Nonetheless, these surpluses have gone abroad, mostly to the US, where savings have collapsed and consumption is at unprecedented levels in relation to income. The bulk of the surpluses went into government bonds bought by the central banks of developing countries. Such funds represent a form of lending by several poor countries to the US state. However, significant volumes also appear to have gone into securitised assets, thus ultimately supporting the explosion of securitisation and subprime lending.

One implication of this is that the crisis is truly global. Deeply problematic assets are held by financial institutions across the world now. It is not simply the US. We cannot at the moment know the extent to which this has occurred. It will only become clear as the crisis unfolds.

The financial crisis is probably a milestone in the reversal of these deeply pathological global flows of capital. My expectation is that American savings will rise quite significantly in the near future. The spending spree in the US will effectively come to an end. Already the US external deficit is declining as the US balance of trade is improving and US exports are rising. The proximate cause of this, of course, is that the value of the dollar has collapsed.

The implications across the world are not easy to gauge. But it seems clear that the dollar will continue to pay a price, and this will have implications for American hegemony. Already the very large sovereign funds of the oil producers—which manage the surpluses accumulated in the last two or three years as oil prices have gone through the roof—are making noises about diversifying away from the dollar, buying assets denominated in yen or euros. If this were to happen on a large scale, then the position of the dollar as the prime reserve currency would suffer greatly.

Interestingly, it looks as if the US ruling class does not consider that to be the main danger it faces at the moment. To me this is the most striking aspect of what the Federal Reserve chairman, Ben Bernanke, has done in the past couple of months. Faced with a domestic crisis and a precariously placed dollar, he chose to abandon the dollar. This is an indication of the fear that the US ruling class feels at the moment—fear that the domestic economic situation is out of control and that they might as well run the risk of the dollar sliding and losing some international purchase if they are to preserve the domestic economy. Whether they are right in making this judgement is a different issue.

If spending by US consumers falls, won't this have a big impact on economies such as China's, which seems to be based largely on exporting to the US?
I am reluctant to go into that because, to a certain extent, the domestic concerns of China are driven by other determinants. At some point the Chinese ruling class will have to face the problem of insufficient domestic demand. How they are going to do that, I do not know. Possibly the tightening American market will encourage them to redirect their efforts to the domestic economy.

This is the whole discussion in the Financial Times about "decoupling".
My knowledge of the Chinese economy is not that detailed, but I do know that, according to Chinese figures, investment spending is enormous. The possibility of expanding investment further is probably not that great. On the other hand, increasing consumer consumption requires substantial income redistribution, a different approach to welfare, altered provision of public goods and so on. In short, it involves a complete rethinking of how the Chinese state relates to the working class. Thus it poses deep political questions and is not at all easy.

Could you expand on the role of central banks and their connection to the state?
We have lived through three decades of liberalisation and globalisation. What we hear from the financial institutions and everyone associated with them is that the state is insignificant, that the state cannot buck the market, and various other platitudes. But the moment there is a crisis they go cap in hand to the state and ask to be rescued, as has happened in Britain with

the collapse of Northern Rock. So obviously the argument about the state being insignificant is ideological. The real issue is to understand how the state operates today, how its role has changed.

The central banks are very important in this connection. The state and the ruling class have been very clever. Central bank independence—that is, separating monetary decision making from the electoral process which provides some kind of scrutiny—was a clever move on their part. Monetary policy has become the exclusive preserve of specialists and is not for the public to discuss. That is nonsense. Just as tax policy is subject to public debate, popular demands and class struggle, so should monetary policy be.

One thing which is not properly appreciated in this connection is that, despite all the deregulation of the last 20 to 30 years, the monopoly of the central bank over the final means of payment has been unchallenged. There might have been incredible financial innovation, but only the central bank is allowed to issue legal tender, into which all other money ultimately converts. In other words, the free market ideology wants free markets in everything except in money. This is the deepest contradiction at the heart of neoliberalism. If you are a true neoliberal, if you really believe that the market is such a great thing, then you should also let it organise money, because money is a key commodity in a capitalist economy. Why should there be a free market in everything except in money? There is ultimately no logic in neoliberalism. When it comes to this question, mainstream economists simply treat anyone who wants to leave the issuing of money to the free market as a crank. But if you point out that, since there is regulation of money, why not also regulate the economy more generally, you are called "extreme".

And so the money market is completely dominated by the central bank, which issues legal tender and thus supplies other banks with liquidity. That gives the central bank enormous power within the financial system. For central bank money is what all the other institutions must have in order to settle their accounts. It is the ultimate embodiment of value, as Marx said of money more generally. By controlling its supply the central bank can decisively influence interest rates across the economy.

But I should stress that, though the central bank is currently very powerful indeed—probably more than at any other time in the history of capitalism—this does not mean that it can take action at will. The weaknesses of central banks, the limitations on their power, became very clear during the disaster of Northern Rock. The provision of money and liquidity to banks had to obey external pressures from the market, and had to operate within a very narrow frame that carried risks for all involved. I do not think that the Bank of England came out of this with flying colours, its actions probably accentuating the shortage of liquidity and exacerbating the run on Northern Rock.

The Japanese example seems to prove that the ruling class can get into a hole that they find it very difficult to get out of. The second most powerful capitalist class, and a very self-contained capitalist class, spent 15 years not getting out of the hole. There have been vague worries among some of the Financial Times writers about the US ruling class getting into the same situation. Or look at Northern Rock. It's incredible that the British government could lose half the money that it put into Northern Rock. It implies the situation is much more serious than some of us thought in August. You are saying there are limits to what the state can do in this situation.

The central bank is a bank. It might sound far-fetched but central banks can go bankrupt. At the very least, they cannot keep acquiring assets that are worthless because their own balance sheets begin to look very bad. This has a bearing on the Bank of England and Northern Rock. It has made loans to Northern Rock against the security of Northern Rock's assets, which are nothing but various mortgages and other loans that Northern Rock made in the past. If the assets of Northern Rock became worthless, the Bank of England would lose an enormous amount of money. It certainly could not contemplate lending on similar terms to two or three more banks, without seriously compromising its own health.

Now multiply this by a large factor and you will see the problem that Ben Bernanke might potentially face at the Federal Reserve. US banks have acquired so much questionable paper over the past few years that they are now sitting on a mountain of it. They have already written off $50 billion and estimates of further bad debt vary from $200 billion to $500 billion, to wild guesses of trillions of dollars. Depending on how the crisis unfolds, they will need additional finance to deal with the problem. The Federal Reserve cannot directly supply such finance, though it can play a key role in organising. Ultimately, of course, other arms of the state could step in, provide additional finance, forgive loans, and so on. But these are last resort interventions that typically have major political and institutional costs. This is not something that the ruling class wants to face because it reveals the nature of class power very clearly and there are no guarantees of smooth resolution.

To put it differently, central banks are pivotal to the current crisis, but they cannot necessarily see a way out of it in the short run. This is a classic example of contradictory capitalist development. At the moment of the central bank's greatest power one also sees its phenomenal weakness. Bernanke looks like a pathetic windblown man who does not know which way to turn. This is not down to his own personal deficiencies compared to Alan Greenspan. He is certainly far better qualified academically than Greenspan. No, it is the nature of the storm that is surrounding him.

I want to add one last thing, a point that I have made indirectly before. I think that the left should insist that credit and monetary policy constitute a legitimate field of criticism, inquiry, public debate, class struggle and radical demands. Monetary policy is fundamental to contemporary capitalism. Precisely because of the increasing autonomy of the financial system, because it has become so huge, finance has arrogated to itself the making of monetary policy, declaring it a matter for the experts. Meanwhile, the price for the mess created by finance is paid by ordinary people in the US, Britain and elsewhere. The left should stress that ordinary people are entitled to a more rational organisation of financial affairs that takes their own interests to heart. They also have a democratic right to exercise scrutiny and control over credit and monetary policy.

The crisis in Respect

Chris Harman

Two meetings took place in London on 17 November 2007, in venues about two miles apart. One was the 360-strong annual conference of Respect, which was attended by 270 delegates from 49 local branches and 17 student groups. The other, held in opposition to the conference and under the title "Respect Renewal", was a rally of 210 people called by MP George Galloway and a number of notables, including some members of the outgoing National Council and some of Respect's local councillors.[1]

Such splits are not unknown in the history of the working class movement. The founding of the Second International in 1889 also saw two conferences called in opposition to each other on the same day, in the same city, Paris. One was called by the German Social Democratic Party and the French Marxist party of Paul Lafargue and Jules Guesde, and backed by Frederick Engels, Eleanor Marx and William Morris. The other was called by the French reformist "possibilists" and backed by the British Social Democratic Federation of Henry Hyndman for sectarian reasons. Nonetheless, the divisions in Respect have caused confusion among many on the left in Britain and are, no doubt, leading to just as great bewilderment internationally. This article attempts to locate the politics behind the division and draw out some lessons.

1:    Respect Renewal claim a much higher figure, but 210 was the maximum number of people allowed in their hall under fire regulations, and is confirmed by counting the numbers present in photos posted on websites.

The eruption of the crisis

Respect's only MP, George Galloway, precipitated the crisis through a series of attacks on the biggest socialist group within the organisation, the Socialist Workers Party (SWP). This began with a veiled attack on Respect's national secretary, John Rees, who is a leading member of the SWP. Galloway also claimed that Respect had wasted resources by sponsoring a 1,000-strong Defend Fighting Unions conference the previous December and by taking part in the Pride London march (one of Europe's largest LGBT rights festivals) in the summer.

By mid-October 2007 the attacks had escalated into an onslaught against the whole SWP. One document circulated by Galloway and his supporters declared, "Respect is in danger of being completely undermined by the leadership of the Socialist Workers Party." The SWP were "Leninists", who were trying to control Respect "by Russian doll methods", claimed Galloway at a Respect branch committee meeting in the east London borough of Tower Hamlets. Local SWP members Paul McGarr and Aysha Ali were "Russian dolls", "members of a group that meets in secret, deciding on a democratic centralist line". Galloway went on to argue, "Paul and Aysha do believe what they are saying," but, he added, "they would have said it even if they didn't believe it".[2] This set the tone for a concerted attempt to drive the SWP out of Respect, with Galloway's supporters unilaterally declaring on 29 October that John Rees was no longer national secretary of Respect and that Lindsey German, the convenor of the Stop the War Coalition, was no longer Respect's candidate for Mayor of London—despite the fact that a 300-strong members' meeting in July had selected her. Five days later Galloway's supporters changed the locks on Respect's national office, shutting out its full time staff. They announced that they would not recognise Respect's annual conference and were calling their "Respect Renewal" rally for the same date.

Galloway's supporters tried to justify their moves by making a whole series of groundless allegations against the SWP. They claimed the SWP was trying to fix the outcome of the Respect conference; it was "blocking delegates" in Birmingham; it was voting for delegates "at completely unrepresentative meetings" in Tower Hamlets; it was dragging out meetings in the hope that other people who opposed it would leave; it was committing the grave sin of urging its members to stand for election as delegates in local branches of Respect; it had made four of the Tower Hamlets councillors

---

2:   Transcript of the emergency meeting of Tower Hamlets Respect branch committee, Thursday 18 October 2007. From notes taken down by Maggie Falshaw.

"turn their backs on Respect", and was trying to organise a "coup" against the democratically elected leader of the council group and even "trying to do a deal with the Liberal Democrats"; it was claimed that "a fundamental division had occurred in Respect between the leadership of a very small organisation called the Socialist Workers Party and almost everyone else in the party".[3]

The allegations are false, as testified by numerous non-SWP members, including Kumar Murshid, formerly a Labour councillor and adviser to Ken Livingstone, who joined Respect earlier in 2007, and Glyn Robbins, chair of Tower Hamlets Respect. The wording of most of the allegations is remarkably similar to that used by the media against supposed Communists during the Cold War in the 1950s, and by the right in the Labour Party against supposed "Trotskyist infiltrators" in the 1960s and 1980s. The aim was not simply to destroy opposition to a particular direction in which Galloway wanted to pull Respect—a direction that, as we will see, was markedly to the right of the trajectory of Respect when it was launched four years ago. It was also to besmirch the name of the Socialist Workers Party, thereby damaging our capacity to play a part in any united campaign of the left. It was sad to see such methods used by someone like Galloway, who had himself been subject to so much witch-hunting in the past from the media. But, tragically, he was now engaged in what he described to one activist from a Communist background as a "fight against Trotskyism". No doubt he was more circumspect when recruiting some other people to his side, which includes both Ken Loach and Alan Thornett.[4]

Some such people were, regrettably, taken in by Galloway's lies. But serious activists, however much they might disagree with some of the SWP's politics, know that our members do not behave at all as he purports. Indeed, the SWP has a long record of working over a wide range of issues with people and organisations with different views to our own. Even Peter Hain, now a senior government minister, recalled in a radio programme in October 2007 being able to work with us inside the Anti Nazi League in the late 1970s. He described our party as the dynamic driving force, but said we were able to work with people who were committed to the Labour Party. Today members of the SWP central committee play a leading role in the Stop the War Coalition alongside Labour Party members such as Tony

3: The first four of these allegations were contained in the stream of emails sent by Galloway's supporters to Respect members; the last two were in a letter published in the *East London Advertiser*, signed by the leader of the Tower Hamlets councillors' group, Abjol Miah, and Galloway's two full time assistants Kevin Ovenden and Rob Hoveman.
4: Alan Thornett is the leader of the British section of the Fourth International.

Benn and Jeremy Corbyn, as well as Andrew Murray, a member of the Communist Party of Britain, and people who belong to no party.

Unity and honest argument

There is a reason we have such a reputation. It is because we follow the method of the united front as developed by Lenin and Leon Trotsky in the early 1920s, and further elaborated by Trotsky when faced with the rise of Nazism in the early 1930s. This method stands in direct opposition to manipulating votes or rigging meetings. It starts with the understanding that exploitation, war and racism hurt working people, whether they believe in the efficacy of reform to change the system or believe, like us, that revolution is the only way to end its barbarity. This has two important consequences:

(1) Fighting back against particular attacks and horrors depends on the widest possible unity. The revolutionary minority cannot by its own efforts build a big enough movement. Revolutionaries must reach out to political forces that agree with them on particular immediate issues, even if they disagree over the long term solution.

(2) By struggling over these issues alongside people who believe in reform, the revolutionary minority can show in practice that its approach is correct, and so win people to its ideas.

It was this understanding that meant that, throughout its history, the Socialist Workers Party and its predecessor, the International Socialists, has worked alongside other organisations and individuals—through the Vietnam Solidarity Campaign in the late 1960s, the Anti Nazi League in the late 1970s and the mid-1990s, the Miners Support Committees in 1984-5, and the Stop the War Coalition and Unite Against Fascism today. It was the same approach that led us to initiate a campaign in defence of miners' leader Arthur Scargill in the early 1990s when he was subject to a vicious, lying witch-hunt by the media and the Labour right wing—and most of the rest of the left failed to stand up for him.

Of course, people have attempted to throw mud at us in the past. But the mud has never stuck because we have no interest in manipulation. We cannot fight back without persuading other forces to struggle alongside us and we cannot win some of those to revolutionary ideas without reasoned argument. Those who have worked in united fronts alongside us know we have always been open about our politics, while simultaneously building unity with those who do not agree with us. To do otherwise would act against both goals of the united front. It would restrict any united front to the minority who are already revolutionaries, making it ineffective. And it would prevent us from being able to show in practice to people who are not revolutionaries that our ideas are better than the various versions of reformism. It would be like cheating at patience.

Anyone with a particular political approach, whether reformist, revolutionary or even anarchist, organises in practice to put across their point of view, even if they sometimes try to deny doing so. And that means getting supporters together, whether formally or informally. Galloway's supporters in Respect could not have issued a stream of emails with between 12 and 19 signatures, and then called a pubic rally in opposition to the Respect conference, if they had not organised to do so as "a group that meets in secret", whether in smoke-filled rooms or through telephone conversations and the internet. As the saying goes, what is sauce for the SWP goose must be sauce for the Galloway gander.[5]

We have always understood that it is necessary to argue for policies that make united fronts effective. So the founding of the Anti Nazi League (ANL) in 1978 involved arguments against those who did not see confronting the Nazis of the National Front as a central priority. A few of the celebrities who initially supported the ANL when it was organising wonderful anti-Nazi carnivals broke with it when the question arose of stopping the Nazis on the streets. If the SWP had not argued with activists across the country, the ANL would never have been able to inflict a devastating defeat on the National Front.

Much the same applied 23 years later when the Stop the War Coalition was formed in the wake of the 9/11 attacks. There had been a highly successful central London meeting, initiated by the SWP and involving others such as George Monbiot, Jeremy Corbyn, Bruce Kent and Tariq Ali. But the first organising meeting after this nearly descended into a disastrous sectarian bun fight as various small groups tried to impose their own particular demands. It was the capacity of the SWP to draw constructive forces together around minimal demands that enabled the coalition to go forward. If some of the sectarian demands had been imposed (such as treating Islamism as if it were as big an enemy as US imperialism) the coalition would have been stillborn. SWP members argued for an approach involving the maximum number of people

---

5:   This is especially so since some of Galloway's allies in the Islamic Forum of Europe have connections with the Bangladeshi group Jamaat-i-Islami. Founded in pre-Independence India, this group developed as a very tight knit politico-religious organisation in both West and East Pakistan. It was involved in the military suppression of the Bengali liberation movement in 1969, before developing separate Pakistani and Bangladeshi wings, both of which still use force to drive the left from university campuses. Until recently the Bangladeshi Jamaat was in government with the right wing National Party, while the Pakistani Jamaat has been part of the alliance that has governed in coalition with General Musharraf's supporters in one province.

without diluting in any way its opposition to the war being waged by the US and British governments.

Far from SWP members behaving like "Russian dolls", our capacity to debate what needed to be done within our organisation and then to win others to it was a precondition for creating one of the most effective campaigns in British history. In a previous incarnation Galloway used to praise the SWP for our capacity to get things done, in particular building the anti-war movement of which he soon became a leading member.

The politics of building Respect

The united front method also underlay our approach to Respect. Back in 2003 the anti-war movement was at its highest point. We had seen up to two million people demonstrate on 15 February 2003, as well as a series of demonstrations all over 300,000 strong. Many activists concluded that a political expression for the movement was required. We shared this general feeling. We also realised that, unless a political focus to the left of Labour was built, disillusion could lead, as it had repeatedly in the 20th century, to an electoral swing to the right—benefiting the Tories and, even worse, Nazi groups. Our duty to the left as a whole was to try to create a credible electoral focus to the left of Labour. We had tried, with only limited success, to achieve this through the Socialist Alliance, which was to a large extent a coalition of existing left organisations (including some that were very sectarian and abstained from the movement against the war). The scale of opposition to the war provided far greater possibilities for building a broad electoral united front.

The left focus would not be a revolutionary one, but would attempt to draw in the diverse forces of the anti-war movement—revolutionaries, of course, but also disillusioned supporters of the Labour left, trade unionists, radical Muslim activists and people from the peace movement. It was a project that only made sense if we could involve large numbers of people who did not agree with us on the question of revolution. To this end, representatives of the SWP leadership were involved in open and frank discussions with various people interested in the same project. Then the expulsion of George Galloway from the Labour Party precipitated the launch of the project. Again we followed a united front approach. We agreed on a minimal set of points, fully compatible with our long term goals, which were also the maximum acceptable to our allies, and to many thousands of people drawn into activity by opposition to the war. Hence the name given to the new organisation—"Respect: The Unity Coalition". This was not the full blooded socialist position we might ideally have preferred; if it was, it would not have been able to attract all those who wanted some sort of anti-war, anti-racist, anti-neoliberal alternative to New Labour. The initials of Respect summed up the nature of the project—Respect, Equality, Socialism, Peace, Environment, Community and Trade unions—with socialism as one clear point among them.

Once again there was a political fight to get Respect off the ground, and the SWP was essential to this. There was argument inside the SWP, with a few people at a special national party delegate meeting in January 2004 opposing the project or its name. Beyond the SWP there were some on the left who objected to working with Muslims. We had to argue against them, pointing out that Islam, like other religions such as Christianity, has been subject to multiple interpretations—and that the claim that it was innately reactionary was part of the racist ideology being used to justify imperialist wars in Afghanistan and Iraq.

There were also more principled people in favour of working with Muslims, but worried about working with people from organisations influenced by historically right wing versions of Islamism, such as that of the Muslim Brotherhood in Egypt.[6] Against these views we argued that some of those influenced by such organisations were being opened up to new vistas by their involvement in the movement against war, as well as the struggle against Islamophobia, alongside socialists, trade unionists and people of other religious beliefs or none. Only the course of the struggle would show whether particular individuals' horizons had been widened enough for them to be drawn to the left. In any case, as with any united front, what mattered was not chiefly the attitude of the leaders, but whether it was possible to win over their followers, something that would only be discovered in practice.[7] This was important, because their following was growing due to the harsh capitalist policies of supposedly secular governments in the Middle East and South Asia on the one hand, and the spread of Islamophobia in Europe on the other.[8]

We also had to argue with people on the left who objected to working with Galloway, claiming that his past record ruled this out. He had, for instance, never been a member of the Campaign Group of MPs; he refused to accept that Respect MPs should have a salary no greater than the average wage; he had also attacked the SWP in the past, saying at the time

6:   This was, for instance, the position of Tariq Ali and Gilbert Achcar

7:   For the general argument, see Harman, 2002.

8:   This was the tone of my arguments in fraternal debates with Gilbert Achcar at the SWP's Marxism festival in July 2005 and at the *Historical Materialism* conference in December 2006.

of the 1990 poll tax riot that "these lunatics, anarchists and other extremists principally from the Socialist Workers Party were out for a rumble the whole time".[9] But for us, in the summer of 2003, what mattered was not what Galloway might or might not have done in the past, or the level of his salary. The key thing was that he had been expelled from New Labour because he had done more than any other MP to campaign against the war. As such he was a symbol of opposition to New Labour's involvement in Bush's war for very large numbers of people who had previously looked to Labour.

Precisely because the SWP was a coherent national organisation, it was able to carry these arguments in a way in which no one else involved in the formation of Respect was. Galloway clearly agreed with this when he enthusiastically agreed to John Rees being nominated as national secretary of Respect, just as Peter Hain and others had once accepted members of the SWP central committee as national organisers of the Anti Nazi League. Hain and Galloway both recognised that a "Leninist" organisation could fight to build unity among people with an array of different political perspectives in a way that a loose group of individuals could not.

We showed our commitment to this over a four-year period. So in the London Assembly and European elections of 2004 we strove to ensure that the Respect lists were much broader than the SWP, even in areas where the SWP members were a large proportion of Respect activists. There were sometimes sharp arguments inside the SWP about making sure non-SWP members were candidates. We recognised this was essential to making Respect into a real "unity coalition". In line with this approach we worked as hard for George Galloway in the 2004 elections to the European Parliament as we did for Lindsey German, a leading SWP member who stood for the London Assembly. And we worked as hard in parliamentary by-elections that summer for Muslim convert and journalist Yvonne Ridley in Leicester as we did for John Rees in Birmingham.

It was the willingness of SWP members to work in this way that produced the first electoral breakthrough for Respect in Tower Hamlets when local trade unionist Oliur Rahman became a councillor with 31 percent of the vote. Soon afterwards SWP member Paul McGarr beat New Labour when he came second in the mainly white Millwall ward in the borough with 27 percent of the vote. No one mentioned "Russian dolls" back then.

In the 2005 general election the diversity of Respect in the east London boroughs of Tower Hamlets and Newham found expression in the candidates for the parliamentary seats in the boroughs. The four

---

9:    Quoted in Morley, 2007, p201.

candidates were Lindsey German, George Galloway, Oliur Rahman and Abdul Khaliq Mian. SWP members showed their commitment to Respect as a broad coalition by working for all the candidates, but especially for George Galloway, who was elected as an MP on a Respect ticket. In Birmingham our members worked very hard for Salma Yaqoob.[10]

The pattern was repeated in the council elections of 2006. We fought for lists of candidates that were mixed in terms of ethnicity, gender and religious beliefs. In Birmingham, Respect stood five candidates—two Muslim women, a Muslim man, a black woman and a female member of the SWP. In Tower Hamlets and Newham, SWP members argued for a mixture of Muslim and non-Muslim candidates in the different wards wherever possible, and others usually accepted our argument. Respect won 26 percent of the vote and three council seats in Newham, 23 percent of the vote and 12 seats in Tower Hamlets and a seat for Salma Yaqoob in Birmingham.

Defending Respect as a project for the left

But, just as with the Anti Nazi League in the late 1970s and Stop the War Coalition in 2001, the very success of Respect led to political arguments— and SWP members had to try to find ways of dealing with them. One argument flowed from the 2006 election results. The successful candidates were all from a Muslim background, despite Respect winning substantial white working class votes (and a mere couple of hundred votes stopped non-Muslim candidates winning in Tower Hamlets). This was used by opponents of Respect to spread the idea that it was a "Muslim party".[11]

Another problem flowing from the success of Respect was familiar to people who had been active in the past in the Labour Party, but was completely new to the non-Labour left—opportunist electoral politics began to intrude into Respect.

Problems had already become apparent during Galloway's successful 2005 election campaign in the Bethnal Green & Bow parliamentary constituency. As John Rees writes, there was "a huge alliance aimed at unseating New Labour's Oona King", who was massively unpopular because of her outspoken support for the war on Iraq. But:

> Galloway's uncritical promotion of anyone that might get him more votes pulled around the campaign, and promoted within it, individuals and forces very distant from the left. Labour councillor Gulam Mortuza was feted…

10:    For the character of the Respect election campaign, see Taylor, 2005.
11:    The interviews in Taylor, 2005, give a very different picture.

Local elder Shamsuddin Ahmed was promoted to vice-chair of Respect for his support. Local millionaire restaurateur and property developer Azmal Hussein became a key figure in Tower Hamlets Respect. Abjol Miah, a young member of the Islamic Forum Europe, was celebrated as "the general" of the campaign. Mohammed Zabadne, a millionaire building contractor, was invited to speak at the victory rally and organised the first victory social a week later.[12]

Socialists did their best to deal with these unhealthy developments. They struggled against the non-left interlopers. By and large the left won. Mortuza turned against Galloway when the left blocked his bid to become "president" of Tower Hamlets Respect, leaving Respect and returning to Labour. Shamsuddin Ahmed was not selected for the council seat he wanted in 2006, left Respect and stood for the Liberal Democrats. Mohammed Zabadne soon became tired of left wing politics and broke with Respect. The willingness of socialists to argue against those who saw Respect simply as a vehicle for their own political careers was vindicated—but two years later this was used by Galloway to denounce, by implication, the SWP.[13]

The pressure to shift Respect in a dangerous direction persisted. There is a model of politics increasingly used by the Labour Party in ethnically and religiously mixed inner-city areas—promising favours to people who pose as "community leaders" of particular ethnic or religious groupings if they agree to use their influence to deliver votes. As three local SWP members and Respect activists in Tower Hamlets explain:

The Labour Party held office locally by making deals with, and promises to, key figures in local communities who then delivered "their" votes at election times. Sometimes this was mediated through organisations, religious bodies and individuals which reflected the local population at any time (Jewish, Irish, especially Catholic Irish around the docks, and others). Of course this tradition tended to replace principled politics with, at best, opportunism... With the arrival of Bengalis in east London this old reformist tradition simply adapted itself to the new situation, and has been a central part of Labour's *modus operandi* in recent decades.[14]

This is what is known in US cities as Tammany Hall politics, or "vote

---

12: John Rees, "Respect: Anatomy of a Crisis", SWP *Preconference Bulletin 3* (December 2007).
13: Galloway complained of "tensions" caused at one Respect meeting to select council candidates in his document "The Best of Times, the Worst of Times", which triggered the crisis.
14: Shaun Doherty, Paul McGarr and John McLoughlin in SWP *Preconference Bulletin 2* (November 2007).

bloc" or "communal" politics when practised by the pro-capitalist parties of the Indian subcontinent. It is something the left has always tried to resist. But it was this that began to appear in Respect in Tower Hamlets. There were arguments around this issue in the run-up to the 2006 council elections:

> On the selection panel...we were continually being told that "strong" candidates were needed in the most winnable wards. This was a thinly veiled code for selecting Bengali men with a standing in the local area. Of course we recognised that after years of Labour clientalism it was important for the preponderance of candidates in these wards to be ethnic Bengalis. But we also argued that there needed to be a balance across the spread of candidates that reflected all the different elements in Respect's coalition. In order to have a unanimous recommendation from the selection panel we in fact agreed to allow three male Bengali candidates in some wards (all wards had three seats), at the urging of people such as Azmal Hussain and Abjol Miah. Against considerable opposition we did, however, argue that a Bengali woman should stand in Whitechapel, one of our strongest wards, as should John Rees... Despite all of the compromises we made, when the agreed list was put to a members' meeting Abjol strongly objected to John's inclusion in Whitechapel, and although we won the vote we decided to make a tactical retreat from what had been a unanimously agreed position of the selection panel.

It later turned out that two of the Respect councillors selected on this basis did not share the political basis on which Respect had been formed:

> One defected to Labour and one resigned. Both felt slighted that their personal ambitions were not being satisfied. Both were Bengali men with some standing in their wards. One was the candidate who replaced John Rees in Whitechapel. Another was, in fact, one of the people hand picked by Abjol and Azmal as the only possible choice in Shadwell.[15]

Arguments also took place in Birmingham in the run-up to the 2007 council elections. The candidate supported by Salma Yaqoob had been in the Conservative Party until just three months before. He had been planning to stand against Respect as an independent in a neighbouring ward. When SWP member Helen Salmon argued against adopting him as

15:    Shaun Doherty, Paul McGarr and John McLoughlin in SWP *Preconference Bulletin 2* (November 2007).

Respect's candidate, Salma Yaqoob said Helen Salmon "had a problem with Asian candidates".[16] Then came the selection meeting for King's Heath—an ethnically and religiously mixed ward. Salma Yaqoob had previously suggested that Helen Salmon should be the candidate. But in the week prior to the selection meeting about 50 people were recruited to Respect in the ward (at a time when there were only about 70 paid-up Respect members in the whole of south Birmingham). An Asian Muslim recruitment consultant was put forward as an alternative candidate at the last minute and he was selected by 30 votes to 20. The overall outcome of the argument in Birmingham was a complete change in the character of Respect's list of candidates in 2007 compared to the list of year before. There was now a slate made up entirely of men from Pakistani backgrounds.

Typical of the reaction of many local people in Birmingham, Muslim as well as Hindu, Sikh, African-Caribbean and white, must have been that of the sister of one Pakistan-born SWP member who said that she had voted Respect previously, but would not do so again because it was a "communalist party".[17] No doubt one of the other parties spread this slander, but events on the ground could be seen as confirming it. Principled socialists had no choice but to argue against such developments. They represented a fundamental shift by sections of Respect away from the minimal agreed principles on which it had been founded—a shift towards putting electability above every other principle, a shift that could only pull Respect to the right. So Socialist Worker ran a short piece criticising what was happening in Birmingham and, a week later, a letter by Salma Yaqoob in response.

Further developments in Tower Hamlets also forced principled socialists to take a stand. In the summer of 2006 another bad Labour Party tradition began to come into Respect—the attempt to influence internal decisions by the use of "pocket members"—members paid for and manipulated by individuals within a party. Former left wing Labour councillor Kumar Murshid has explained how this worked on the ground:

One thing that caused me to move away from Labour was the culture of political division and "pocket members" that took hold in the party. You get one or two people with 50 or 100 pocket members who come into political

---

16: Helen Salmon, Pete Jackson and others, SWP *Preconference Bulletin 2* (November 2007).

17: Information provided by Talat Ahmed.

meetings to decide positions or nominations. They grab power without any support in real terms—and the politics just gets thrown out the window.[18]

Balwinder Rana argues that the same methods have been used by the Labour Party in Southall, west London: "When an election is coming up, they go door to door, getting membership and paying their membership dues from their own pockets".[19] Now attempts were made to use similar methods at Tower Hamlets Respect members' meetings. One wealthy member turned up with dozens of membership applications and a wad of money to sign people up at the reduced rate for the unemployed so they could vote at a meeting to decide who would head the Respect group on Tower Hamlets Council.

Arguments also took place within the newly elected Respect group on the council. Four councillors, including Respect's first elected councillor, trade unionist Oliur Rahman, and its two women councillors, objected to what they saw as right wing positions taken by the majority of the group, and the failure of this majority to use their positions to agitate and campaign for Respect's positions. None of the objectors were at that point in the SWP, although two soon joined. The issues became sharper late in the summer of 2007 when one of the Respect councillors resigned his seat in Shadwell, triggering a by-election. A Respect selection meeting got heated when a young woman, Sultana Begum, dared to stand against a middle aged man, Harun Miah. The SWP members and the four left wing councillors decided that Sultana Begum had the sort of fighting spirit best suited to represent Respect. Making this choice was one of the alleged "crimes" of the SWP referred to by Galloway—even though SWP members, after losing the vote at the selection meeting, worked flat out to win the seat for Respect, and were even thanked by the successful candidate.

Our real "crime", it seems, was that we argued our politics openly and vigorously, and refused to be dragooned into being "Russian dolls" for George Galloway's friends.

The mystery of Galloway's turn

For some, the mystery in this account may be why Galloway turned so suddenly against the SWP. We can only surmise what his motive might have been. But his record is clear. He behaved marvellously immediately after his election by going to the US Senate and denouncing the war in front of

---

18: Interview in *Socialist Worker*, 17 November 2007.
19: Speech at Respect conference.

the world's television cameras. But after that his role rapidly became rather different to that of the "tribune of the oppressed". There were complaints that he tended to leave much of his constituency work in Tower Hamlets to those whose salaries he paid out of his MP's allowances.

Then, at the beginning of 2006, he dealt a blow to everyone who was preparing to campaign for Respect in the local elections: he absented himself from politics for weeks to appear in the despicable "reality TV" show *Celebrity Big Brother*. Every active supporter of Respect was faced at work with taunts from the right and with people on the left saying they would never vote for Respect again. The SWP had to decide how to react to this. The pressure was particularly acute during these weeks because leading Respect members such as Ken Loach and Salma Yaqoob were keen to denounce Galloway. Fortunately, as a "Leninist" organisation of "Russian dolls" we had our annual conference just as *Celebrity Big Brother* started and were able to agree on a general reaction, which our members then tried to argue. We pointed out that appearing on the TV progamme was stupid and an insult to those who had worked to get him elected, but that it was not in the same league as dropping bombs to kill thousands of people in Iraq and Afghanistan. We defended Galloway at meetings of the Respect leadership, in an article putting the case in *Socialist Worker* and through statements on television by John Rees and others. We never, of course, got any thanks from Galloway for this.

It is probably fair to say that, had SWP had not defended Galloway during the *Big Brother* affair, Respect would have disintegrated at that stage. Nevertheless, there is no doubt that the *Big Brother* farce hit our vote that May. Galloway never once acknowledged the damage he did. On the contrary, in the months after the fiasco he began to use his "celebrity" to build a career as a radio talkshow host, interspersed with television appearances and, again insulting to Respect activists, appearing as guest presenter on *Big Brother's Big Mouth* in June 2007. Yet he had the gall just two months later to complain that the SWP was "undermining" Respect. Meanwhile he had achieved the dubious record of being the fifth highest earning MP, after the former ministers William Hague, David Blunkett and Ann Widdecombe, and the Tory columnist and candidate for mayor of London, Boris Johnson. Some tribune of the people!

Despite his increasing preoccupation with his media career throughout most of 2006 and the first half of 2007, Galloway was still capable of letting us have occasional glimpses of his old skills at denouncing imperialism. He remained an asset to the left, even if a diminishing one, and we in the SWP reacted accordingly. We never imagined he would suddenly attack us for resisting those who were pushing sections of Respect in the direction of electoral opportunism. So we continued to try to get him to speak on Respect platforms, even if media commitments limited his availability, and we defended him against a further attempted witch-hunt.

When he suddenly did launch his attack with the document of mid-August, anyone capable of looking a little below the surface could see it was directed against us. The document appeared when New Labour unexpectedly began to hint there might be a general election within four or five weeks. Galloway had said he would not stand for re-election to his seat in Bethnal Green & Bow, but he did show a desire to stand in the other Tower Hamlets constituency. That required him to win votes. So his document was based, in part, on electoral arguments. Respect had done poorly in the Ealing & Southall parliamentary by-election. For those with a modicum of political analysis, this could be explained by the timing (it was called at two and half weeks notice), by the fact that it was in the middle of the short-lived "Brown bounce" as the new prime minister came into office and by our lack of roots in the area. But Galloway contrasted it with the success of Respect in the Shadwell ward by-election in Tower Hamlets, drawing the conclusion that the only way to win seats was to follow the methods which had begun to take root in parts of Birmingham and Tower Hamlets. There was no future in appealing to workers on the basis of class or anti-war arguments (despite the victories of SWP members Michael Lavalette and Ray Holmes in council elections in May) and instead there had to be a shift towards courting "community leaders". The SWP was resisting such a turn, and so it had to be attacked.

Breaking points

The attack on the SWP was centred on the area where Galloway and his ally Abjol Miah hoped to be Respect parliamentary candidates, Tower Hamlets. There was an explosive meeting in mid-October to elect delegates to the annual conference. The question of "pocket members" raised its head again. Scores of people attended who activists had never seen before. As Kumar Murshid wrote in a letter to one of Galloway's supporters, Azmal Hussain, who chaired the meeting:

The fact that you and your colleagues mobilised so many members to come to the meeting yesterday was fantastic, except that most everyone I spoke to did not really know why they were there or what they wanted. I put to you that this is precisely the problem when your energies are given to the pursuit of positions and supposed power as opposed to political issues around which we need to define ourselves and our party.

The Respect rules stipulated that nominations for delegates had to be received in advance of the meeting. In all, 46 nominations had been received and there were a number of vacant places. An account by SWP members tells what happened next:

> Just before the vote was about to be taken Kevin Ovenden [paid parliamentary assistant to Galloway] brought in a second handwritten list. This list contained names of people who were not fully paid up members of Respect, people who had not been asked if they wished to stand, people identified by only one name and one member of Newham Respect who was proposed from "George's office". After the chair, Azmal Hussain, refused to put a compromise proposal to the vote the meeting became chaotic and the chair and a number of others left. Jackie Turner, Tower Hamlets Respect secretary, took over in the chair with the agreement of the meeting and the original nominations were ratified and it was agreed to discuss with the proposers of the second list how the remaining places could be filled.[20]

George Galloway, who was not at the meeting, put his name to a denunciatory email claiming the SWP had "systematically undermined" the meeting, ignoring democratic procedures so as to take control of the conference delegation.[21] When the SWP and the left councillors defended themselves, he accused us of aggression. At the "Russian dolls" meeting two nights later he told some of our members (including his 2005 election agent) to "fuck off". Some of his supporters made it clear they wanted to drive us out of Respect. They attempted to do so at another Tower Hamlets meeting the following week. But seeing that they did not have a clear majority, Azmal Hussain, in the chair, refused to take any votes against or abstentions on their resolution and then tried to end the meeting when people objected.

One very disturbing feature of this meeting was the attitude of Galloway's supporters towards women members of Respect. Rania Khan, at 25 the youngest councillor, recalls:

20: Shaun Doherty, Paul McGarr and John McLoughlin, SWP *Preconference Bulletin 2* (November 2007).

21: Email to members of Tower Hamlets Respect by Azmal Hussain, George Galloway and others, 16 October 2007.

We had about 50 women that night and they had valid membership cards but they were not allowed to take part. It was raining and cold outside and they had small children with them, and someone who was close to the council group leaders said to one of the women queuing up outside, "My wife doesn't come. Why are you here?"[22]

This was not the first time such attitudes had been displayed towards Respect members, and particularly young women. Lufta Begum says that Respect council group leader Abjol Miah "shouted at me".[23] Paul McGarr says, "Some of the young Muslim women have been repeatedly insulted and bullied." He adds that he does not see this as a particular characteristic of Muslim men—it was how women would have been treated by Labour officials in the mining village he grew up in 40 years ago. The point, however, is that the left have always sought to resist such behaviour.

Up to this point the SWP had done its utmost to reach a compromise that would prevent the split in Respect coming out into the open. Our only precondition was that principled socialists had to have the right to argue within Respect's democratic structures against opportunism and Tammany Hall communalism. But the behaviour of Galloway and his supporters in Tower Hamlets showed that compromise would not work. There was only one possible way of keeping Respect alive in its original form—for the SWP and others on the left to fight flat out. The left councillors were so angry by this point that no one could dissuade them from breaking with the rest of the Respect group on Tower Hamlets council. As Lufta Begum says, "John Rees said to us, don't resign the whip at present. But we could not endure it any more".[24]

Resigning the whip did not, as Galloway's supporters claimed, mean them leaving Respect. There is a long tradition in British politics of elected representatives losing or rejecting the "whip" (ie the discipline of the parliamentary or council group) of a party without leaving the party itself.

The internal discussion in the SWP
Galloway and his supporters have portrayed the SWP as a closed "Leninist" group in which a small number of people at the centre dictate to the members, who then are frogmarched into manipulating wider meetings. The picture does not correspond to the way the SWP really works. This was shown by

22: Interview with Rania Khan, 17 November 2007.
23: Speech at Respect conference.
24: Speech at Respect conference.

the way we reacted to the attacks on us from late August onwards.

Once it became clear just how serious Galloway's attacks were, we circulated his first document and our reply to our members, and called a meeting for all London members. The meeting was chaired by an experienced member, who had argued for an alternative slate for the central committee to the one proposed by the outgoing leadership at the 2006 party conference. There was open debate, with alternate speeches from those who supported and those who opposed the central committee's interpretation of events. And there was not the slightest hint of intimidation, with a strict ban on heckling. A series of members' meetings in each locality followed and then a national delegate meeting. Again those who disagreed with the leadership's position were able to speak without hindrance—including three non-delegates who were invited as the only observers so they could make their points. At the end of the meeting a vote was taken in support of the leadership's reply to Galloway's arguments and it was carried overwhelmingly in a room containing more than 200 people; there were only two "noes" and four abstentions. Arguments on both sides in the debate within the party were then printed in an internal bulletin; all the arguments within Respect were circulated to party members; further local aggregate meetings took place and then another national meeting, attended by about 250 people, which voted with two against and a handful of abstentions to endorse a central committee document.[25]

One particularly sad thing in this whole sorry saga was the behaviour of three SWP members, who had every right to put their arguments to the party, and had done so at the meeting of London members, in the party's internal bulletin and at the first national delegate meeting. Two of these members, who had both been in the party for a number of years, had taken employment as Galloway's assistants. They chose to ignore the overwhelming feeling at the SWP's national meeting and not only lined up with him, but also helped orchestrate the attacks on the SWP and the left councillors in Tower Hamlets.[26] The third, a former member of the Militant organisation, was asked by the central committee not to stand

25: This article is based on that document. I have changed some of the wording to make sense to a wider audience than SWP members and I have put in additional material dealing with events since the meetings. The original document is available on the SWP website: www.swp.org.uk

26: As the bitterness of Galloway's attacks on the SWP increased we argued that working for him was becoming incompatible with loyalty to other SWP members. They rejected the suggestion and were clearly on Galloway's side at National Council meetings of Respect and local meetings in Tower Hamlets. Their abandonment of the SWP was proved when they rejected the offer to appeal to the party's disputes committee against the central committee's decision to expel them.

for the position of national organiser of Respect, but insisted on putting himself forward for this job. We had no choice but to part company with the three and terminate their membership of the SWP. The vote at the second national meeting held by the SWP endorsed this decision.

No one reading the account of the succession of meetings and discussions we organised should be able to conclude that our "Leninism" or "Trotskyism" is undemocratic. Thousands of people with a record of activity in the working class, anti-war and anti-racist movements had access to all the different arguments and followed them attentively before coming to a conclusion. They decided overwhelmingly that they would not be "Russian dolls" for Galloway as he tried to turn Respect into a vehicle for furthering the political careers of people who shared few of its original values.

The conclusion of our discussions was that it was necessary to try to continue to build Respect according to the original conception as a left focus reflecting the diversity of the forces involved in the anti-war movement. This could only be done by opposing the attempts by Galloway and his allies to stifle accountability of elected representatives, to prevent Respect members from challenging moves towards opportunism and to drive the biggest group of organised socialists from positions of influence in Respect. To this end, every effort had to be made to ensure that the Respect annual conference took place with delegates elected on a democratic basis. It was while we were deciding on this approach that news came through that Galloway's supporters were trying to sabotage the conference by calling their own rally on the same day. Galloway's rally consisted to a very large extent of speeches denouncing the SWP.

Results and prospects

Respect has not been the only attempt to build a left alternative to a rightward moving social democratic party. We have seen similar attempts with the Scottish Socialist Party, P-Sol in Brazil, the Red-Green Alliance in Denmark, the Left Bloc in Portugal, Die Linke in Germany, the efforts to find a single anti-neoliberal candidate for the presidential elections in France in 2007 and the formation of Rifondazione Comunista in Italy. Neither has Respect been the only case in which the project has suddenly been endangered by the behaviour of leading figures.

The Rifondazione leadership in Italy moved very quickly from intransigent opposition to the centre-left to joining a centre-left government implementing the policies it once opposed.[27] The majority of the

---

27: Trudell, 2007.

leadership of the Scottish Socialist Party gave evidence in a libel trial against the party's best-known figure, Tommy Sheridan.[28] The Portuguese Left Bloc was thrown into disarray in the autumn of 2007 by the decision of José Sá Fernandes, a left wing independent activist elected to Lisbon council with the Bloc's support, to make a deal with the Socialist Party. The Red-Green Alliance in Denmark was paralysed in the run-up to the November 2007 elections by a media campaign directed against the organisation's decision to choose a young Muslim woman as one of its main parliamentary candidates. There are continuing tensions inside the German party Die Linke over the participation of some of its East German members in local government coalitions with the social democrats. The attempt to put forward a single presidential candidate for the anti-neoliberal left in France, backed by nearly half of the Ligue Communiste Révolutionnaire (LCR), came to nought. The French Communist Party claimed its own candidate represented the movement, while José Bové, himself claiming to be the "unity candidate", attacked the Communist Party and the LCR, only to agree later to be adviser on "food sovereignty" to the right wing Socialist Party candidate Ségolène Royal.

None of this means that the attempt to create a left focus is in itself misplaced. The meagreness of the reforms offered by Labour and other social democratic parties has created a huge political vacuum to their left, which the forces of the revolutionary left are too weak to fill more than partially by themselves. It is this which creates the need for a gathering of left forces wider than the revolutionary left organised through a united front. But the very thing that makes such political united fronts potentially able to attract wide support—the involvement of well known non-revolutionary political or trade union figures—necessarily means they are unlikely to last indefinitely in the face of changing circumstances without intense arguments breaking out over their direction. Figures who believe in the path of reform rather than revolution can often put up very strong and principled opposition to what a particular government is doing at a particular point in time. But their very commitment to the path of reform means that they can suddenly drop some of their principles in favour of opportunistic attempts to advance within the existing structures of society.

Galloway, for instance, has been open about his commitment to the path of reform. He has said that the Labour government would have been

---

28:    Gonzalez, 2006.

very different "if John Smith were still alive".[29] On television and radio programmes he has often demonstrated a strange faith in the capacity of the police to deal with crime, and has declared his commitment to the unity of the British state, which he sees New Labour as undermining.[30]

Such views meant that at some point he was likely to be attracted to opportunistic methods that revolutionary socialists would have to resist. The same was true of Bové in France, of Sá Fernandes in Portugal and of Rifondazione's leader Fausto Bertinotti in Italy. It also cannot be ruled out in the case of the most important West German leader of Die Linke, Oskar Lafontaine. This does not mean it has necessarily been wrong to form a political united front with such figures. However, it requires an awareness that the very success of such a project can embolden reformist as well as revolutionary forces, encouraging them to go off in their own direction and to attack viciously those who resist.

The point was made in this journal three years ago that "electoral splits from an existing mainstream reformist party necessarily involve activists who reject the policies of current governments, but who have not broken with the whole conception of parliamentary socialism".[31] This would inevitably mean that "when the going gets tough there is pressure among activists whose political background has been in mainstream reformism to fall back on the methods of parliamentary alliances". It was necessary for revolutionaries to go through "the experience of trying to build an alternative with people who are still at least half influenced by reformist ideas—but also do not hide their distinct views and take every opportunity to win people to them through their publications, their meetings and one to one arguments".

The assumption then was that the "pressure" towards opportunism would arise when there were openings for supposed influence at the governmental level, as with Rifondazione in Italy and previously with the Alliance Party in New Zealand. What was unexpected was the much lower level of temptation required for prominent figures to break with declared principles. The examples of the Scottish Socialist Party, of Buffet and Bové in France, and of Galloway have taught us all a hard lesson.

This does not, however, mean that the method of the political united front is wrong. It is likely to continue to be essential in the period ahead

---

29:    This is what he said on one occasion in the presence of Colin Barker. John Smith was the leader of the Labour Party in the early 1990s after Neil Kinnock and before Tony Blair.

30:    *Question Time*, on BBC1, 25 October 2007, available on George Galloway's website.

31:    Harman, 2004.

as the way to channel the bitterness against social democrats abandoning the interests of their traditional supporters. But it is necessary always to remember that any particular configuration may be of limited duration, with some forces turning their backs on it even as new ones open up fresh possibilities.

This also means it is wrong to conceive of the left focus taking the form of a "broad party", united over the whole range of policies, rather than a coming together in a coalition of independent political forces and traditions—some revolutionary, some reformist. There is no way that reformists and revolutionaries can agree on all their political objectives without dishonesty and manipulation on one side or on both. The LCR in France has a different attitude to the role of working class in the struggle to change society to that of Bové or Buffet. George Galloway and the "community leaders" in Tower Hamlets or Birmingham have a quite different attitude to those of us who are consistent revolutionaries. Unity to fight mainstream parties is one thing. An agreed programme on how to change society is another.

These arguments also apply in important forms of day to day activity. In Britain trade union leaders sympathetic to Respect agree with revolutionaries on opposition to anti-union laws, but they may well be opposed to urging particular groups of workers to take unofficial action in defiance of them. In Germany union leaders who support Die Linke have not agreed with the correct decision of some Die Linke branches to back a strike by an independent train drivers' union.

Where revolutionaries are very few in number, their options for united action may be restricted to working in a much bigger organisation where left reformism predominates, while being able to do little more than make propaganda for their own views within it. But where the revolutionary and reformist forces are more evenly balanced, revolutionaries have a duty to argue and agitate independently, even as they work with others in the political united front. This has one very important practical implication. It means a revolutionary press that does not restrict its arguments to those shared by its reformist allies. Only in this way can it provide a coherent Marxist view of the world and not fudge over what needs to be done in each concrete, immediate struggle.

These lessons are going to continue to be important. The few dozen people who think of themselves as revolutionaries but have joined the Respect Renewal breakaway will learn this lesson the hard way. They will face a choice between having to avoid speaking on a whole range of issues or saying things that upset one or other of its component parts. They will be faced on a daily basis by Galloway, with his disdain for what ordinary supporters think about his media performance and his opinions of issues such as crime, by those Tower Hamlets councillors whose main concern is their own careers, by those who mistakenly believe the only way to win the votes of Muslim workers is to keep quiet in the face of male chauvinist attitudes, and by those who despite their denials have tried to play the communal card in the past and will do so again in future. We can only hope that at some stage principle wins in the battle with opportunism.

Meanwhile, the main body of Respect faces the continued challenge of trying to build a consistent left focus. That will be harder after the breakaway. But wider political developments are likely to offer new opportunities in the medium term. The crisis in Respect arose, in part, because the immense feeling against the war was not matched by a corresponding increase in the level of industrial struggle, allowing union leaders to use their influence to endorse New Labour. And the crisis came to a head in the late summer because the "Brown bounce", however short-lived, worried those whose only concern was short term electoral success. But New Labour is now facing renewed problems as Gordon Brown reveals his true face, not only through his commitment to Bush's wars in Iraq and Afghanistan and threats against Iran, but also through his attempt to hold down public sector wage rises below inflation, and his continuation of Blairite policies in education and the health service. The breakaway of the Galloway group from Respect may have been a blow to the attempt to provide a left focus for those disillusioned by New Labour. But revulsion at Brown's policies should provide plenty of opportunities to recover from it.

References

Gonzalez, Mike, 2006, "The Split in the Scottish Socialist Party", *International Socialism 112* (autumn 2006), www.isj.org.uk/index.php4?id=247

Harman, Chris, 2002, *The Prophet and the Proletariat*, second edition (Bookmarks).

Harman, Chris, 2004, "Spontaneity, Strategy and Politics", *International Socialism 104* (autumn 2004), www.isj.org.uk/index.php4?id=12

Morley, David, 2007, *Gorgeous George: The Life and Adventures of George Galloway* (Politico's).

Taylor, Ian, 2005, "Respect: the View from Below", *International Socialism 108* (autumn 2005), www.isj.org.uk/index.php4?id=137

Trudell, Megan, 2007, "Rifondazione Votes for War", *International Socialism 113*, (winter 2007), www.isj.org.uk/index.php4?id=284

Material Girls

Women, men and work

Lindsey German, £12.99

A major new study of women and capitalism today

Women's lives have been transformed over the past half century. Women have entered the workforce on a scale unprecedented outside of wartime. The family has been reshaped around the full time women workers and is no longer centred on full time housewives. New circumstances have given rise to new attitudes towards women's role in society: to marriage, children and sex— and much of it for the better.

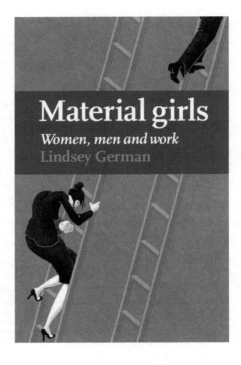

But far from escaping inequality, most women are still at the bottom of the pile. Why, at the beginning of the 21st century, does the promise of liberation remain unfulfilled? Why has the revolution in women's lives stalled?

The battle for women's liberation urgently needs to be renewed. But, argues Lindsey German, it will only succeed by linking up with wider struggles to change society as a whole.

Lindsey German is the author of *Sex, Class and Socialism* and most recently of *Stop the War: The Story of Britain's Biggest Mass Movement*. She is the national convenor of the Stop the War Coalition.

To order call 020 7637 1848 or visit www.bookmarks.uk.com

The united front

Joseph Choonara

The "united front" is a strategy. It is the answer revolutionaries give to a very general question: how should workers committed to the revolutionary overthrow of capitalism relate to those who believe that the system can be reformed and does not need to be overthrown? For most of the past century the consciousness of most workers has been reformist rather than revolutionary; organisations committed to reform, rather than revolution, have dominated the workers' movement. Because of this the strategic problem of the united front has been posed again and again. But because it is posed in a wide range of contexts and periods, the precise form taken by the united front varies.

In his biography of Lenin, Tony Cliff highlights the distinction between strategy and tactics:

> The concept of tactics applies to measures that serve a single task or a single branch of the class struggle. Hence Lenin speaks about the tactics needed, say, during the January days of 1905... He also speaks about trade union tactics, parliamentary tactics, and so on. Revolutionary strategy encompasses a combination of tactics which by their association and growth lead to the working class conquest of power.[1]

Those who view the united front as just a tactic, as a specific form of organisation that can simply be applied to any given situation, are likely to

---

1: Cliff, 1986, pp253-254.

go astray when trying to understand what connects the united front in different historical or geographical contexts. The forms assumed by the united front flow from the context—the key tasks facing the working class, its consciousness, the balance of forces between reformist and revolutionary organisations, and so on.

For Leon Trotsky, whose name, more than any other, is associated with the united front, the broad strategy could encompass a huge range of possible forms:

> Just as the trade union is the rudimentary form of the united front in the economic struggle, so *the soviet is the highest form of the united front* under the conditions in which the proletariat enters the epoch of fighting for power.[2]

I will return to the question of the soviet as a form of united front. What is of interest here is what soviets, trade unions and contemporary united fronts such as the Stop the War Coalition might have in common. The basic characteristics of the united front are as follows:
• It draws together workers—revolutionary and non-revolutionary—in common struggle. These struggles can range from the basic defence of workers' conditions under capitalism (trade unions) to the creation of a workers' state from below (soviets).
• It represents a set of demands acceptable to both revolutionaries and sections of the working class who are not yet revolutionary.
• The forces involved remain independent forces. Revolutionaries are able to pursue goals independent of the united front, and articulate their wider political vision.
• It is also a site of struggle—within the united front reformist and revolutionary currents can argue about strategy and tactics. Indeed, there will always be a battle of ideas, and debate over strategy and tactics, within the united front.
• The superior ideas and methods of struggle put forward by the revolutionaries should allow them to win some of the reformist workers involved in the united front to revolutionary politics.

The clearest theory of the united front was developed by the generation of Marxists, including Trotsky, Lenin and Antonio Gramsci, who took part in the revolutionary upsurge that followed the First World War. This was a period in which mass revolutionary organisations had to operate

---

2:   Trotsky, 1989, p132 (Trotsky's emphasis).

alongside mass reformist organisations. After the initial upsurge of struggle ended in the early 1920s, the revolutionaries were forced to deal with a period of defensive struggle. Because the working class was on the defensive, the question of working class unity, and hence of the united front, was posed extremely sharply.

Precursors

Trotsky justified the united front strategy by quoting no less an authority than Karl Marx and Frederick Engels's *Communist Manifesto*:

> The Communists do not form a separate party opposed to other working class parties. They have no interests separate and apart from those of the proletariat as a whole… The Communists…are on the one hand, practically, the most advanced and resolute section of the working class parties of every country, that section which pushes forward all others; on the other hand, theoretically, they have over the great mass of the proletariat the advantage of clearly understanding the line of march, the conditions, and the ultimate general results of the proletarian movement.[3]

These passages, written before the emergence of mass reformist parties, capture the essence of the task faced by revolutionaries. They must advance the wider interests that unite the working class, and do so as the most resolute and advanced section of that class. In practice Marx and Engels engaged in a range of organisations—from the embryonic Communist League, with a few hundred members, which took part in the wave of European revolutions in 1848, through to the First International, which drew in everything from British trade unions to secret socialist societies.[4]

Towards the end of their lives Marx and Engels were to argue against the emergence of what they saw as "anti-proletarian" currents of thought in the German Social Democratic Party (SPD), the largest workers' party of their day:

> It is representatives of the petty bourgeoisie who are here making themselves heard, full of anxiety that the proletariat, under pressure of its revolutionary position, may "go too far". Instead of determined political opposition, general

---

3:   Marx and Engels, 1977a.
4:   For a brilliant summary of Marx and Engels's attitudes to the party, see Molyneux, 1978.

mediation; instead of struggle against government and the bourgeoisie, an attempt to win them over and persuade them.[5]

Here their argument was against "alien influences" within essentially healthy bodies, and Marx and Engels continued to stress the need for united workers' parties drawing in and representing the whole working class. It was in Russia that this conception of the workers' party would be challenged.

Lenin, operating under conditions of repression and illegality, hit upon a very different form of organisation. His Bolshevik Party was not a party of the whole working class, but of the most advanced revolutionary workers. These workers could form a homogenous force, and the centralised organisation of the Bolsheviks gave them considerable ability to fight for a strategy within the wider working class. However, even for Lenin this was a form of organisation appropriate only to Tsarist Russia. Until 1914 few Marxists seriously challenged the general applicability of the broad socialist party model.

Two things changed this. First, the leaders of socialist organisations across Europe rushed to support their own national ruling classes when the First World War broke out. This betrayal, especially by the German SPD, stunned even Lenin. The SPD continued to use Marxist rhetoric, but in practice it had developed in a different direction, stressing a gradual awakening of working class consciousness and a slow, piecemeal transition to socialism. It had developed a range of institutions, along with layers of functionaries and parliamentarians, which sought to negotiate with capitalism, rather than overthrow it. The second factor was the victory of the 1917 Revolution in Russia, which provided the clearest insights into the advantages of the Leninist revolutionary party *and* the need for the united front.

The united front in 1917

Russia did not have the kind of mass reformist parties that were developing in Germany, Britain and elsewhere. However, reformist consciousness remained dominant in the working class. Any working class compelled to sell its labour power, dictated to in the workplace by bosses and managers, will contain a mixture of ideas—some based on struggle and solidarity, some based on resignation and acceptance of ruling class ideas. Not only this, but because the specific experiences of individual workers differ, the

---

5:    Marx and Engels, 1977b.

consciousness of the class will contain great unevenness.

Lenin's concept of the party is the beginning of the solution to this problem. It draws together the workers with the most advanced ideas and arms them with the theoretical tools, arguments, strategies and tactics to lead other workers. The united front is the other crucial element of the solution.

The Russian Revolution began, as revolutions do, with an explosion of popular anger. The "spontaneous" February 1917 Revolution was in contrast to the "conscious" insurrection carried through in October that year:

> The February insurrection is called spontaneous... In February nobody laid out the road in advance, nobody voted in the factories and barracks on the question of revolution, nobody summoned the masses from above to insurrection. The indignation accumulated for years broke to the surface unexpectedly, to a considerable degree, even to the masses themselves. It was quite otherwise in October. For eight months the masses had been living an intense political life. They had not only been creating events, but learning to understand their connections. After each action they had critically weighed its results.[6]

During the prolonged revolutionary period stretching from February to October the working class learned from numerous advances and retreats. One episode is of crucial importance. From July onwards Alexander Kerensky headed the provisional government, the "official" state power in Russia, with the support of the moderate left parties, the Mensheviks and Social Revolutionaries. His government sought to ride out the revolutionary wave while continuing the slaughter of the First World War and attempting to restore capitalist stability to Russia. Above all this meant destroying the influence of the soviets—mass democratic organs of workers' power that had sprung up in February. This policy also meant imprisoning or driving underground the leaders of the Bolshevik Party. At first Kerensky worked in alliance with the right wing commander in chief of the army, Lavr Kornilov, but in late August Kornilov broke with Kerensky and moved against the stronghold of the revolution, the city of Petrograd. His aim was to overthrow Kerensky and establish himself as Russia's "strongman". Trotsky explains how the Bolsheviks responded:

> What course did the Bolshevik Party take? Not for an instant did it hesitate to conclude a practical alliance to fight against Kornilov with its jailers... Everywhere committees for revolutionary defence were organised,

---

6:   Trotsky, 1977, p1126.

into which the Bolsheviks entered as a minority. This did not hinder the Bolsheviks from assuming the leading role: in agreements projected for revolutionary mass action, the most thoroughgoing and boldest revolutionary party stands to gain always. The Bolsheviks were in the front ranks; they smashed down the barriers blocking them from the Menshevik workers and especially the Social Revolutionary soldiers, and carried them in their wake... In the midst of Kornilov's campaign, Kerensky appealed to the sailors of the cruiser Aurora, begging them to assume the defence of the Winter Palace. These sailors were, without exception, Bolsheviks. They hated Kerensky. Their hatred did not prevent them from vigilantly guarding the Winter Palace. Their representative came to the Kresty Prison for an interview with Trotsky, who was jailed there, and they asked: "Why not arrest Kerensky?" But they put the query half in jest: the sailors understood that it was necessary first to smash Kornilov and after that to attend to Kerensky.[7]

Trotsky captures the essence of the united front. The strategy of working with the masses, while winning them away from reformist ideas, meant the Bolsheviks proving in practice that it was they who could most consistently defend the revolution from Kornilov. They achieved this through forming joint organisations with the Mensheviks and Social Revolutionaries. Lenin, writing in the midst of the battle to defend the revolution, stressed the other aspect, the need for the Bolsheviks to maintain their independence within this united front, and the continued need for ideological struggle:

Even at the present time, we are not duty bound to support the Kerensky government. That would be unprincipled. It is asked: then we are not to fight against Kornilov? Of course we are. But that is not one and the same thing. There is a limit to this; it is being transgressed by many Bolsheviks who fall into "conciliationism" and allow themselves to be driven by the current of events. We shall fight, we are fighting against Kornilov, but we do not support Kerensky; we are uncovering his weaknesses...we are varying the forms of struggle against Kerensky...by explaining the weaknesses and vacillations of Kerensky to the people (who are fighting against Kornilov).[8]

It was in the struggle against Kornilov that the Bolsheviks won over

---

7:    Trotsky, 1989, pp121-122 (note that Trotsky here refers to himself in the third person).
8:    Quoted in Trotsky, 1975, p108.

the bulk of Russian workers. The struggle to defend the conciliators had exposed the conciliators. This allowed the Bolsheviks eventually to win a majority in the soviets, previously dominated by the Mensheviks and Social Revolutionaries. But even at the high point of the revolution, the October insurrection, the united front remained crucial. Trotsky describes the relationship of the party and the soviet:

> Whereas the soviets in revolutionary conditions—and apart from the revolution they are impossible—comprise the whole class with the exception of its altogether backward, inert or demoralised strata, the revolutionary party represents the brain of the class. The question of conquering the power can be solved only by a definite combination of party with soviets—or with other mass organisations more or less equivalent to soviets.[9]

As Russia moved towards the completion of the revolution, a very sharp question arose: who would lead the insurrection? Should it be organised through the soviets or through the Bolshevik Party? Initially Lenin argued that the Bolshevik central committee should call the insurrection.[10] Although the Bolshevik Party played a central role in carrying through the insurrection, Trotsky was clear that it had to be called by the military revolutionary committee—an elected body of the soviet—rather than the party alone:

> Would it not have been simpler...to summon the insurrection directly in the name of the party? This form of action undoubtedly has weighty advantages. But its disadvantages are hardly less obvious. In those millions upon whom the party legitimately counted it is necessary to distinguish three layers: one which was already with the Bolsheviks on all conditions; another, more numerous, which supported the Bolsheviks in so far as they acted through the soviets; a third which followed the soviets in spite of the fact that they were dominated by Bolsheviks.[11]

The revolution was carried to completion by a united front. The Bolsheviks had to forge an alliance with non-Bolshevik workers, soldiers and peasants, including those who followed the soviets *despite* the Bolsheviks. Trotsky continues:

9:   Trotsky, 1977, p1126.
10:   Bone, 1974, p101.
11:   Trotsky, 1977, p1127. I am grateful to Colin Barker for drawing this quote to my attention.

Those standing for the Bolsheviks as a party were above all industrial workers, with the hereditary proletarians of Petrograd in the front rank. Those standing for the Bolsheviks in so far as they had a legal soviet cover were a majority of the soldiers. Those standing for the soviets, independently and regardless of the fact that...Bolsheviks dominated them were the more conservative groups of workers—former Mensheviks and Social Revolutionaries, who dreaded to break away from the rest of the masses—the more conservative parts of the army even including the Cossacks, and the peasants who had freed themselves from the leadership of the Social Revolutionary party and were adhering to its left flank.[12]

Trotsky's argument was based on a careful assessment of the consciousness of the masses:

According to the report of Ensign Berezin, at an October military conference of the Bolsheviks in Moscow the delegates were saying: "It is hard to know whether the troops will come out at the summons of the Moscow committee of the Bolsheviks. At the summons of the Soviet they might all come out.".... At a conference of 16 October in Petrograd, Boky made this report in the name of the party committee: In the Moscow district "they will come out at the summons of the Soviet, but not of the party"; in the Nevsky district "all will follow the Soviet". Volodarsky thereupon summarised the state of mind in Petrograd in the following words: "The general impression is that nobody is eager to go into the streets, but all will appear at the call of the Soviet." Olga Ravich corrected him: "Some say also at the call of the party.".... Attempts to lead the insurrection directly through the party nowhere produced results.[13]

Based on his assessment, Trotsky draws conclusions about the forces that can be brought into action by a united front:

The party set the soviets in motion, the soviets set in motion the workers, soldiers, and to some extent the peasantry. What was gained in mass was lost in speed. If you represent this conducting apparatus as a system of cog-wheels— a comparison to which Lenin had recourse at another period on another theme—you may say that the impatient attempt to connect the party wheel directly with the gigantic wheel of the masses—omitting the medium sized

---

12: Trotsky, 1977, p1127.
13: Trotsky, 1977, pp1128-1129.

wheel of the soviets—would have given rise to the danger of breaking the teeth of the party wheel, and nevertheless not setting sufficiently large masses in motion.[14]

The Comintern: generalising the experience

The Third International, formed in March 1919 and known as the Comintern, was the child of the 1917 Revolution. It was formed as revolts that accompanied the end of the First World War convulsed much of Europe. Initially it was made up of a handful of small parties. But a series of splits in reformist organisations meant that "by early 1921, parties affiliated to the Comintern had the support of the majority of politically conscious European workers in six countries (France, Italy, Norway, Bulgaria, Yugoslavia and Czechoslovakia) and of a substantial minority in others (Germany, Sweden and Poland)".[15] Unfortunately, by this time the revolutionary tide was ebbing.

The first phase of the German Revolution, which broke out in November 1918, had been brought to an end as the SPD and the German high command crushed the newly formed Communist Party in Berlin, and then moved against workers' and soldiers' councils that had been established in an echo of events in Russia. The great wave of struggle known as the *biennio rosso* (two red years) in Italy had also been halted. In April 1920 the most advanced section of the working class, in the city of Turin, were left to fight alone by the reformist dominated Italian Socialist Party (PSI). In September, amid a growing wave of factory occupations, the PSI again stood by and allowed the revolutionary moment to pass. Victory in either Italy or Germany would have altered the balance of class forces across the whole of Europe. Defeat meant a shift in the interests of the old ruling classes.

This formed the context for the third congress of the Comintern in summer 1921. Already that year the gap between the strategic needs of the moment and the practices of the fledgling Communist Parties had been highlighted by events in Germany. Here the leadership of the party, ill-advised by impatient advisers from the half-formed international, misjudged the situation completely and tried to turn a localised strike movement into an unprepared and disastrous rising in March 1921. "The inevitable collapse of the adventure was followed by savage repression. The KPD [the

---

14:   Trotsky, 1977, p1130.
15:   Hallas, 1985, p33.

German Communist Party] was outlawed. Membership fell catastrophically to 150,000 or less and thousands of militants were imprisoned".[16]

Surveying the situation—and critical of the advice given to the German Communists—Lenin and Trotsky decided it was necessary to educate the Communist Parties in the art of retreat, and that the united front was the key tool for the task. This process began at the third congress and was continued through to the fourth, held in November and December 1922. Faced with the shift in the balance of class forces, workers could feel the urgency of demands for unity. The strategy of the united front, if correctly applied, could forge that unity, while simultaneously winning workers away from reformism and preparing for a new wave of struggle.

Trotsky spelt out most clearly what was required in his report "On the United Front", written in early 1922 and aimed at the French Communists:

> If the Communist Party had not broken drastically and irrevocably with the [reformist] social democrats, it would not have become the party of the proletarian revolution. It would have forever remained a parliamentary safety-valve attached to the bourgeois state. Whoever does not understand this, does not know the first letter of the ABC of Communism. If the Communist Party did not seek for organisational avenues to the end that at every given moment joint, coordinated action between the Communist and the non-Communist (including social democratic) working masses were made possible, it would have thereby laid bare its own incapacity to win over—on the basis of mass action—the majority of the working class. It would degenerate into a Communist propaganda society but never develop into a party for the conquest of power.
>
> It is not enough to possess the sword, one must give it an edge; it is not enough to give the sword an edge, one must know how to wield it. After separating the Communists from the reformists it is not enough to fuse the Communists together by means of organisational discipline; it is necessary that this organisation should learn how to guide all the collective activities of the proletariat in all spheres of its living struggle. This is the second letter of the alphabet of Communism.[17]

Separation of the revolutionaries from the reformists is merely the starting point. The revolutionaries must enter into struggle alongside

16: Hallas, 1985, p64.
17: Trotsky, 1974a, p93.

reformists in order to win a majority in the working class. But should the united front extend only to reformist workers, or should it include reformist leaders too? "The very posing of this question," argued Trotsky, "is a product of misunderstanding":

> If we were able simply to unite the working masses around our own banner or around our practical immediate slogans, and skip over reformist organisations, whether party or trade union, that would of course be the best thing in the world. But then the very question of the united front would not exist in its present form. The question arises from this, that certain very important sections of the working class belong to reformist organisations or support them. Their present experience is still insufficient to enable them to break with the reformist organisations and join us.[18]

The approach to the reformist leaders poses a dilemma for them. "The reformists dread the revolutionary potential of the mass movement; their beloved arena is the parliamentary tribune, the trade union bureaus, the arbitration boards, the ministerial ante-chambers".[19] This places revolutionaries at a distinct advantage if the reformists accept the appeal for unity, allowing them to win previously reformist workers towards revolution. But if the reformist leaders refuse unity it will expose those leaders' lack of seriousness in defending the interests of workers.

Finally, Trotsky warns the Communists:

> Any sort of organisational agreement which restricts our freedom of criticism and agitation is absolutely unacceptable to us. We participate in a united front but do not for a single moment become dissolved in it. We function in the united front as an independent detachment. It is precisely in the course of struggle that broad masses must learn from experience that we fight better than the others, that we see more clearly than the others, that we are more audacious and resolute.[20]

Experience of the united front

By 1922 the German Communist Party had begun to heal some of the wounds inflicted by the disastrous adventure of March 1921. The strategy

18: Trotsky, 1974a, pp93-94.
19: Trotsky, 1974a, p94.
20: Trotsky, 1974a, p96.

of the united front was key to the recovery. As Pierre Broué records in his monumental history of the German Revolution, during discussions between the reformist SPD and the Communist KPD "the SPD presented itself as the most obstinate in refusing joint activity, and the KPD as the most determined in seeking agreements".[21] While the appeals to the leadership of the reformist organisations met with resistance, they paid off in the workplace, where factory councils began to re-emerge as a powerful force in 1922. "By the autumn of 1922, the Communists had won sufficient influence in several thousand factory councils to be able to hold and politically dominate a national congress of the factory councils that November".[22] The Communists were also able to win influence during a railway strike in spring that year, during which the government sought to ban public sector strikes. The Communists appealed to the reformist parties and trade union federations to support action against the ban. The failure of the reformist organisations to support the action established the Communists as the most serious class fighters in the eyes of many workers.

The German Communists also pressed for united action on directly political issues, the most serious of which was the rise of the far right. On 24 June 1922 a government minister, Walter Rathenau, was assassinated by right wing former army officers:

> The murder produced a huge uprising of working class anger. The social democrats could no longer ignore the Communist calls for unity. All over Germany their members were marching alongside Communists against the far right. They would tear up their party cards unless their leaders made some gesture towards unity.[23]

For a while there was formal agreement between the SPD and the Communists to oppose the far right. Then, with the SPD rank and file appeased, the leadership broke off negotiations:

> The rebuff did not prevent the Communists again and again raising the question of united action—usually linking the question of self-defence against the far right with united action against inflation, demanding the seizure of industrial property by the state and under the control of factory councils.

21:   Broué, 2006, p607.
22:   Broué, 2006, pp609-610.
23:   Harman, 1997, p236.

The KPD's appeals were addressed to the leaders of the social democratic organisations, but they were intended also for the ears of the SPD rank and file. The Communist organisations in the localities set about drawing these into the joint activity that the SPD leaders refused.[24]

These tactics saw the German Communists grow by about 40,000 members from mid-1921 to late 1922 to reach a total of around 220,000. In the same period the SPD lost a similar number of members. But the lessons were learnt in a one-sided manner. The German Communists showed none of the tactical flexibility—the ability to read the mood of the masses and balance of class forces, and respond with appropriate changes of direction—that Lenin raised to the level of an art.[25] The leaders of the party had reacted violently against the ultraleft madness of the "March action", but now swung the other way, giving "the united front approach a distinctly rightist slant".[26]

The year 1923 saw an intense political crisis as French troops occupied the Rhineland, a deep economic crisis marked by unparalleled inflation and an upsurge in workers' struggles, giving new life to the factory councils, which formed an approximation to the Russian soviets. By June that year the Communists had gained a further 70,000 members through the united front approach, and managed to polarise the SPD into a left and a right wing. The situation was rapidly becoming revolutionary. But the Communist leadership was unable to shift from its defensive posture to begin to test the balance of forces by coordinating an offensive thrust. It was taken by surprise when a general strike, to a large extent led by Communist shop stewards, brought down the right wing Cuno government in August 1923. At that point they agreed in principle with the need to make a revolution, but had no sense of how to connect the day to day struggles of workers with the prospect of insurrection. What preparations happened were technical and military, rather than politically preparing workers for an uprising.

The pace of events was forced when General Müller moved against Saxony, where the militancy of the workers' movement had produced a government of the socialist left including revolutionary Communist ministers. The Communists relied on the leaders of the left of the SPD to

---

24:   Harman, 1997, p236.
25:   This flexibility in strategy and tactics is the main theme of Tony Cliff's, *Lenin: Building the Party* (1986), which is due to be reprinted later in 2008 and deserves to be read by a new generation of Marxists.
26:   Hallas, 1985, p91.

support a call for a new general strike, which everyone knew had insurrectionary implications. The left SPD leaders, still committed to reformism, refused to do so and the expected German-wide revolution was aborted. The German bourgeoisie seized the opportunity to restabilise its rule, even if only for a few years, and politics in Europe as a whole shifted further to the right.[27]

Gramsci and the united front

Against this background Antonio Gramsci, the most outstanding leader of the Italian Communist Party, sought to apply the idea of the united front in the Italian context. His *Lyons Theses*, written early in 1926, three and a half years after Mussolini's seizure of power, argued:

> With its strategy and tactics, the party "leads the working class"…the principle that the party leads the working class must not be interpreted in a mechanical manner. It is not necessary to believe that the party can lead the working class through an external imposition of authority…the capacity to lead the class is related, not only to the fact that the party "proclaims" itself its revolutionary organ, but to the fact that it "really" succeeds, as part of the working class, in linking itself with all the sections of that class… The "united front" of anti-fascist and anti-capitalist struggle which the communists are striving to create must aim at being an organised united front, ie at being based on bodies around which the masses as a whole can regroup and find a form… In Italy, the united front tactic must continue to be utilised by the party, insofar as it is still far from having won a decisive influence over the majority of the working class and the working population.[28]

There was little opportunity to put this into practice. By autumn that year Gramsci had been arrested. But the theme of the united front resonates through his famous *Prison Notebooks*. For instance, his concept of contradictory consciousness reflects this preoccupation:

> The active man-in-the-mass has a practical activity, but has no clear theoretical consciousness of his practical activity, which nonetheless involves understanding the world in so far as it transforms it. His theoretical consciousness can indeed be historically in opposition to his activity.

27:   For a detailed account of the "German October" see chapter 13 of Harman, 1997.
28:   Gramsci, 1990, pp367-373.

One might almost say that he has two theoretical consciousnesses (or one contradictory consciousness): one which is implicit in his activity and which in reality unites him with all his fellow workers in the practical transformation of the real world; and one, superficially explicit or verbal, which he has inherited from the past and uncritically absorbed.[29]

The working class have elements of passivity and acceptance of the status quo, but also elements of solidarity and struggle. The revolutionary party has to forge unity with workers, despite this contradictory consciousness, to draw out the positive element through "practical transformation of the real world".

Trotsky and resisting the Nazis

One very important by-product of the defeat of the revolutionary wave in Western Europe was the rise of Stalinism in an isolated Russia. That in turn led to the imposition on the Western Communist Parties of policies that bore little connection to the realities of the class struggle.[30] From 1928 to 1934 this meant the policies of the notorious "third period", involving the revival of the worst "ultra-left" positions. The Comintern executive decreed in July 1929, "In countries where there are strong social democratic parties, fascism assumes the particular form of 'social-fascism'".[31] Such an analysis led the German Communist leaders to make light of the real fascist threat of the Nazis, treating them as no greater a danger than the SPD. Communist militants did fight the Nazis heroically in cities such as Berlin, but their leaders' policies meant they did so in isolation from the wider working class movement.

Trotsky was almost as cut off from mass struggle as Gramsci, though through exile rather than imprisonment. Nonetheless he wrote a series of brilliant analyses of the struggles against fascism across Europe. Here are to be found some of his sharpest articles on the united front. With increasing urgency he attacked the notion that the social democrats were the main enemy:

Today the social democracy as a whole, with all its internal antagonisms, is forced into sharp conflict with the fascists. It is our task to take advantage of

---

29:   Quoted in Harman, 2007, pp109-110.
30:   For the degeneration of the Soviet Union see Binns, Cliff and Harman, 1987; Cliff, 1974. For the degeneration of the Comintern see Hallas, 1985, chapters 5, 6 and 7.
31:   Quoted in Hallas, 1985, p127.

this conflict and not to unite the antagonists against us. The front must now be directed against fascism... It is necessary to show by deeds a complete readiness to make a bloc with the social democrats against the fascists in all cases in which they will accept a bloc... The overwhelming majority of social democratic workers will fight against the fascists, but—for the present at least—only together with their organisations.[32]

The advice was ignored. In 1933 the Nazis took power, defeating the most powerful Communist Party in the world and exacting a terrible revenge on one of the most militant working classes in the world. The defeat had two causes: the social democratic leadership refused to fight and the Communists failed to force the SPD to form a bloc against the right. In the wake of the 1933 defeat the Communists did call, unsuccessfully, for a general strike. But for three years they had told workers that the SPD was the main enemy, and that the fascists were not a threat. Even now the Communists and the Comintern remained trapped in their theory. So after Hitler's seizure of power the Comintern leadership could still argue that the "current calm after the victory of fascism is temporary. Inevitably, despite the fascist terror, the revolutionary tide will grow".[33]

The popular front
If Germany showed the danger of not fighting for unity, the late 1930s would show a different danger—the wrong kind of unity. In 1934 the mood of Socialist and Communist militants, horrified by the victory of the Nazis in Germany the year before, forced their leaders into united action against attempts to bring far right governments to office in France and Spain. There were huge demonstrations on the streets of Paris in February and a rising in Asturias in Spain in October. But at this point a new line emerged from Stalin in Moscow, that of the "popular front". This meant Communists seeking alliances not just with the social democrats, but also with "liberal" mainstream capitalist parties. Any notion of political struggle was subordinated to Moscow's foreign policy goal—the formation of a military alliance with French imperialism, and hopefully British imperialism as well.

The French Communists now pressed for a "People's Front" to contest elections. This alliance did not simply include the working class parties; it also included the Radicals, a party of the bourgeoisie that straddled

---

32:   Trotsky, 1975, pp104-105.
33:   Quoted in Harman, 1989, p256.

the centre-right as well as the centre-left. Trotsky, with increasing urgency, argued that it was the Radicals who held the whip hand:

> The "People's Front" represents the coalition of the proletariat with the imperialist bourgeoisie, in the shape of the Radical Party and smaller tripe of the same sort... The majority of Radical voters do not participate in the struggle of the toilers and consequently in the People's Front. Yet the Radical Party occupies in this front not only an equal but a privileged position; the workers' parties are compelled to restrict their activity to the programme of the Radical Party.[34]

The popular front was popular, precisely because it drew on the thirst for unity against the growing threat of the right. It won the elections in June 1936 overwhelmingly and the social democrat leader, Leon Blum, formed a government. There were no Communist ministers in the government; the Communist Party accepted its exclusion for fear of scaring the French ruling class.

The limitations of the popular front soon became evident. The election was followed by a sharp upturn in class struggle in France. There was an explosion of strikes and occupations, involving more than six million workers. Trotsky, in exile in Norway, was inspired to write an essay entitled "The French Revolution has Begun".[35] The ruling class was forced to make concessions to maintain control, but this alone was not enough. Blum put pressure on Maurice Thorez, leader of the rapidly expanding Communist Party, to end the strike. The Communists' "new authority was used not to develop, but to end the movement. 'It is necessary to know when to end a strike,' declared Thorez".[36]

The squandered opportunity led to further moves to the right, with the Communists calling for the transition from a "People's Front" to a French Front, including right wing nationalists. The Communists backed a succession of increasingly conservative governments as the workers' movement went into decline, until deputies elected on the popular front ticket voted to ban the party. Finally in June 1940 parliament, with a popular front majority, voted "to install the quasi-fascist regime of Pétain and Laval".[37] There was a similar pattern of popular front, concessions to the

---

34:   Trotsky, 1974b, pp99-100.
35:   Trotsky, 1974c.
36:   Hallas, 1985, p146.
37:   Hallas, 1985, p147.

right and defeat in even more dramatic circumstances in the Spanish Civil War.[38] In both cases the Communists under Moscow's influence had tied the fate of workers to sections of the ruling class, allowing revolutionary moments and mass struggles to burn out, and the right to triumph.

Reviving the united front

As it grew into a serious, if small, revolutionary organisation in the early 1970s, the International Socialists in Britain, forerunner of the Socialist Workers Party, sought to apply the legacy of the Comintern before its corruption by Stalinism. Duncan Hallas, writing in this journal as the Wilson government of the mid-1970s presided over a sharp rise in unemployment, cuts in real wages and attacks on the welfare state, spelt out the need for a united front of opposition: "All these bring to the fore the problem of left wing unity to defeat the developing right wing offensive." Possible allies in this united front included "the Labour left wing, the remaining trade union lefts, the Communist Party and the revolutionary left".

He also spelt out what the united front *wasn't*:

> It is not a substitute for a revolutionary party. The united front tactic can never, under any circumstances, mean the subordination of revolutionary politics and organisation to reformist politics and organisation. It presupposes the existence and independence of a revolutionary *force*. The bigger that force, the greater the united front possibilities. It is not a "let's forget our differences and unite" approach. On the contrary; the united front tactic always and inevitably involves a political struggle to *compel* reformists and centrists to live up to their own pretensions, to break some of their ties with the capitalist establishment (both direct and through the trade union bureaucracy) and to engage in a *fight*, alongside revolutionaries, for objectives they themselves profess to support. It is not a union of revolutionary groups. The whole point is to involve workers and workers' organisations who accept the immediate objectives but not, at present, revolutionary politics as a whole.[39]

It is this method of pushing for unity that underlay the approach of the Socialist Workers Party to the Anti Nazi League, the miners' support

---

38: For the story of the Spanish Popular Front, see Durgan, 2007, and Hallas, 1985, pp148-155.
39: Hallas, 1976.

groups and, more recently, the Stop the War Coalition. In each case it meant a preparedness to work with leading figures in reformist organisations and tendencies. But it also meant maintaining our own arguments, our own capacity to agitate independently, and our own press and organisation. That is the approach we put forward today in relation to Respect and to other united fronts such as Unite Against Fascism and Defend Council Housing.[40]

40:    For more on Respect and the Socialist Alliance that preceded it as applications of the united front strategy, see Chris Harman's article in this journal; Rees, 2001; and Rees 2002.

References

Binns, Peter, Tony Cliff and Chris Harman, 1987, *From Workers' State to State Capitalism* (Bookmarks).

Bone, Ann (translator), *The Bolsheviks and the October Revolution: Central Committee Minutes of the Russian Social Democratic Labour Party (Bolsheviks) August 1917-February 1918* (Pluto).

Broué, Pierre, 2006, *The German Revolution 1917-1923* (Merlin).

Cliff, Tony, 1974, *State Capitalism in Russia* (Pluto), www.marxists.org/archive/cliff/works/1955/statecap/

Cliff, Tony, 1986 [1975], *Lenin: Building the Party* (Bookmarks).

Durgan, Andy, 2007, *The Spanish Civil War* (Palgrave).

Gramsci, Antonio, 1990, *Selections from Political Writings 1921-1926* (University of Minnesota), www.marxists.org/archive/gramsci/spw2-contents.htm

Hallas, Duncan, 1976, "On the United Front", *International Socialism* (first series), number 85, January 1976, www.marxists.org/archive/hallas/works/1976/01/unitedfront.htm

Hallas, Duncan, 1985, *The Comintern* (Bookmarks), www.marxists.org/archive/hallas/works/1985/comintern/

Harman, Chris, 1989, introduction to part four of *Fascism, Stalinism and the United Front* (Bookmarks).

Harman, Chris, 1997, *The Lost Revolution: Germany 1918-1923* (Bookmarks).

Harman, Chris, 2007, "Gramsci, the Prison Notebooks and Philosophy", *International Socialism* 114 (spring 2007), www.isj.org.uk/index.php4?id=308

Marx, Karl, and Frederick Engels, 1977a [1848], *The Communist Manifesto*, in David McLellan (ed), *Karl Marx Selected Writings* (Oxford University), www.marxists.org/archive/marx/works/1848/communist-manifesto/

Marx, Karl, and Frederick Engels, 1977b [1879], "Circular Letter to the Leaders of the SPD", in David McLellan (ed), *Karl Marx Selected Writings* (Oxford University), www.marxists.org/archive/marx/works/1879/09/18.htm

Molyneux, John, 1978, *Marxism and the Party* (Pluto).

Rees, John, 2001, "Anti-capitalism, Reformism and Socialism", *International Socialism* 90 (spring 2001), http://pubs.socialistreviewindex.org.uk/isj90/rees.htm

Rees, John, 2002, "The Broad Party, the Revolutionary Party and the United Front", *International Socialism* 97 (winter 2002), http://pubs.socialistreviewindex.org.uk/isj97/rees.htm

Trotsky, Leon, 1974a [1924], *The First Five Years of the Communist International*, volume two (New Park), www.marxists.org/archive/trotsky/1924/ffyci-2/

Trotsky, Leon, 1974b [1935], "Committees of Action—not People's Front", in *Whither France?* (New Park), www.marxists.org/archive/trotsky/1936/whitherfrance/ch03.htm

Trotsky, Leon, 1974c [1936], "The French Revolution has Begun", in *Whither France?* (New Park), www.marxists.org/archive/trotsky/1936/whitherfrance/ch03c.htm

Trotsky, Leon, 1975, *The Struggle Against Fascism in Germany* (Pelican).

Trotsky, Leon, 1977 [1930], *The History of the Russian Revolution* (Pluto), www.marxists.org/archive/trotsky/1930/hrr/

Trotsky, Leon, 1989 [1931], "What next? Vital Questions for the German Proletariat", in *Fascism, Stalinism and the United Front* (Bookmarks), www.marxists.org/archive/trotsky/germany/1932-ger/

Slums, resistance and the African working class

Leo Zeilig and Claire Ceruti

M ike Davis's book *Planet of Slums* provides a brilliant account of the rapid growth of urban areas and megaslums, created by the hammer blows of the global restructuring of the world system since the 1970s.

Though Davis's principle arguments concern the extraordinary growth of "megacities", he also raises vital questions about the role of the working class in a world transformed by "market reforms" since the mid-1970s.[1] This article focuses on some of Davis's claims about the working class, and concentrates exclusively on the situation in sub-Saharan Africa. There are two important reasons for this. One is that Structural Adjustment Programmes (SAPs), implemented across the developing world, have had their most devastating effect here. The other is that Davis's assertion that, with the growth of the African slum, "myriad groups" of the informalised poor have dislodged the African working class is open to doubt.

Davis's argument

Africa has seen the "supernova growth of a few cities like Lagos (from 300,000 in 1950 to 13.5 today)" and "the transformation of several small towns and oases like Ouagadougou, Nouakchott, Douala, Kampala…and Bamako into sprawling cities larger than San Francisco or Manchester".[2] As

---

1: Davis, 2006, p7.
2: Davis, 2006, p8.

cities stretch out to include small towns and previously rural villages, we are confronted with "the emergence of polycentric urban systems without clear rural/urban boundaries". [3]

Historically, Davis argues, the movement to urban centres was meant to reflect the growth of manufacturing and the concomitant increase of wage labour—Marx's industrial proletariat. This development was also meant to see a growth in agricultural productivity to feed swelling cities through the application of large-scale modern farming techniques. But the opposite has occurred. "Urbanisation without industrialisation is an expression of an inexorable trend: the inherent tendency of silicon capitalism to delink the growth of production from that of employment". [4] The culprit, Davis explains, is the twin evils of the 1970s debt crisis, and the IMF and World Bank's restructuring of Third World economies. So today urbanisation becomes synonymous with falling wages, factory closure and massive unemployment.

Davis asks, "How has Africa as a whole, currently in a dark age of stagnant urban employment and stalled agricultural productivity, been able to sustain an annual urbanisation rate (3.5 to 4 percent) considerably higher than the average of most European cities (2.1 percent) during the peak Victorian growth years"? [5] Though cities are no longer hubs of formal employment, under the pressures of IMF and World Bank enforced agricultural deregulation millions flee rural poverty for urban slums. In Kenya, for example, 85 percent of the population growth in the ten years after 1989 was soaked up in the slums of Nairobi and Mombasa. Some sub-Saharan African countries have literally been turned into mass slums. In 2003, 99.4 percent of the population were "slum-dwellers" in Chad and Ethiopia.

While the poor have been consigned to the global slum, the wealthy have built fences and gun towers around their neighbourhoods. There are almost 300,000 registered private security guards defending these gated compounds and approximately 2,500 private security firms in South Africa alone. [6]

In tandem with the growth of the megaslum has been the collapse of formal employment, which Davis blames on "a new wave of SAPs and self-imposed neoliberal programmes", which have "accelerated the demolition of state employment". [7] While salaries of the jobs that have remained in

---

3:    Davis, 2006, p10.
4:    Davis, 2006, p14.
5:    Davis, 2006, p15.
6:    "We Guard Millions, But Are Paid Peanuts", *Green Left Weekly*, April 2006.
7:    Davis, 2006, p163.

the formal sector have shrunk almost to invisibility, there has been a massive growth of informal work. This is work that lives outside the factory and office, and might involve people trying to survive by selling vegetables in markets or CDs to passing motorists. Since 1980, says Davis, "economic informality has returned with a vengeance, and the equation of urban and occupational marginality has become irrefutable and overwhelming: informal workers, according to the United Nations, constitute about two thirds of the economically active population of the developing world".[8]

Slums, in Davis's account, symbolise the total reconstitution of class structures in the Third World. Unemployed slum-dwellers are not the urban proletarian powering political transformation. At the end of *Planet of Slums* we are left with a question: "To what extent does an informal proletariat possess that most potent of Marxist talismans: 'historical agency'?"[9] But to what extent, in the picture drawn by Davis, are they a "proletariat" at all? In the world of neoliberal slums there is "no monolithic subject", but "myriad acts of resistance", that emerge from a chaotic plurality of "charismatic churches and prophetic cults to ethnic militias, street gangs, neoliberal NGOs and revolutionary social movements".[10]

What's going on?

Traditionally the African working class has been a small proportion of the global proletariat. So, in 1995, 40 percent of the world's estimated 270 million industrial workers were found in OECD countries, but only 5 percent in Africa.[11] But even these figures, more than ten years old, exaggerate the global share of industrial workers on the continent. Though there has been a global increase in wage labour, with the restructuring of production there has also been an explosion of unemployment. Chris Harman describes this unevenness: in "most regions (although not in most of Africa) there is also a growth of the number involved in wage labour of a relatively productive sort in medium to large workplaces. But even more rapid is the expansion of the vast mass of people precariously trying to make a livelihood through casual labour".[12]

In Africa there has been a dramatic "informalisation" from the 1970s, exacerbated by the unravelling of the corporatist state—often triggered by IMF-led SAPs. Ten years of these programmes meant that by 1991 a

8:    Davis, 2006, p176.
9:    Davis, 2006, p201.
10:   Davis, 2006, p201.
11:   Quoted in Harman, 2002, p23.
12:   Harman, 2002, p25.

number of African countries saw a fall in formal wage employment: an estimated 33 percent in the Central African Republic, 27 percent in Gambia, 13.4 in Niger and 8.5 percent in Zaire (today's DRC). In the same period the government in Zimbabwe pursued policies involving privatisation and the closure of state companies deemed unprofitable by Western donors, the IMF and the World Bank. More than 20,000 jobs were lost between January 1991 and July 1993. In 1993 unemployment had reached a record 1.3 million from a total population of about ten million. Tor Skalnes reported 25,000 civil service jobs lost by 1995, while "inflation rose and exports declined".[13]

In South Africa, the "success" story of the continent, official unemployment was 16 percent in 1995 and rose to 31.2 percent in 2003, but if those who have given up the hunt for work are included the figure rises to 42 percent. Formal employment collapsed in many "traditional" sectors. During the 1990s the number of jobs contracted 47 percent in mining, 20 percent in manufacturing and 10 percent in the public sector.[14]

One graphic example of deindustrialisation elsewhere on the continent is the textiles and clothing industry. Much of the original growth in this sector in the 1960s and 1970s was a result of governmental policies of producing local substitutes for previously imported goods. Textiles and clothing expanded until the sector comprised between 25 and 30 percent of those formally employed. When the World Bank and IMF insisted that governments "open" their economies to foreign imports, the resulting job losses were devastating. In Ghana in the late 1970s the industry employed 25,000 people; by 2000 only 5,000 were employed. A similar picture emerges in Zambia, where only 10,000 worked in the sector in 2002, down from 25,000 or more in the early 1980s.[15]

When the Kenyan economy was prized open in the 1990s, new and secondhand clothes (*mitumba*) from the US and the EU, together with the increases in the cost of electricity, made it almost impossible for Kenyan manufacturers to function. An industry that had been relatively healthy in the 1980s, employing approximately 200,000, almost collapsed. Approximately 70,000 factory and mill jobs disappeared. By 2004 fewer than 35,000 people were employed in Kenya's clothing export sector.[16]

The growth of the informal sector has been a direct result of the

---

13:   Zeilig, 2007, p107.
14:   Quoted in Bond and Desai, 2006, p239.
15:   Quartey, 2006, p136.
16:   Otieno, 2006, p19.

collapse of traditional industries. Whether this has led to the collapse of previously solid class identities or to their reformulation is open to question. But where the working class does exist it has played a cohesive role in relation to the "myriad" groups fighting neoliberalism. It is not the case that the formally employed are cut off from informal workers by their "privilege", or that they live in "formal housing" away from the mass of slum-dwellers.

There has been a long academic debate about the nature, and even existence, of an African working class. Even the left wing scholar Basil Davidson, who spent a lifetime defending progressive social movements on the continent, could write dismissively that the working class was unable "to achieve the solidarity and coherence that could have moved them towards empowering socialist political movements".[17] Ruth First argued that African patterns of development had created a hybrid class (the "peasantariat"), founded on a linked rural and urban identity.[18]

At times Davis's slightly apocalyptic account repeats this questioning of the capacity of a Third World, or African working class, to play its "historical role". It may have done so in the past, but now, under the impact of neoliberalism, it is once again a hybrid slum-dweller, unable to lead new social movements on the continent. Yet actual class reconfiguration does not suggest a working class entirely dislodged from its "historical agency".

The case of Soweto

Davis's account is problematic as Africa is not, uniquely or universally, a space of undifferentiated deindustrialisation where the working class has been uprooted from formal employment. To take one example, Davis writes about Soweto's "backyards" and how "residents have illegally constructed shacks that are rented to younger families or single adults".[19] Soweto is South Africa's largest township, home to an estimated two million residents, twice the number of those recorded in a survey eight years ago.[20] It is a place of phenomenal diversity, including wealthy suburbs serviced by modern shopping malls and a golf course, as well as "respectable" working class communities in modest apartheid-era housing. These areas sit cheek

---

17:   Davidson, 1992, pp232-233.
18:   A combination of rural and urban certainly played a part in the formation of the working class in most parts of Africa in the 19th and 20th centuries—from migrant labour in the mines in southern Africa from the 1900s, to labour in oil extraction and processing in the Niger Delta from the 1970s. See Iliffe, 1983.
19:   Davis, 2006, pp44-45.
20:   See Morris, 1999.

by jowl with squatter camps and informal settlements that seem to exemplify Davis's descriptions of Southern slums.

But recent research conducted by the Centre for Sociological Research (CRS) in Johannesburg suggests a reality quite different from the fashionable view that unemployment in South Africa has "polarised the labour market by increasing the resources to some of the 6.6 million in the core who are formal, permanent workers while at the same time reducing the resources" to the rest.[21] The research suggests far more fluidity between the "core" of 6.6 million and the rest. In a Soweto-wide survey of more than 3,000 people in 2006, respondents were asked to describe their lives.[22]

The pie-chart (figure 1) presents a picture of life ravaged by unemployment in Soweto. Some 50.1 percent of the respondents in the survey were not in formal employment. This requires some explanation. "Partial workers" are people who explained that they did not work but occasionally did piecework, while "fill-ins" were those who were engaged in small businesses, similar to the "petty bourgeoisie", but they explained that they would accept work if they were offered. These "businesses"—in the much celebrated "entrepreneurial" world of the new South Africa—might be hawking sunglasses or bootleg videos by the side of the road, or perhaps more often in Soweto selling a few fruit and vegetables on the pavement. None of these people, a full 26 percent, are counted in the official unemployment statistics. These figures present a devastating verdict on the laisser-faire policies of both Nelson Mandela and Thabo Mbeki's governments.

But do these statistics imply that mass unemployment has created a new class of the wageless poor excluded from the world of work, with the working class now a small and privileged group living outside the township-slum whose interests are separate from the majority of the urban poor? A closer look reveals something quite different. If we examine the Sowetan household we see an extraordinary mixing up of the different and seemingly divided groups of the poor. For example, in only 14.3 percent of households were there no employed people. This means that less than a sixth of households were entirely unemployed or self-employed. We can go even further. In 78.3 percent of households there was a mix of adults who were employed, self-employed and unemployed. There is no impenetrable wall between work and unemployment, as the "poor" and "middle class" live side by side, as family members and friends. Poverty and relative prosperity are connected in the household.

21:    Quoted in Ceruti, 2007, p22.
22:    *Classifying Soweto*, research conducted by the CRS, Johannesburg, South Africa.

Figure 1: Soweto's labour force
Produced by CSR, November 2007

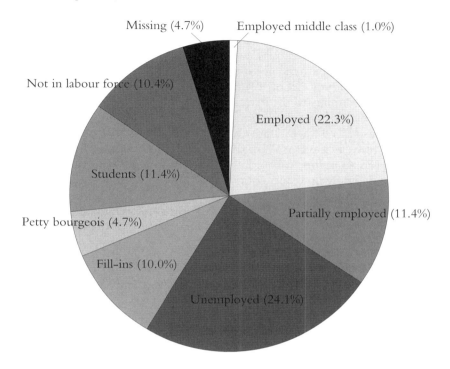

What does this mean in terms of people's lives? To take one case study, "Mr Khumalo…was a teacher and now works as a driver. He lives with his wife, who is a nurse, and his three children. One child is at university. He supports his brother and his sister. His brother has been unemployed for two years after the factory closed." Mr Khumalo described himself as "working class…trying to push to be middle class". The employed and the unemployed are integrated at the level of the household. "These stories show that the polarisation of the labour market, far from making the stable employed into a privileged layer, may have the reverse effect of increasing the responsibilities on their wages".[23] The effect is to destabilise the formally employed.

23:   Ceruti, 2007, pp22-23.

Soweto is also an extraordinarily mixed urban space. The majority of people do not live in shacks. The table below (figure 2) shows the spread of housing types across Soweto. Some 75.7 percent live in a range of formal housing, from council housing to recently built government housing. But there is still a chronic shortage of housing in Soweto. A shocking 23.7 percent of people live in "informal" shacks, hostels or "backrooms" (often corrugated iron extensions tacked onto the side of brick houses). In addition, new housing has simply not been built since 1994 in anything like the quantities required (or promised). According to the statistics below, RDP houses, as this housing shock is popularly labelled (known after the Reconstruction and Development Programme introduced briefly after 1994), account for only 4.2 percent of the total housing types in Soweto. This also reflects the fact that most RDP houses are built outside township boundaries, and not in spaces where people need them—close to family networks, work opportunities and facilities. Although the unemployed, partial workers and fill-ins are more likely to be found in the shacks and slums of Soweto, people from each group are found in all housing types (with the exception of hostels). This is not a picture of an informal proletariat living exclusively, or even mainly, in shacks and slums.

Figure 2: What kind of houses do people live in?
Produced by the CSR, November 2007

Housing type	Percent
Unrenovated council house	34.8
Renovated council house	19.9
Council house with major rebuild or extension	6.1
Bond house	10.7
RDP house	4.2
Backyard shack	6.9
Backyard room	6.3
Other shack/mkhukhu	7.6
Hostel	2.9
Brick house	0.4
Other	0.4

Put simply, and limited to Soweto, these figures tell us that the jobless and formally employed are not hermetically sealed off from each other, in terms of either the household or neighbourhood. Nor are they clustered in the "informal" slum settlements of Soweto. The graph below (figure 3) shows that employed and partial workers also live in shacks, though in smaller numbers than the self-employed, while the majority of the self-employed, like the majority in all these categories, live in a brick house of some kind.

There is, in addition, an important level of complexity to the concepts of unemployment and informality. In Soweto there are several distinct categories among the labour force included under the umbrella of "informality". So the unemployed are those completely out of work, who do not vend, sell or "fill in" on temporary jobs, and this group was 21.92 percent of the population; "partial workers" are those who do occasional piece-work and may work full time for a week or a month *interspersed with periods of unemployment*. This means that Davis's wageless informal proletariat, made up of those who struggle precariously as vendors and in small businesses, resemble the "fill-ins" and the "petty bourgeoisie", who make up a mere 14.65 percent of the total labour force.

This is not to deny that the effects of unemployment have had a dramatic and devastating effect on the poor. The implication from the survey is that almost all families have been shaken by the hurricane of job losses. This has important consequences for social unrest. If there is no clear divide in the world of unemployment, informal work and formal employment, the potential for a crossover of protests exists. The explosion of "service delivery" uprisings in South Africa over the past four years has seen communities erupt in riots and protests against the lack of basic services. In 2005, for example, there were 881 recorded protests.[24] Though the number of protests may have dropped off from this high point, the levels remain impressive. The public sector general strike in June 2007 was the largest strike since the end of apartheid, pulling many people into trade union action for the first time. The potential cross-fertilisation of these struggles—of community and workplace—does not live only in the mind of activists, but, as the survey suggests, expresses the real household economy of contemporary South Africa.

Soweto seems to point to a confused reality. The South African township and slum might be viewed as a meeting point for trade unionists, university students, graduates, the unemployed and informal traders. Though the spectre of unemployment affects all layers of society, these

24:    Quoted in Ceruti, 2007, p20.

Figure 3: Where do different sections of Soweto's labour force live?

Graph produced by the CSR, November 2007

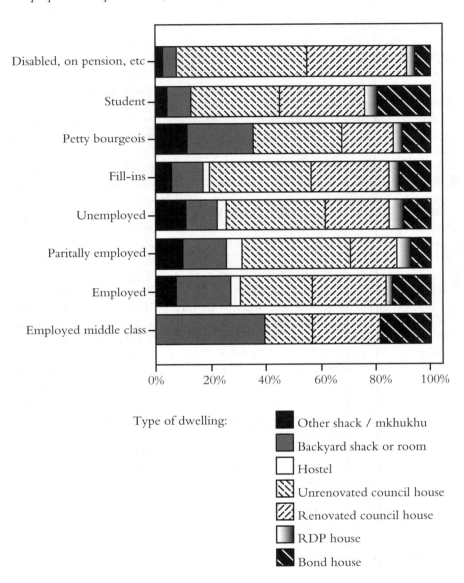

Type of dwelling:

- ■ Other shack / mkhukhu
- ■ Backyard shack or room
- □ Hostel
- ▨ Unrenovated council house
- ▨ Renovated council house
- ▨ RDP house
- ◪ Bond house

groups are not permanently cut off from each other and can be found in the same household supporting each other. Though we can not easily generalise from the experience of Soweto, there seems a reasonable chance that the mix of the formally and informally employed at the level of the household, and their intermingling fates, in diverse urban spaces could also be found in other Southern cities.

Femi Aborisade also sees an inclusive process at work. Even where the household combination of formal and informal employment is absent, "others have come to realise that the lot of the workers determines their own lot and that indeed they have a common interest. When workers are not paid or are poorly paid the poor peasant farmers and the poor petty traders (mainly women) know from their own experiences that their sales suffer. In an age of increasing unemployment, there are several dependants on the worker, and they have come to appreciate that their interests and that of the worker (who sustains their survival) are the same".[25] These relationships perpetuate cultural diversity within class formations, where a dual consciousness may exist among people who have maintained a relationship (and social rules) from their rural world.

Wage labour and neoliberalism

The current wave of global restructuring has devastated the continent with dramatic unevenness. Davis's picture of Africa's "dark age" of deindustrialisation and agricultural stagnation cannot be simply replicated across the continent. Davis presents Kinshasa (capital of the DRC) as an apocalyptic vision of the future city-slum made up of an almost entirely informalised population. But the particular circumstances in the DRC—including war waged almost without end since 1998—will not be easily reproduced in Africa (and even less so across the developing world). While there are important areas of near complete collapse, in other parts of the continent there has been the important growth of wage labour recently, linked to the global commodity boom.[26] These processes of capitalist growth on the continent are inherently contradictory, uneven and temporary—if that boom blows, so can those jobs. The memory of the last collapse in formal employment and the reality of mass unemployment weigh heavily on the minds of those urban workers. While this insecure world of wage labour helps determine (and discipline) their behaviour, there is no question that the African proletariat exists.

25: Quoted in Zeilig, 2002, p96.
26: See Renton, Seddon and Zeilig, 2007.

Capitalism consigns huge numbers of the population to idleness, but it can pull many of these people back into wage labour when there is expansion. In limited, though significant, areas on the continent this has been the recent experience. The constant ebb and flow into the labour force has become one of the permanent features of wage labour under neoliberal capitalism. What this suggests is that there are many people outside of the formally employed who have some experience of a workplace, however irregularly. This contact with wage-labour will affect their understanding of solidarity and the "class struggle". The same could also be said for those retrenched in the jobs massacres over the past decade.

Though the rapid deindustrialisation of Africa is indisputable, recent countervailing tendencies have seen the development of certain industries and the creation of jobs in areas previously decimated by the economic crisis. In recent years there has been an impressive recovery of many of the jobs lost in the textiles and clothing sector discussed above. Take Lesotho, where most formal sector jobs are in the rag trade. In 2006 Hong Kong and Taiwanese textiles firms in the country repackaged themselves as "ethical" manufacturers for a US market; thousands of jobs were created.[27] Though approximately 5,000 jobs were lost in the clothing sector in Madagascar in 2005, new markets were found and the sector was expected to grow through 2007-8.[28] Nor is job growth only found in the textile industry.

The new scramble for Africa has seen renewed interest in the continent's oil reserves and minerals, which has also had the effect of creating employment in extractive industries. One notable actor in these developments is China, whose role on the continent has received substantial, if inaccurate, discussion.[29] Chinese investment on the continent has grown by giant steps. The volume of trade has increased from $3 billion in 1995 to $55 billion in 2006. Though this figure amounts to only 10 percent of Africa's total trade (compared to 32 percent with the EU and 18 percent with the US), it is projected to keep growing to $100 billion by 2010.[30]

Chinese involvement in African mining has seen previously abandoned mines reopened. Though the Chambishi copper mine was the site of the worse mining disaster in Zambian history in 2005, when 52 workers were killed, it also represents an area of formal sector expansion. When the mine was purchased by a Chinese state-owned enterprise in 1998,

27:   "Textiles No Longer Hanging By A Thread", *IRIN*, 3 July 2006.
28:   See "Madagascar: Outlook For 2007-08: Economic Growth", the *Economist* Intelligence Unit, 7 March 2007.
29:   But see Sautman and Hairong, forthcoming 2008.
30:   See Sautman and Hairong, forthcoming 2007.

employment was boosted to 2,200 from 100.[31] However, in the new privatised world of contemporary Zambia nothing is the same. Formal jobs rarely return in the same shape, and few of the miners who are now employed in the reopened Zambian copper mines have pensionable contracts, a situation that contrasts dramatically with the previous practices.[32] Today mining communities have been ravaged by HIV/Aids, and little exists in the way of healthcare. Housing that was provided for miners does not exist on any meaningful scale, and townships, where most workers now live, are without proper services. The effect of years of privatisation has also meant that the partial "recovery" has not benefited the national state. So when copper was $2,280 a ton in 1992 the state-owned mining sector earned the Zambian government $200 million from 400,000 tons of production. In 2004 at similar production levels but with copper selling at an increased price of $2,868, only $8 million was provided by private mines to the state treasury.[33] There is no more eloquent example of the catastrophic effect of privatisation on the continent.

Other jobs have been created in diverse sectors and countries from the investment of Chinese money across the continent. A private Chinese conglomerate in Nigeria involved in manufacturing, construction and other projects has 20,000 employees. State-owned Chinese firms in Nigeria have created 1,000 to 2,000 workers making shoes and textiles, while the Urifiki Textile Mill in Tanzania, another Chinese state-owned factory, has 2,000 workers. The controversy surrounding the involvement of the China National Petroleum Company in Sudan does not interest us here, but its claims of job creation do. The company has made the bellicose assertion that it has provided jobs for "more than 100,000 Sudanese while contributing to other employment sectors as the oil industry has grown".[34] Even with the obvious exaggerations these are significant figures.

None of this evidence is presented to suggest that Africa's contemporary economic position is positive. On the contrary, the continent remains an overwhelmingly marginal recipient of the flows of Foreign Direct Investment, and many regions remain economically devastated. The effect of almost 30 years of IMF and World Bank led structural adjustment has created bomb-craters of destruction across the continent that cannot be easily filled. But the picture is not one of Davis's universal collapse and

---

31:   Christian Aid, 2007, p21.
32:   See Larmer, 2006.
33:   Christian Aid, 2007, p22.
34:   Quoted in Sautman and Hairong, forthcoming 2008.

near-apocalypse. The continent has seen economic growth and job creation, and will continue to do so—even if the growth remains uneven and inherently parasitical.

Recomposition of class and protest

The recomposition of class is undeniable, but it has not always led to a weakening of solidarity or the "class struggle". In the late 1970s the global crisis meant that loans turned into debts and national adjustment, and restructuring became a requirement for further loans. More and more African states saw their macroeconomic policies shaped by the conditions imposed by IMF and World Bank boffins. The result was an epoch of social unrest that Davis describes.[35]

This started in Egypt in 1977, when the government's decision to raise food and petrol prices as part of a programme of financial stringency under the auspices of the IMF provoked fierce rioting in major cities across the country. As has been described by David Seddon and John Walton, the first wave of struggle was based on wide coalitions of the popular forces, though the working class was usually centrally involved through the trade union movement.[36] The impact of unrest depended on the participation of the wider groups, including the lumpen-proletariat of the slum, unemployed youth, elements of the new petty bourgeoisie and university students. Directed predominantly towards current economic reforms and austerity measures, they also contained elements of a critique of regime legitimacy and deployed notions of social justice. In most cases they served to redefine the terrain of struggle and to provide the basis for the emergence at a later stage of political movements aimed at changing governments rather than just policies. The point to highlight is that these protests involved a frequently very well organised and formally employed working class.

A second wave of protests broke out at the start of the 1990s. This wave of popular protest, now more explicitly political and with more far-reaching aims and objectives, spread across the continent like a political typhoon. From 1989 protests rose massively across sub-Saharan Africa. There had been approximately 20 annually recorded incidents of political unrest in the 1980s; in 1991 alone 86 major protest movements took place across 30 countries. By 1992 many African governments had been forced to introduce reforms and, in 1993, 14 countries held democratic elections. In a four-year period from the start of the protests in 1990 a total of 35 regimes

---

35: Davis, 2006, p161.
36: Walton and Seddon, 1994.

had been swept away by protest movements and strikes, and in elections that were often held for the first time in a generation.[37]

Again these revolts are not only meaningful as new forms of "post-formal" resistance, but equally as ones often led by a formally employed working class. The social chaos that had been whipped up by the structural adjustment storm did bring new political forces into play, but they did not displace trade union organisation. On the contrary, it was more often than not unions—together with and frequently "leading" a variety of other forces—which forced regimes onto the defensive in Burkina Faso, Burundi, Cameroon, the Central African Republic, Chad, Comoros, Congo, Côte d'Ivoire, Gabon, Ghana, Guinea, Kenya, Lesotho, Madagascar, Mali, Mauritania, Nigeria, Swaziland and Zaire. Even when governments were not replaced, the pattern was similar across the continent, and trade unions, according to John Wiseman, "sought not simply to protect the work-place interests of their members but have endeavoured to bring about a restructuring of the political system".[38] During this second wave of protests in the 1990s trade union movements displayed greater independence and militancy than at any time in their history on the continent, and they did all of this in a world transformed by neoliberalism. Even in Kinshasa, the capital of Congo-Zaire that Davis privileges in his account as typical of life in the city-slum, the early 1990s saw a political movement heavily influenced by trade unions that threatened to remove Mobutu in what has been described as the Congo's "second revolution".[39]

Nowhere on the continent were these transformations clearer than in the struggles that shook Zimbabwe from 1996. Initially the struggle was expressed in strike action and spread from workplace to student protests and community struggles. Public sector strikes were punctuated by "bread riots", as poor neighbourhoods near Harare exploded in rioting in January 1998, while students fought against the privatisation of catering facilities. All these elements combined with a growth in political demands. The disparate voices coalesced around the central, indeed leading, role played by the Zimbabwe Congress of Trade Unions (ZCTU). In many ways this typified Davis's characteristion of "myriad acts of resistance"—but with a working class (often deindustrialised and weakened) still playing a central role.

The struggle formed the backdrop for the formation of the Movement for Democratic Change (MDC) which almost toppled the

---

37:   Zeilig and Seddon, 2002, p16.
38:   Wiseman, 1996, p49.
39:   See Renton, Seddon and Zeilig, 2007.

regime in elections in 2000. The case is put most forcefully by the former student leader at the University of Zimbabwe, Brian Kagoro, referring to a period of activism in the mid-1990s:

> So you now had students supporting their parents on their student stipends which were not enough, because their parents had been laid off work. So in a sense as poverty increases you have a reconvergence of these forces. And the critique started...around issues of social economic justice, [the] right to a living wage...students started couching their demands around a right to livelihood.[40]

Myriad forces converged across numerous countries, and spoke of both the devastation of structural adjustment but also the explosive consequences of this destruction. Groups previously separated from each other found that solidarity was an instinct born of common experiences. Students no longer simply dipped into the social world outside their campus, as they passed through university in transition to formal sector employment. Along with other groups also once conceived as privileged (teachers, civil servants and "professionals"), students became an intimate part of the urban poor and unemployed. As early as 1994 Mahmood Mamdani wrote that "previously a more or less guaranteed route to position and privilege, higher education seemed to lead more and more students to the heart of the economic and social crisis".[41]

Pauperisation across the whole continent has been "the heavy artillery with which it batters down all Chinese walls" between different social groups.[42] But it has not triggered the total informalisation of the African proletariat, which still exists and still has the potential to lead movements for social transformation.

Contemporary social movements bring together heterogeneous groups that relate to a formally constituted working class. However, these movements—and the processes of class formation—can only be fully understood in the context of popular struggles, and the actual moments of protest and resistance. The answer to Davis's brilliant, though gloomy, account is in the real course of events. As Alex Callinicos puts it, commenting on a series of strikes in Africa, "Sub-Saharan Africa...is host to many great slum settlements—but is also the site of a series of major

---

40:   Interview with Brian Kagoro, 23 June 2003, Harare, Zimbabwe.
41:   Mamdani, 1994, pp258-9.
42:   Marx and Engels, 2003, p8.

mass strikes. This year started with a general strike in Guinea-Conakry...
South Africa and Nigeria, have been hit by major strikes...these struggles...confirm that the organised working class is a powerful social and
political actor in Africa".[43]

The dynamic reality of class struggle on the continent reveals a
working class, albeit reformulated, playing a central role both in the movements for democratic change and in the narrowly defined "economic"
struggles that punctuate daily life on the continent.

43: "Swelling Cities Of The Global South", *Socialist Worker*, 3 July 2007.

References

Bond, Patrick and Ashwin Desai, 2006, "Explaining Uneven and Combined Development in South Africa", in Bill Dunn and Hugo Radice (eds), *Permanent Revolution: Results and Prospects 100 Years On* (Pluto).

Ceruti, Claire, 2007,"'Divisions and Dependencies among Working and Workless", *South African Labour Bulletin*, volume 31, number 2.

Christian Aid, 2007, A Rich Seam: Who Benefits from Rising Commodity Prices (Christian Aid).

Davidson, Basil, 1992, *The Black Man's Burden: Africa and the Curse of the Nation-State* (James Currey).

Davis, Mike, 2006, *The Planet of Slums* (Verso).

Harman, Chris, 2002, "The Workers of the World", *International Socialism 96* (autumn 2002), http://pubs.socialistreviewindex.org.uk/isj96/harman.htm

Harrison, Graham, 2002, *Issues in the Contemporary Politics of Sub-Saharan Africa: the Dynamics of Struggle and Resistance* (Palgrave).

Iliffe, John, 1983, *The Emergence of African Capitalism* (Macmillan).

Larmer, Miles, 2006, *Mineworkers in Zambia: Labour and Political Change in Post-colonial Africa* (Tauris Academic Studies).

Mamdani, Mahmood, 1994, "The Intelligentsia, the State and Social Movements in Africa" in Mamadou Diouf and Mahmood Mamdani (eds), *Academic Freedom in Africa* (CODESRIA).

Marx, Karl and Frederick Engels, 2003 [1848], *The Communist Manifesto* (Bookmarks).

Morris, Alan, 1999, *Change and Continuity Survey of Soweto in the Late 1990's* (University of the Witwatersrand).

Otieno, Gloria, 2006, *Trade Liberalization and Poverty in Kenya: A Case Study of the Cotton Textiles Subsector* (Kenya Institute for Public Policy Research and Analysis).

Quartey, Peter, 2006, "The Textile and Clothing Industry in Ghana", in Herbert Rauch and Rudolph Traub-Merz (eds), *The Future of the Textile and Clothing Industry in Sub-Saharan Africa* (Friedrich-Ebert-Stiftung).

Renton, David, David Seddon and Leo Zeilig, *The Congo: Plunder and Resistance* (Zed).

Sautman, Barry and Yan Hairong, forthcoming 2007, "Friends and Interests: China's Distinctive Links with Africa", *African Studies Review*, volume 50, number 3.

Sautman, Barry and Yan Hairong, forthcoming 2008, "The Forest for the Trees: Trade, Investment and the China-in-Africa Discourse", *Pacific Affairs*, volume 81, number 1.

Seddon, David and Leo Zeilig, 2005, "Class and Protest in Africa: New Waves", *Review of African Political Economy 103*.

Walton, John and David Seddon, 1994, *Free Markets and Food Riots: the Politics of Global Adjustment* (Blackwell).

Wiseman, John, 1996, *The New Struggle for Democracy in Africa* (Avebury).

Zeilig, Leo (ed), 2002, *Class Struggle and Resistance in Africa* (New Clarion).

Zeilig, Leo and David Seddon, 2002, "Marxism, Class and Resistance in Africa", in Leo Zeilig (ed), *Class Struggle and Resistance in Africa* (New Clarion).

Zeilig, Leo, 2007, *Revolt and Protest: Student Politics and Activism in sub-Saharan Africa* (Tauris Academic Studies).

Theorising neoliberalism[1]

Chris Harman

A new word entered the vocabulary of the left in November 1999 with the momentous protest against the World Trade Organisation in Seattle—"neoliberalism".[2] Just as the movement that erupted at that protest defined itself as being against "globalisation" (or "corporate globalisation"), so it came to describe itself as "anti-neoliberal". The far left took over this terminology, often describing economic policies it opposed as "neoliberal".

But there was an ambiguity in the term "neoliberal". Did it refer to a way of running the capitalist system that could be changed with a change in government policy, or did it refer to something intrinsic to the present phase of capitalism that only challenging the system as whole could overcome? And was this present phase really described by the right wing "libertarian" anti-statist ideology of the neoliberals or was it a much more complex system of attacks?

Many of the most influential thinkers in the post-Seattle movement accepted the first answer to both questions. Leaders of Attac in France said their organisation was not "anti-capitalist", but merely wanted to stop short term financial flows disrupting national economies.[3] Bernard Cassen, founder of Attac, wanted a "protectionist" national economy

---

1:   This article is based on research for a forthcoming book. I would appreciate suggestions and constructive criticism. Please email chrisharman@swp.org.uk
2:   It is not to be found in earlier works dealing with the same phenomenon, such as Harvey, 1989, or Harman, 1995.
3:   Pierre Tartakowsky, speaking at a fringe meeting at the National Union of Students conference in Blackpool, April 2000.

organised along capitalist lines. Susan George would occasionally speak about capitalism, but could also write of "the harmful consequences of globalisation", as if this were something separate from, and intrinsically worse than, capitalism.

When it came to explaining what had changed since the 1960s, the emphasis tended to be on the victory of one ideology over another, rather than changes in the inner functioning of the global economic system. This was put very clearly by the French sociologist Pierre Bourdieu. He argued, "The main issue is neoliberalism and the retreat of the state. In France neoliberal philosophy has become embedded in all the social practices and policies of the state".[4] This was "the effect of a shared belief...which has created a climate favourable to the withdrawal of the state and so submission to the values of the economy".[5]

The logic of this position was that all that was needed to reverse the unpleasant policies pursued by capitalist governments and corporations was a shift in ideology or politics at the top of society. Pressing for this could involve alliances with particular capitalist groups. Susan George spelt this out in theory, writing that "sometimes the allies may even be... transnationals" such as those in the insurance industry.[6] Bernard Cassen applied this in practice by giving electoral support to the former French defence minister Jean-Pierre Chevènement.

Such approaches contrasted sharply with the analyses of those of us who saw the faults falling under the rubric "neoliberalism" as flowing from the logic of capitalism at a certain stage in its development. This did not prevent us joining with the wider movement in agitating against those faults. As I wrote at the time, "Hundreds of thousands, perhaps millions of people are beginning, for the first time, to challenge the global system. They come from a vast range of backgrounds and experiences, and bring with them the differing ideas that have developed there".[7] The different approaches were, however, bound to work themselves out in practice at some point. I added, "The movement will not be able to develop beyond a certain point unless such arguments are resolved".[8]

Developments over the past two years show that the arguments are indeed becoming important in practice. Alex Callinicos and Chris Nineham have written about the debilitating divisions that emerged in the World

4:   Interview in *Socialist Review* 242 (June, 2000).
5:   Bourdieu, 1998, pp6-7.
6:   George, 1999, p184.
7:   Harman, 2000, p55.
8:   Harman, 2000, p55.

Social Forum movement that arose out of Seattle,[9] while Daniel Bensaïd and Pierre Rousset have pointed out:

> The "pillars" of the alterglobalisation—the Brazilian Workers Party and Rifondazione Comunista—lead or actively participate in centre-left governments , implementing openly social liberal policies. This evolution in less than six years is full of consequences. The problem does not lie in the suddenness of the conversions… The lack of resistance that they have encountered within their own parties must focus attention both on the limits of the anti-neoliberal rhetoric and the profound resignation that it has partially masked.[10]

For this reason it is necessary to take up once again the analysis of the relationship of neoliberalism to capitalism—and by implication, of anti-neoliberalism to anti-capitalism.[11]

Marxist analyses of neoliberalism

A number of Marxist analyses have attempted to come to terms with neoliberalism, for instance Gerard Duménil and Dominique Lévy's *Capitalism Resurgent*, François Chesnais's *La Mondialisation du Capital* and, probably most influentially, David Harvey's *The New Imperialism* and *A Brief History of Neoliberalism*.

These works contain a mass of useful information about the world today. But they are also marked by the same ambiguity over neoliberalism to be found in the non-Marxist writings within the movement. All make reference to the problems faced by capitalism in the 1970s that led to a new period of crises. But they suggest that it is not capitalism as such that is to blame; rather it is a particular regime of capitalism. So Duménil and Lévy say that the new period was heralded by a fall in the rate of profit from which the system has not yet fully recovered,[12] but then go on to describe the advance of neoliberalism as a "coup" (no less) by "finance capital" in the late 1970s.[13] This coup supposedly overturned the "Keynesian" approach of industrial capital, which had been based on accumulation through a "compromise" with working class organisations on the terrain of the welfare state.[14]

Chesnais's tone is often similar. He also refers to a "coup d'etat" in

---

9:   Callinicos and Nineham, 2007.
10:   Bensaïd and Rousset, 2007, p25 (my translation).
11:   I did so at some length seven years ago, see Harman, 2000.
12:   Their explanation is different to Marx's. See my comment in Harman, 2007a.
13:   Duménil and Lévy, 2004a, p86.
14:   Duménil and Lévy, 2004a, p186.

the late 1970s. He writes that "industrial capital" has been forced to subordinate itself to "money capital".[15] Chesnais is a revolutionary socialist, but the implication of his argument is that, if "industrial capital" still dominated "finance capital", capitalism today would not be experiencing a "mediocre or poor dynamic of investment" or "the destruction of industrial employment...and strong pressures which weigh on those jobs which remain".[16]

Essentially the same arguments are to be found in David Harvey's work. He presents a picture of capitalism in the US, Western Europe and Japan before the mid-1970s expanding on the basis of "a class compromise between capital and labour". This meant an acceptance that:

> The state could focus on full employment, economic growth and the welfare of its citizens, and that state power should be freely deployed alongside of, or if necessary, intervening in or substituting for market processes to achieve these ends. Fiscal or monetary policies usually dubbed "Keynesian" were widely deployed to dampen business cycles and to ensure reasonably full employment.[17]

He calls this "embedded liberalism" and argues that it "delivered high rates of economic growth in the advanced capitalist countries in the 1950s and 1960s" and that a "social and moral economy was fostered through the activities of an interventionist state".[18]

He recognises that this system broke down in the mid-1970s. This was, he argues, caused by "a crisis of over-accumulation", which he sees as persisting into the present.[19] But he goes on to imply, again and again, that an alternative was possible within the existing system.

Capitalists, he argues, adopted the neoliberal approach because their class power had been diluted under Keynesianism and was threatened in the mid-1970s. Their response was determined by their need for a "restoration

---

15: Chesnais, 1997, p74. The passages from Chesnais are my translations.

16: Chesnais, 1997, p304.

17: Harvey, 2005, p10.

18: Harvey, 2005, p11.

19: Harvey's account is based on a passage in the third volume of Marx's *Capital*. But, for Marx, over-accumulation occurs at one phase of the slump-boom cycle. When the boom reaches its height, capital accumulation exceeds the resources of labour power needed to sustain it by providing surplus value to maintain the rate of profit. This leads to the production of more commodities than the system can absorb. In Marx's account the resulting crisis removes over-accumulation. For Harvey overproduction seems to be a permanent condition, but he does not explain how this is possible. To do so he would have to examine the nature of the capitalist cycle today and its impact on the rate of profit.

of class power"[20]—or even because "neoliberalism creates conditions for class formation".[21]

One particular expression of this reassertion of class power has been the domination of finance over industry: "There was undoubtedly a power shift away from production to the world of finance… In a conflict between Main Street and Wall Street, the latter was to be favoured." Harvey continues, "One substantial core of rising class power under neoliberalism lies, therefore, with the CEOs, the key operators on corporate boards, and the leaders of the financial, legal and technical apparatuses that surround this inner sanctum of capitalist activity." And while they rise in power, the unfortunate shareholders are among those who suffer: "The power of the actual owners of capital, the stockholders, has been somewhat diminished".[22]

From this it follows not simply that there is an alternative within capitalism, but also that this alternative might actually be more favourable to capitalism: "Paradoxically, a strong and powerful social democratic and working class movement is in a better position to redeem capitalism than is capitalist class power." This, he writes, might "sound a counter-revolutionary conclusion" but "it is ordinary people who suffer, starve, and even die in the course of capitalist crises rather than the upper classes".[23]

In *The New Imperialism* Harvey suggests how a reformed capitalism might work:

> The United States could downgrade if not turn away from its imperialist trajectory by engaging in a massive redistribution of wealth within its borders and redirection of capital flows into the production and renewal of physical and social infrastructures… A massive counterattack within the US as well as in the other core countries of capitalism against the politics of neoliberalism and the cutting of state and social expenditures might be one of the only ways to protect capitalism internally from its self-destructive and crisis prone tendencies.[24]

A very similar approach is to be found in Duménil and Lévy, who argue that the "Keynesian view of the history of capitalism, including its current problems…is very sensible" and "one can only regret that the

---

20:   Harvey, 2005, p16,

21:   Harvey, 2005, p72. See also p36 and p76.

22:   Harvey, 2005, p33. In making this argument, Harvey goes in the opposite direction to most of those who emphasise finance capital. They focus instead on a shift towards "shareholder power".

23:   Harvey, 2005, pp152-153.

24:   Harvey, 2003, pp75-76.

political conditions of recent decades have not made it possible to stop the neoliberal offensive and put to work alternative policies...in the context of other social alliances".[25] The logic of this argument is that left wing socialists might be justified in joining centre-left governments such as those in Brazil and Italy. Compromising on anti-capitalism can, it would seem, permit a challenge to neoliberalism.

The nature of neoliberalism

What is the real character of neoliberalism? The question is not as easy to answer as it might seem.

At one level neoliberalism is an ideology. Literally "neoliberalism" means the "new liberalism", and "liberalism" in its continental European (as opposed to North American) sense means "free market economics". As such it is a resurrection of the orthodox "laissez faire" economic ideology that prevailed until the great slump of the 1930s. This ideology contended that free market economies will run smoothly, steadily producing more wealth. Any problems that arise are supposedly a result of "unnatural monopolies" (especially in the labour market), which prevent the free movement of prices and wages pulling supply and demand together. State intervention is seen as distorting the economy and has to be restricted to defending private property, national defence and, in the monetarist version of neoliberalism, overseeing the money supply. The ideology is backed by supposed rigorous "neoclassical" economic theory, which purports to show mathematically that free markets always "clear"—that is, all labour will be employed producing goods that are all sold.[26]

Economic "liberalism" of the old sort fell into disrepute as an ideology by the end of the Second World War. In fact, it had already begun to be superseded as a practice by the beginning of the 20th century, when, as Rudolf Hilferding, Nikolai Bukharin and Lenin pointed out, "free market capitalism" began to give way to monopoly capitalism and its product, imperialism. State intervention was seen as necessary to provide the infrastructure for capitalist production (railways had long been nationalised in Germany, and in Britain conservative governments nationalised the electricity grid and the airlines). The subsequent organisation of the national economy for war, first in Germany and Japan, then in Britain and the US,

---

25:   Duménil and Lévy, 2004a, p201.
26:   Some neoliberals reject the part of neoclassical theory that rules out crisis, basing themselves on the so-called "Austrian school" that sees crises as an indispensable part of the "creative destruction" of the system. See Harman, 1996a, and Chang, 2002.

showed that state intervention could provide a basis for renewed profitability and accumulation.

It was against this background that a new orthodoxy emerged, preaching state intervention as the way to protect capitalism against itself. The new orthodoxy based itself on the ideas of the British economist John Maynard Keynes, who in the 1930s partially revised the neoclassical ideas he had previously backed wholeheartedly.[27] As Al Campbell has noted, after the Second World War "capital adopted Keynesian ideas because it believed that the various restrictions and regulations would be beneficial to the process of capital accumulation at that historical moment, particularly in comparison with the poor record of accumulation presented by its recent experience without those restrictions during the Great Depression".[28]

There was always some resistance to the new Keynesian orthodoxy. A minority of economists, notably Friedrich von Hayek and Milton Friedman, continued to hold on to the old doctrine. Campbell claims that "most finance capital never accepted the Keynesian compromise", but that it accounted for only 15 percent of capital.[29] Governments and big corporations accepted Keynesian ideology, not because it was imposed upon them by working class strength, but because increased economic activity by the state was accompanied by much higher levels of profitability in the US and major European states than under the pre-war ideology of economic liberalism.

Keynesianism as an ideology reflected the reality of capitalism in the period after the Second World War. National economies were increasingly dominated by near-monopolies that worked with the state to struggle for global dominance against near-monopolies based in other national economies. The result was a seemingly relentless trend towards increased state involvement in capitalist accumulation that had begun in the 1880s. To those of us who were taught economics in the early 1960s, Keynesianism was *the* explanation for the sustained economic growth of the post-war years. Yet as Robin Matthews pointed out long ago, the economic expansion of post-war Britain did not depend on Keynesian "remedies" for recurrent crises or on higher levels of government investment than in the pre-war years.[30]

An important by-product of the statified capitalist economy (and of its arms spending in particular) in the industrially advanced countries was

---

27: For the shift to various versions of Keynesianism, see Harman, 1996a.
28: Campbell, 2005, p189.
29: Campbell, 2005, p188.
30: Matthews, 1968, p556. See also Tomlinson, 1981.

full employment and therefore a degree of working class strength, which, in the late 1950s and 1960s, capital had to make concessions to. But to see these concessions as causing the statification or the long boom is to get things completely the wrong way round.

Keynesianism as an economic practice, rather than an ideology, was not put to the test until the first serious economic crisis in 40 years erupted in the mid-1970s—and it proved incapable of dealing with it. Capitalists were faced with a combination of recession and rising prices known as "stagflation". The Keynesians were at a loss. As one, Francis Cripps, put it, they suddenly realised that "nobody really understands how the modern economy works. Nobody really knows why we had so much growth in the post-war world".[31] Within three or four years Keynesianism had been replaced as the orthodoxy by reborn versions of the ideas it had pushed aside four decades earlier. This was not a question of states somehow coming to accept a wrong set of ideas:

> There was a structural crisis of capitalism. That is, the policies, practices and institutions that had been serving well capitalism's goal of capital accumulation ceased to do so. More narrowly, one can say that capitalism abandoned the Keynesian compromise in the face of a falling rate of profit, under the belief that neoliberalism could improve its profit and accumulation performance.[32]

In its first phase this rebirth of old ideas took the form of "monetarism". Milton Friedman, the central figure in monetarism, claimed that any problems with the free market system were caused by governments' inept control of the supply of money. But this version of free market economics proved unworkable in less than a decade, and the emphasis shifted to versions like those of von Hayek and Robert Lucas, which were even more critical of state intervention than Friedman's.[33] The ideas were popular with supporters of capitalism for a number of reasons.

Neoliberalism as a ruling ideology
Partly there was simple apologetics. Powerful voices had emerged from the popular struggles of the late 1960s and early 1970s challenging the legitimacy of capitalism. The mainstream defence against such voices had been

---

31: The *Guardian*, 26 September 1983.
32: Campbell, 2005, p189.
33: Friedman's contention that the state had an important role to play in managing the money supply was seen as almost tantamount to Keynesianism by some of the "new classical economists". See Garrison, 1992.

that Keynesian state intervention had proved capitalism could satisfy people's needs. Now that claim fell apart in the face of economic crisis. The argument had to be turned upside down. State intervention was now presented as the problem rather than the solution.

This was especially pleasing for those who dealt in finance rather than production, because under the new orthodoxy any way of making money was necessarily beneficial. Neoliberalism saw sitting at home receiving interest or dividend payments as an incentive to production, and therefore a valuable social activity. As Nikolai Bukharin had pointed out long before, it was "the economic theory of the leisure class".[34]

But more than apologetics was involved. There was a sense of desperation within capitalist circles in the mid-1970s. The first signs of crisis in their system coincided with growing assertiveness among workers. There had already been attempts to counter this in the late 1960s and early 1970s. Wage controls were imposed in Britain in 1966-70, 1971-2, 1973-4 and 1975-9; and in the US in 1971. Left wing supporters of Keynesianism tend to forget that these were an integral part of the post-war orthodoxy. But wage controls were not effective. They might work for a year or two, but they built up resentment among workers, which encouraged militancy even where it had hardly existed before, and they eventually fell apart amid waves of strikes.

The reborn free market approaches presented by Friedman and Hayek seemed to offer a way out. They claimed that the economy would resolve its own problems if it were freed from "distortions" to the market—whether these came from state intervention or from trade union interference with the "flexibility" of the labour market. Free trade would prevent national monopolies distorting prices, and unemployment would settle at the "natural rate" necessary to prevent wages eating into profits.

Ruling class ideologies are rarely just lies cynically spread in order to win the acquiescence of the ruled. They are sets of beliefs that give the ruling class a sense of its own importance, sanctify its rule in its own eyes as well as in the eyes of others and provide it with confidence that it can deal with any apparent flaws in its own system. Keynesianism fulfilled this role during the post-war decades in the advanced Western countries, as did Stalinism in the "Communist" states and "developmentalism" in Latin America, as well as the post-colonial states of Africa and Asia. But it became increasingly clear from the mid-1970s onwards that state intervention could

---

34: Bukharin, 1927.

not prevent economic crises in any of the world's regions.[35] Neoliberalism succeeded in filling the ideological gap. As such it appealed not just to finance capital, but to productive capital as well.

Neoliberalism in practice

It is important to differentiate between the claims of any ideology and what those who hold it actually do. There is rarely a direct correlation between the two. Yet many commentators, on the right and left alike, continue to make claims about neoliberalism that simply do not fit the empirical record of the past three decades.

First, there is the widespread belief that neoliberalism involves a retreat of the state. This is falsified by a glance at the rate of state expenditure in the advanced capitalist countries.

Figure 1: Ratio of total government tax revenue to GDP across 21 developed countries (percentage)[36]

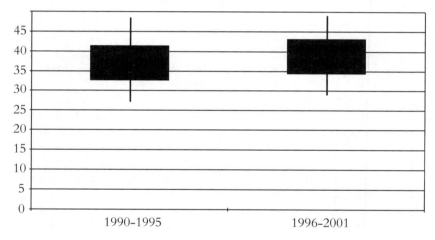

1990–1995   1996–2001

35:   The Czechoslovakian recession of the 1960s, followed by the Polish crisis of the mid-1970s showed that even the most extreme forms of state intervention could not sustain accumulation indefinitely. See Harman, 1977.

36:   United Nations Economic and Social Council, basic data on government expenditure and taxation, February 2004.

Figure 2: US state spending as a proportion of GNP

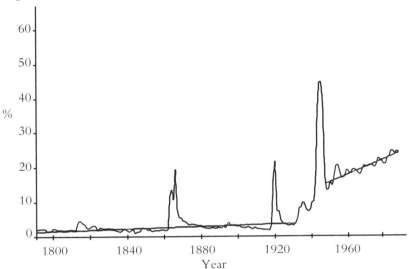

As I have pointed out before in this journal, multinational corporations continue to be rooted in states.[37] The biggest have half their assets, markets and labour forces located in a single home state, to which they look to protect their interests. Capitalism can no more do without the state today than it could in the Keynesian period. State intervention has been used to drive through attacks on workers, as with Margaret Thatcher's anti-union laws or the use of the police against the miners' strike of 1984–5. But it has also repeatedly been used to protect sections of capital against the effects of crisis in a way supposedly ruled out by neoliberal ideology. The US state helped bail out Chrysler when it came close to going bust in 1979; it took charge of negotiations in the 1980s to prevent US banks being dragged under by unpayable debts from Latin American countries. In 1998 it propped up the Long Term Capital Management hedge fund and, most recently, through the Federal Reserve central bank, it has tried to limit the damage caused to the financial system by the subprime mortgage crisis. Indeed, states have intervened more to deal with crises since the 1970s than in the 1960s and 1950s for the simple reason that the crises have been much more severe.

37:    Harman, 2007b.

It is true that the inability to stop crises using old "Keynesian" techniques has led to short term attempts to leave things to the market in the belief that "creative destruction" will allow "efficient" capitals to benefit from the weakening or elimination of "inefficient" ones. This is what the Volcker shock—the raising of US interest rates at the end of the 1970s—was supposed to do; it is what the Thatcherites tried to do with high interest rates and restriction of the money supply in 1980-4; it was also, in effect, what the USSR's ruling *nomenklatura* embarked on when faced with the great economic, social and political crisis that developed from the mid-1980s onwards. But on each occasion those that survived these attempts turned back to reliance on the state.

The US may be the advanced country where the neoliberal ideology is most entrenched. But it has financed government spending by the "Keynesian" method of borrowing through most of the neoliberal period in a way that it did not do in the Keynesian era. For the US ruling class neoliberalism, in the sense of letting the market rip apart established capitals, is something to be imposed on weaker national capitalisms to the benefit of US capital, not something to be allowed to happen without restriction in the US itself.

The same logic has been followed in Western Europe, Japan, China and, after the wave of not very creative destruction under Yeltsin, Russia. By contrast, the most thorough attempts to implement neoliberal practices have been in the poorer countries of the Global South. Here local ruling classes that entrenched their rule during the "developmentalist" post-war years embrace genuinely neoliberal measures promoted by the International Monetary Fund and World Bank in the hope of becoming junior partners to capitals operating from the industrially advanced countries.[38] But even in these cases tensions can arise, leading to some reassertion of the role of the national state. Certain Latin American countries have taken a "neodevelopmentalist" turn—complete with Keynesian economic advisers—mixing "Keynesian" and "neoliberal" practice in the aftermath of devastating economic, social and political crises.[39]

For these reasons, "neoliberal" is not in reality an accurate description of the operation of capital today. We are not faced with a reversion of the system to the free market capitalism that came to an end more than a century ago. Rather we face a system that attempts to deal with its problems by restructuring on an international scale of the units of the system that

38:    For more on this, see Harman, 2003.
39:    Katz, 2007.

emerged in the course of the 20th century—units that Marxists called "monopoly capitalisms", "state monopoly capitalisms", or "state capitalisms". States continue to play a central role in trying to facilitate or regulate this, even if the internationalisation of production makes this much more difficult that in the immediate post-war decades.

Finance and neoliberalism

Duménil and Lévy justify their claim that government economic intervention in the past three decades has been in the interests of "finance capital" by referring to the high long term rates of interest that Paul Volcker imposed in 1978, while he was chair of the US Federal Reserve. These high rates were, they argue, "maintained through the 1980s and 1990s".[40] This ignores the empirical reality. When high interest rates started seriously hurting industry in 1982 Volcker cut them, and the real trend of long term interest rates in the second half of the neoliberal period has been down, not up.

Figure 3: Ten-year treasury constant maturity rate
Source: The US Federal Reserve

40:    Duménil and Lévy, 2005, p13.

The whole claim that there are two distinct sections of capital—finance capital and industrial capital—is open to challenge. Many important financial institutions not only lend money, but also borrow it, since they are involved in "intermediation" between lenders and borrowers. What matters for them is not the absolute level of interest rates but the gaps that open up between different rates, particularly between long term and short term rates. And industrial concerns lend as well as borrow. Typically they accumulate surpluses between bouts of new investment, which they lend out in return for interest.

One important phenomenon over the past quarter of a century has been a long term decline in the proportion of surplus value going into new productive investment, which is a result of profit rates throughout the system not being fully restored to their early 1970s level. Saving by capital is greater than productive investment[41]—and industrial capitalists have turned to financial ventures in an attempt to use their surpluses profitably. If a greater section of capital is focused on finance than in the past, this is not because something called finance capital has taken control from industrial capital. It is because industrial capital has attempted to restore its profit rates through "financialisation". At the end of the day this is a blind alley for it, since only productive labour can produce the new value out of which expanded profits can come. It is not that Wall Street has taken over from Main Street, as Harvey asserts. It is that both face problems today that they did not in the immediate post-war decades.

Accumulation by dispossession

David Harvey's account of neoliberalism focuses on features that, he claims, lead to a new model of capitalist accumulation—accumulation by "dispossession", "primitive accumulation", and the absorption by capital of "non-capitalist" sectors and societies. Accumulation by dispossession is, he argues, "the dominant form of accumulating relative to expanded reproduction"[42] and takes a wide range of forms:

• "The privatisation of land and the forcible movement of peasant populations"; "the conversion of...common, collective, state, etc...property rights ...into exclusive property rights".
• "The commodification of labour power and the suppression of alternative forms of production and consumption".
• "The monetarisation of exchange and taxation, particularly of land".

41:   There is a detailed examination of these trends in Terrones and Cardarelli, 2005.
42:   Harvey, 2003, p153.

• The reduction of "whole populations to debt peonage".
• "The dispossession of assets by credit and stock manipulation".
• "The patenting and licensing of genetic material, seed plasma and all manner of products".
• The "buying up" of assets that have been devalued through crisis "at fire-sales prices", with crises being "orchestrated, managed and controlled to rationalise the system" to "permit accumulation by dispossession to occur without sparking a general crisis".
• "The rolling back of regulatory frameworks designed to protect labour".[43]

Harvey's list includes a range of unpleasant features of contemporary capitalism. But merely describing these as "dispossession" does not explain the present stage of the system. "Dispossession" is simply a long word meaning theft. When Pierre-Joseph Proudhon used the phrase "property is theft" in the 19th century, it was an anti-capitalist rallying cry, capable of expressing people's indignation at the system; so too is Harvey's phrase "accumulation by dispossession". But sloganising against theft is not the same as providing a serious analysis, any more than it was when Marx criticised Proudhon in 1847.

The problem with Harvey's analysis is all the more serious because it includes features that have always accompanied capitalist accumulation, like the "dispossession" of some capitals by others in the course of the recession-boom-recession cycle, as well as attacks on wages and working conditions. It also includes methods that some capitalists use to expand their profits at the expense of other capitalists such as "the dispossession of assets by credit and stock manipulation". This cannot enable the capitalist class as a whole to accumulate more. As Marx put it:

> The class of capitalists taken as a whole cannot enrich itself as a class, it cannot increase its total capital, or produce a surplus value, by one capitalist's gaining what another loses. The class as a whole cannot defraud itself.[44]

What applies to the dispossession of some capitalists by others even applies to certain forms of dispossession of non-capitalist sectors of the population. For instance, the widespread third world phenomenon of forcibly driving the urban poor from inner cities to make fortunes for property developers involves the further oppression of some of the poorest sections of the population. But it does not, in itself, create new value or surplus

---

43:   These methods are referred to in Harvey, 2003, pp145-147.
44:   Marx, 1987.

value for the capitalist class as a whole. The rents charged on luxury flats or office blocks are paid for out of already existing surplus value in the pockets of rich individuals or capitalist corporations.[45]

"Primitive" accumulation

Harvey argues that dispossession means that "primitive accumulation", which Marx saw as important at the time of the rise of capitalism, continues to be a central feature of the world today—indeed, it seems, a more important feature than accumulation through the exploitation of labour power. But for Marx primitive accumulation was not simply the building up of fortunes by early capitalists through robbery. It was, centrally, robbery of land from peasants, which then forced them to seek employment as wage workers. Its specificity did not lie in exploiting classes increasing their wealth by force (something that has happened in all sorts of class societies). Crucially, it permitted the development of a specifically capitalist way of expanding this wealth by creating a class of "free" workers with no choice but to sell their labour power to those now in control of the means of production.

This form of "primitive" accumulation does continue today. Old landowners in Egypt, agrarian capitalists in Brazil, local Communist Party bosses in China and recently established capitalist farmers in India are continually trying to grab the land of local peasants, and where they succeed a new proletariat is created. But Harvey is mistaken in claiming this only characterises recent decades. As Terry Byres has noted, primitive accumulation occurred in the colonial empires that persisted into the post-war decades, although it was "far less successful in its separation of the producers from the means of production than domestic primitive accumulation was in Western Europe…it had also left a large stratum of poor peasants in possession of land".[46]

While recent decades have seen the crudest forms of primitive accumulation, "it is not obvious that capitalist transformation is proceeding successfully" except in the case of East Asia.[47] For Byres, the only large country where primitive accumulation has added substantially to capital accumulation as such is China, where "from 1978 onwards, millions were driven off the land, ie were effectively dispossessed and proletarianised".[48]

45: This point is made in Fine, 2006.
46: Byres, 2005, p84.
47: Byres, 2005, p87.
48: Byres, 2005, p88.

No account of primitive accumulation should leave out the most important in the 20th century—the seizure of the land from the USSR's tens of millions of peasant families through Stalin's "collectivisation" of agriculture from 1929 onwards. Harvey refers to this, but cannot include it in his account of the pre-neoliberal capitalist era, since he sees Stalinist-type regimes as attempts "to implement programmes of modernisation in those countries that have not gone through the initiation into capitalist development".

For Harvey, Marx's account of "primitive accumulation" is less important than an idea drawn from Rosa Luxemburg. She argued that a shortage of demand for capitalism's products meant the system could only continue to expand by cannibalising the pre-capitalist world around it. Harvey writes, "The idea that some sort of 'outside' is necessary for the stabilisation of capitalism…has relevance." He argues that capitalism's problem is "over-accumulation" and that this can be solved by eating up "non-capitalist social formations or some sector within capitalism that has not yet been proletarianised".[49]

But what is there "outside capitalism" to allow "accumulation by dispossession" on the necessary scale? Harvey's answer is that the state constitutes this "outside"—whether it is the state of the so-called "non-capitalist countries", the developmental state in much of the Third World, or the state sector in advanced capitalist countries. Since these are all, for him, non-capitalist, a shift of their resources into private hands can provide new resources for capitalist accumulation. In making this argument, Harvey chimes with the "common sense" of a good portion of the left internationally, but it is a mistaken common sense.

Already in the 1870s Engels understood that nationalisation does not in itself produce something outside capitalism:

The modern state, no matter what its form, is essentially a capitalist machine, the state of the capitalists, the ideal personification of the total national capital. The more it proceeds to the taking over of productive forces, the more does

---

49:    Harvey, 2003, p141. Another of his "fixes" is investment in long term infrastructure projects within capitalism. It is these that he sees as absorbing "excess" capital and labour during the early post-war decades, although without explaining how they maintained the profitability of capital. His argument in some ways resembles that of Baran and Sweezy in *Monopoly Capital*—but unlike them Harvey hardly mentions the huge sums spent on arms in *A Short History of Neoliberalism*, *The New Imperialism* or his earlier *The Condition of Postmodernity*. It is this omission that allows him to conceive of a peaceful "spatial fix" for capitalism today. For an acute criticism of his argument, see Fine, 2006, pp143-144.

it actually become the national capitalist, the more citizens does it exploit. The workers remain wage workers—proletarians. The capitalist relation is not done away with. It is rather brought to a head.[50]

In the period following the Second World War all serious Marxist analyses had to take into account intervention by states, not only to support private capitalists, but also to undertake capital accumulation in their own right. For instance, the German Marxist Joachim Hirsch described how:

> As the development of the productive forces progresses, the maintenance of the process of accumulation demands, on the one hand, forms and individual capitals of an order of magnitude which capital, to some extent, is no longer capable of bringing forth itself directly in its reproduction process, and which can only be realised through the intervention of the state apparatus. On the other hand, this very process creates the necessity for counteracting state interventions to guarantee a relative equilibrium in the process of reproduction as a whole.[51]

To read Harvey, you would think that the existence of a substantial state sector slowed down accumulation during the post-war decades. But that was a time with a higher rate of accumulation than today, so much so that is has been baptised "the golden age of capitalism". As Ben Fine notes, "The boom…was sustained by the opposite of the factors that Harvey now takes to be instrumental in current accumulation, not least the extension of nationalised industries and the economic role of the state more generally".[52]

The real rationale for privatisation
There has been a trend towards privatisation of nationalised industries across much of the capitalist world for the past quarter of a century, just as there was a trend in the opposite direction through much of the 20th century. How are we to explain this? A number of distinct factors are involved.

The first moves to privatise state owned industries in the 1980s were often a pragmatic response to "the fiscal crisis of the state"—the pressure on government finances as recession cut into tax revenues, and unemployment forced up dole and social security payments. Selling off state holdings in profitable companies, and then whole state owned corporations, brought

---

50:   Engels, 1897, pp71-72.
51:   Hirsch, 1987, pp 81-82.
52:   Fine, 2006, p145.

in lots of cash and provided short term relief for governments' problems. It was this that motivated the 1974-9 Labour government to sell shares in Burma Oil and BP.

Combined with this was a belief that state monopolies, removed from the pressure of competition, were not pushing their workers hard enough. This ties in with a wider notion that is often repeated today, even by some on the left—that the period of state economic interventionism was somehow based on a "Fordist" compromise between employers and workers (a view which should be refuted by the actual behaviour of the Ford Motor Company).[53] The logic of this view was that breaking up state owned monopolies and opening them to the market would force their managers to be much harder on the workers, and would intimidate the workers into accepting worse conditions. Certainly the approach of privatisation often encouraged managers to force through methods to push up productivity. And once privatised, it was easy for companies to "contract out" a range of activities, so breaking the links that tie weak groups of workers to potentially more powerful ones. Ben Fine argues that "privatisation has been an important way in which the relations between capital and labour have been reorganised" and is connected to so-called "labour market flexibility".[54]

But this motivation for privatisation could clash with its use as a short term solution to the state's financial problems. For the state to make a lot of money out of privatisation, the privatisers had to have a prospect of monopoly profits. The breaking up of firms to shake up managers and frighten workers would do away with the monopoly. In practice most firms were sold intact, and left in a position of being able to charge monopoly prices to other sections of capital.[55] The state then had to appoint "regulators" to try to do by decree what the market was meant to do.

At the same time, privatisation is not absolutely necessary to create the illusion of the automatism of the market. The breaking up of state run institutions into competing units (NHS trusts, foundation hospitals, city academies, "self-governing" colleges, "agencies") can try to achieve the same goal; so can "market testing" within particular entities. So too can deregulation aimed to produce competition between different nationally based, and often still state owned, companies. This is what the European Union is trying to do to a whole range of industries such as electricity and

---

53: See for instance, Dunn, 2004, pp63-64 and 66-67.
54: Fine, 1999, p42.
55: Witness the bitter complaints of Ryanair's ultra-Thatcherite boss Michael O'Leary against BAA's monopoly charges for using London's main airports.

postal services. The end result of privatisation in a country like Britain can be that whole sections of "privatised" services such as electricity, water and rail can be run by foreign state owned companies.

These last examples refute Harvey's portrayal of privatisation somehow crossing a magic line from "non-capitalist" to "capitalist" production. They do fit in with his description of neoliberalism as concerned with "class power", although describing this as a "restoration", let alone a creation, of class power is to massively exaggerate the weakness of the capitalist class in the pre-neoliberal period. There is also considerable debate about how effective privatisation has really been. Keynesian pro-capitalist analysts have produced studies suggesting zero or very few gains to "efficiency" from privatisation compared to changes such as new technology that could have been introduced just as effectively, perhaps even more effectively, in a nationalised concern.

Class power is involved in privatisation in another way. A powerful ideological myth sustaining capitalist rule within bourgeois democracies is that the state represents the whole of the population. To sustain this myth the ruling class has to concede a margin of influence to the mass of people over the behaviour of the state through elections. This was not a problem when the general level of profitability allowed it to grant real reforms. Indeed, state possession of industries could help sustain the myth that the state was neutral in relation to class forces, so stabilising capitalism politically as well as economically. But when capitalism entered a long period of crises three decades ago a risk arose that people would expect the state controlled section of industry to protect them against the impact of these crises. Separating industry off from the state and subjecting it to the market can depoliticise the attacks on workers that accompany the crisis, shifting the blame to the seemingly automatic, natural forces of the market.

So Gavriil Popov, the free market economist who was mayor of Moscow during the tumultuous years 1989 to 1992, argued:

> If we cannot soon denationalise and privatise property, we will be attacked by waves of workers fighting for their own interests. This will break up the forces of perestroika and put its future in question... We must seek new mechanisms and institutions of political power that depend less on populism.[56]

This Russian example challenges Harvey's ideas that "non-capitalist

---

56:   Quoted in *Socialist Review*, December 1990.

states" were transformed into capitalist ones to the benefit of the world system as a whole between 1989 and 1991. Far from this seeing the "creation" of a new class, many of the same people continued to control industry and the state. Faced with a great social crisis, they sought to find a way out by restructuring the economy under their control, and to protect themselves, through forms of privatisation giving the impression of ownership by the mass of people (for instance, privatisation by distributing vouchers, which favoured industrialists and apparatchiks who could then buy them up on the cheap). Some of the old ruling class gained from this and some lost out. But it can hardly be argued that the result was a great boost to accumulation either in the former USSR or worldwide—accumulation rates worldwide fell in the 1990s to even lower levels than in the 1980s.[57]

The almost "giveaway" privatisations of 1980s Britain, when firms and housing stock were sold below their real value, had the additional ideological advantage of winning support from sections of the middle class and some workers. However, this was not nearly as powerful a force as those who talked in the mid-1980s about "authoritarian populism" used to claim. For instance, one 1980s study found that workers who bought their council houses were no more likely to vote Tory than those who had not.[58] Harvey overstates the case when he writes that under Thatcher "middle class values spread more widely to encompass many of those who had once had a firm working class identity".[59]

There are two more factors involved in the trend towards privatisation. Many commentators hold that it makes restructuring through mergers and acquisitions across national boundaries easier. As Ben Fine has argued, restructuring internationally "has posed a problem to state owned industries which are confined to domestic ownership alone".[60] For capitalists involved in such activities, there is always the suspicion that a state owned partner will be getting tax concessions and subsidies from its government which will distort its balance sheets—and that if the merged company faces economic difficulties that government will come under political pressure to try to pass the buck to the foreign partner.

This element in the logic of privatisation is particularly appealing to those best placed to gain from it. Privatisation imposed on Third World countries by the International Monetary Fund and the World Bank as

---

57:   See the figures in Terrones and Cardarelli, 2005.
58:   Heath, Jowell and Curtice, 1985.
59:   Harvey, 2005, pp61-62.
60:   Fine, 1999, p42.

the price of deferring debt repayments can be of considerable benefit to American and European capital. Harvey quite rightly makes this point. He is, however, mistaken when he gives the impression that this form of "accumulation by dispossession" is somehow central to profit making.

An indication of where capital can best gain profits is given by the global flows of foreign direct investment. Two thirds of these are to the advanced countries, and the biggest chunk of the rest is to one destination only—China. The fact that those non-Western countries with financial surpluses (China, the Gulf oil states, etc) have been using them to finance "private equity" takeovers of Western firms suggests that they know where most of the lucre still lies.[61]

Finally, privatisation is very profitable for some capitalists. It cannot in itself create more surplus value. Only increasing the exploitation of workers or peasants can do that. Otherwise all that is involved is diverting surplus value from one capitalist to another. But it does benefit particular capitalists. Their material interests are very much connected with the propagation of neoliberal ideology, and they set out to woo, bribe and browbeat politicians into pushing privatisation further.

How effective is neoliberalism for capitalism?
There is always a certain danger in propagandising and agitating against repeated capitalist offensives. In stressing the harm they do it is very easy to overestimate their success and to underestimate the obstacles confronting them. It is also easy to forget that these obstacles come not only from popular resistance, but from contradictions within capitalism itself. A picture is presented of a defeated working class, no longer capable of withstanding the onslaught on its conditions. The typical worker is said to suffer precarious employment, with the threat continually hanging over his or her head of the firm simply shutting down and moving abroad.

61:    Duménil and Lévy have completely distorted the picture in one of their widely read articles. They assert that "in 2000, US financial investments (treasury bills, bonds, commercial paper, stock shares, direct investment, etc) in the rest of the world amounted to 3,488 billion dollars. The corresponding income was 381 billion dollars, that is, a return of nearly 11 percent. It is interesting to note that this income was approximately equal to the total after-tax profits of all corporations in the United States, excluding such flows from abroad—that is a ratio of 100 percent" (Duménil and Lévy, 2004b). This is a complete misuse of figures, since it ignores foreign investments in the US and the counterflow of income from the US to capitalists and states abroad. Inward investment into the US has for some years been considerably greater than outward investment from it—even if the outward investment is on average more profitable. Duménil and Lévy recognise this elsewhere, giving figures showing income flows into and out of the US balancing each other. See the graph reproduced in Harvey, 2005, p191.

So John Holloway asserts, "Capital can move from one side of the world to the other within seconds".[62] Hardt and Negri's *Empire* claims, "Capital can withdraw from negotiation with a given local population by moving its site to another point in the global network... Entire labouring populations have thus found themselves in increasingly precarious employment situations".[63] For Harvey, capital relocates production as one of the "spatial temporal fixes" through which it responds to over-accumulation: "The geographical mobility of capital permits it to dominate a global labour force whose own geographical mobility is constrained".[64] With technological change "offshore production became possible and the search for profit made it probable. Wave after wave of deindustrialisation hit industry after industry and region after region within the US".[65] This, he claims, enables capital to impose increasingly precarious forms of work on workers:

> In the neoliberal scheme of things short term contracts are preferred in order to maximise flexibility... Flexible labour markets are established... The individualised and relatively powerless worker then confronts a labour market in which only short term contracts are offered on a customised basis. Security of tenure becomes a thing of the past. Under neoliberalisation, the figure of "the disposable worker" emerges as prototypical upon the world stage... Disposable workers—women in particular—survive both socially and affectively in a world of flexible labour markets and short term contracts, chronic job insecurities, lost social protections, and often debilitating labour, amongst the wreckage of collective institutions that once gave them a modicum of dignity and support.[66]

This picture is not unique to left critics of neoliberalism. It is also to be found in the writings of those who have abandoned the left to embrace some version of the "Third Way". Some of the phrases in Harvey could almost come from the writings of Anthony Giddens or Manuel Castells.[67] Castells, for instance, writes of:

62: Holloway, 1995, p125. Holloway does at one point recognise that productive capital is loss mobile than money capital, but then goes on to ignore the effect of this distinction on the relations between capitals and states.
63: Hardt and Negri, 2001, pp296-297.
64: Harvey, 2005, pp168-169.
65: Harvey, 2003, p64.
66: Harvey, 2005, pp169-170.
67: See Giddens, 1998; Giddens, 2002; Castells, 2006.

Structural unstability [sic] in the labour markets everywhere, and the requirement for flexibility of employment, mobility of labour, and constant reskilling of the workforce. The notion of the stable, predictable, professional career is eroded, as relationships between capital and labour are individualised and contractual labour conditions escape collective bargaining.[68]

So many different voices tell the story that, it seems, no amount of counter-evidence can stop people believing in it.[69] For instance, Harvey, writing 18 years ago, admitted that such counter-evidence exists, referring to the empirical work of Anna Pollert who "challenges the ideas of flexibility in labour markets and labour organisation and concludes the 'discovery of the flexible workforces is part of an ideological offensive which celebrates pliability and casualisation and makes them seem inevitable'".[70] His response was simply to dismiss such evidence out of hand: "I do not accept this position. The evidence for increased flexibility (subcontracting, temporary and self employment, etc) through the capitalist world is simply too overwhelming to make Pollert's counter-examples credible".[71] He did not himself provide such evidence, and does not in his later books either.

I have challenged the sorts of claims Harvey takes for granted before and do not intend to lay out the evidence once more here.[72] But certain important points need to be made:
• Financial capital may be very mobile, but industrial capital is fixed in buildings, machinery and a material infrastructure required to sustain it. It cannot move at a moment's notice. Harvey at least recognises that,[73] but does not let it ruin his story of the relentless spread of precariousness.
• The major source of recent job losses has not been the contracting out of work abroad. Tim Koechlin has analysed US investment and concludes that between 1991 and 2004 foreign direct investment by US companies only amounted to 7.4 percent of total productive investment by those companies, and investment in "developing countries" to only 2.5 percent.[74] Another study shows that between 1993 and 1998 US manufacturing employment "increased from 16.8 to 17.6 million and almost regained the 1989 peak

---

68: Castells, 2006, p9.
69: See for instance, the article by the journalist John Harris, "The Slow Death of the Real Job is Pulling Society Apart", the *Guardian*, 19 October 2007.
70: Harvey, 1989, p190.
71: Harvey, 1989, p191.
72: See Harman, 1996b; Harman, 2002. See also Dunn, 2004, and Bellofiore, 1999.
73: Harvey, 2003, p100.
74: Koechlin, 2006.

of 18 million". This was followed by "the largest slump in manufacturing employment in post-war history". This was not caused by a flood of imports of either goods or services, but rather "the result of inadequate growth of domestic demand in the presence of strong productivity growth" and the "weakness of US exports" due to "the high US dollar".[75]

• Capital cannot manage without workers who have certain skills, and prefers workers who have some sense of responsibility for the job. It takes employers time to train people and they are rarely keen to lose them if they can avoid it. They therefore do not always treat workers as "disposable", even when it comes to semi-skilled and unskilled labour. This is true just as much in less developed countries as in the advanced industrial ones.[76]

• The empirical evidence for Western Europe does not justify a picture of a uniform, relentless spread of precarious jobs. There was a "substantial" increase in the number of such jobs in the early 1990s, but the relative proportions of permanent jobs (82 percent) and non-permanent jobs (18 percent) remained almost unchanged between 1995 and 2000. There are also huge variations between countries. Despite Britain being supposedly the most neoliberal country in Europe, one measure of precarious employment shows it as amounting to only 16 percent of jobs in 1992 as compared to 35 percent in Spain.[77] There was actually a decline in the course of the 1990s, so that by 2000 one survey showed only 5 percent of British employees being on temporary contracts.[78] And the number of people who had worked at the same workplace for more than ten years rose from 29 to 31 percent.[79]

• Many forms of work lumped together as "precarious" are long term, permanent jobs. This is true of the great majority of part time jobs, which are by no means temporary. This is also true of many jobs with short term contracts. Often short term contracts are for workers who are in fact permanent, with their contracts regularly being renewed when they expire. They are denied certain employment rights, but that does not mean the employer can easily dispense with their services or prevent them having the power to fight back. After all, there were no such things as formal contracts of employment in Britain before the introduction of redundancy payments

75: Baily and Lawrence, 2004.
76: See, for example, Selwyn, 2007, on Brazilian agricultural workers.
77: Bodin, 2001.
78: Taylor, 2002.
79: These figures are from the Office for National Statistics', *Social Trends 2001*, p88. An excellent, but as yet unpublished, study of the transformation of work by Kevin Doogan provides a similar picture to these figures.

in the late 1960s, and employers had the right to sack workers whenever they felt like it. But this did not prevent the growth of shopfloor based union strength, even among groups such as dockers who were employed on a daily basis.

• Often what is involved is not workers losing the capacity to exert leverage on employers, but employers seeking to undermine workers' belief that they can do so. A study by Kate Bronfenbrenner found that during the economic upturn of the 1990s American workers felt more insecure about their economic future than during the depths of the 1990-1 recession. "More than half of all employers made threats to close all or part of the plant" during union organising drives. But afterwards "employers followed through on the threat and shut down all or part of their facilities in fewer than 3 percent" of cases.[80]

In other words, it is in the interests of employers to overemphasise how precarious jobs are in order to demoralise workers and lower the level of resistance. The task of the left is not to exaggerate insecurity, but to point to the counter-factors that provide workers with continued strength if they have the confidence to deploy it.

Neoliberalism, the welfare state and the social wage

There is an assumption in most anti-neoliberal writing that we are living through a period of the "withdrawal of state from social provision", as Harvey puts it.[81] But once again empirical evidence does not back up such assertions, particularly for the advanced industrial countries. State expenditure on social provision, like state expenditure in general, has, if anything, tended to rise through the decades since the 1970s (see figure 4).

Since 1995 expenditure on "social protection" by the main European countries has been more or less fixed, going up and down slightly with unemployment levels, and was no lower in the most recent US recessions than previous ones, despite "welfare reform" in the Clinton presidency. An analysis by Anwar Shaikh calculated the "net social wage"—the value of social expenditure from which workers benefit minus the taxes which workers pay—in a number of countries.[82] He found that, for Germany, Canada, the United Kingdom, Australia and Sweden combined, this net social wage was generally higher as a proportion of GNP in the 1980s than in the 1960s and 1970s; the trend was similar in the US (figure 5).

80: Bronfenbrenner, 2000.
81: Harvey, 2005, p161.
82: Shaikh, 2003.

Figure 4: Welfare expenditure as percent of GDP 1979 and 1995[83]

Country	1979	1995
Australia	13.2	16.1
Canada	14.5	18.0
France	22.0	29.1
Germany	25.4	28.7
Italy	21.2	22.8
Sweden	25.1	34.0
United Kingdom	16.4	22.5
United States	13.8	15.8

Figure 5: Net social wage as percent of GNP

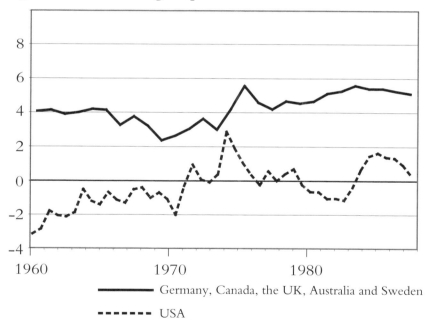

Germany, Canada, the UK, Australia and Sweden

------- USA

83:   Drawn from Swank and Martin, 2001, pp 917-918.

Shaikh's analysis also makes a very important point. The bulk of "social wage" expenditure has always been paid for out of taxes on ordinary wages. In effect, it amounts to a redistribution of wage income within the working class—and in the US in the 1950s and 1960s, when the net social wage was negative, it amounted to workers providing a subsidy to the state rather than vice versa. Noting the variation between countries he writes:

> Unlike the United States, the other OECD countries had generally positive net social wage ratios. Germany and the United Kingdom had the highest ratios, though even they averaged only about 5 percent of GDP and about 8 percent of total wages. Second, Sweden, the very paradigm of a welfare state, had an average net social wage around zero over the boom period.[84]

There have been repeated attempts by governments to cut back on social expenditures over the past three decades. Indeed in Britain struggles against cutbacks began much earlier than that.[85] Yet the expenditures have gone on rising. How is that to be explained?

Part of the explanation has to do with struggles against the cutbacks. So long as governments depend on elections in bourgeois democracies, they cannot completely ignore the impact of their policies on the lives of the mass of the population. So in Britain the prominence of the NHS in successive general elections led New Labour to increase the proportion of GNP going into it. Harvey is right to highlight "the balance of class forces" in determining the degree of neoliberalisation.[86] But that is not the end of the story. There are features built into capitalism that compel it to pay out a social wage even though it resents doing so.

Capitalist ruling classes can only prosper by exploiting people's capacity to work (their "labour power"). That capacity is damaged by illness, accidents and malnutrition. So capitalists have to worry about keeping a fit and able body of workers (ie "reproducing labour power"). That requires healthcare for workers, and benefits to enable workers to survive through periods of unemployment so that they can be fit for exploitation when the economy revives.

Modern capitalism also has to worry about the upbringing of the

---

84:   Shaikh, 2003.
85:   I remember reading about the first cuts in old copies of left wing publications from the early 1950s.
86:   Harvey, 2005, p50.

next generation of labour power, and ensuring it has the right level of education, training and work discipline to be profitably exploited. Hence the way its apologists worry about the "human capital" of the workforce and the amount of educational "value added" by schools. Finally, it is not just a question of physical wellbeing and aptitude. It is also a question of morale. The capitalist wants contented workers to exploit in the same way that a farmer wants contented cows. Workers cannot be expected to labour with any commitment to their work if they expect to starve to death once they reach retirement age. As Marx put it, there is a historically and socially determined element to the cost of reproducing labour power as well as a physiological one.

A pivotal moment in welfare development in Britain was the panic that developed at the time of the Boer War, when it was discovered that a high proportion of those who tried to enlist in the armed forces were not fit enough to fight. Ann Rogers has summarised the upper and middle class reaction:

> The belief that change was necessary if Britain was to compete successfully with Germany and the United States remained central. Whether the argument was formulated by the Fabians or by Liberal imperialists the concentration was on the damage that poverty was doing to society rather than the misery it caused individual workers…the underlying reason for the desire to improve the health of the working class was the need for a healthier labour force in the factories and the army.[87]

This was the background to the granting of old age pensions and the provision of school meals by the Liberal government of 1906.

But labour power is not an object like other commodities, which are passive as they are bought and sold. It is the living expression of human beings. What from a capitalist point of view is "recuperation of labour power" is for the worker the chance for relaxation, enjoyment and creativity. There is a struggle over the social wage just as over the normal wage, even if both are, up to a certain degree, necessary for capital.

This makes it very difficult for capital to redesign the welfare state in a way which would really fit with its narrow economic requirements. That would involve maintaining and even expanding those of its elements that are essential to the maintenance and reproduction of a productive labour force,

---

87:   Rogers, 1993. This article provides an excellent account of the different forces involved in the rise of the welfare state and the current pressures on it.

while curtailing or abandoning "non-productive" expenditure on things like the care of the chronic sick, of the seriously disabled and of retired workers. The competitive extraction of surplus value demands the continuation of part of the welfare state. The political realities of maintaining power through bourgeois democracy rule out dismantling the rest of it.

This is where internal markets, market testing, contracting out, privatisation, encouraging private pensions and all the rest come in. They are mechanisms that are meant to depoliticise the process of social provision, so making it easier to refuse it to those deemed not to deserve it on the one hand, and to clamp down on the workers in the welfare sector on the other.

The political ambiguities of anti-neoliberalism

Why do these arguments matter if we are all agreed that marketisation, privatisation and precariousness are bad things? They matter because mis-analysis leads to serious mistakes when it comes to fighting back. If the centre of accumulation has moved from day to day exploitation to "dispossession", then the focus of the fight shifts from the working class to struggles of those who are marginal to the productive process. The shift in focus is further reinforced if almost all jobs are seen as precarious, with employers being able to dismiss any workers who rebel. This is what Harvey seems to be arguing when he writes that in the post-1973 world "accumulation by dispossession moved to the fore as the primary contradiction within the imperialist organisation of capital accumulation".[88]

Such an analysis puts a stress on "social movements" as opposed to class movements.[89] The writers who have gone furthest in drawing such a conclusion are Laclau and Mouffe who write that the "overdetermination assumed by social struggles in the third world" involves "the construction of political identities having little to do with strict class boundaries".[90] Harvey resists this conclusion, at points insisting that class is central to resistance, but his theoretical framework leaves it open to an interpretation little different from that of Laclau and Mouffe. This has important practical implications. Struggles of social movements tend to rise rapidly and then fall back just as rapidly precisely because they are not based on those whose position within the structures of capitalist production binds them together organically and

---

88: Harvey, 2003, p172.

89: There is a confusion in the use of the term "social movements" in some European countries because it lumps together struggles waged along class lines against exploitation with those against oppression and war that appeal, to some extent, across class lines.

90: Laclau and Mouffe, 1985, p13.

provides them with the power to confront the system. As the saying goes, social movements "rise like a rocket and fall like a stick". What are left behind are skeleton organisations that are too weak to achieve their goals. Those involved are then all too easily tempted to conclude that a struggle cannot lead to victory, and to put their faith in reforms within the existing society, whether through old style reformist and populist parties or through NGOs.

Instructive in this regard are the arguments used by Fausto Bertinotti of Rifondazione Comunista in Italy to justify his turn to a government coalition with the pro-capitalist "centre-left" led by Romano Prodi. His turn came as the wave of demonstrations that occurred between the Genoa G8 protest (July 2001) and the start of the Iraq war (March 2003) began to decline, and in the wake of the failure to gain enough votes in a referendum on workers' rights for it to pass into law. He painted a picture of the popular movements in Italy risking devastating defeats because precariousness had sapped people's capacity to fight back:

> The basic thing that characterises neoliberal globalisation is precariousness. It conditions the time devoted to labour and life, the relations of production and social relations, and which even penetrates into attempts to modify the people's lives.[91]

What was involved in Rifondazione's shift was not just the capitulation—or betrayal—of one individual. Crucial was his capacity to convince many thousands of activists to accept his arguments. This was possible because Rifondazione's activists had long been influenced by certain autonomist and Eurocommunist ideas that held that the working class's strength had been damaged permanently by the mobility of capitalism and the "deindustrialisation" and "precarity" it produced. Social movements were seen as the only way forward, and when they went into decline the only hope seemed to be entering a government which might make at least a little turn away from "neoliberalism". Much the same happened to some of the semi-autonomist left in Argentina after the great revolt of December 2001 to January 2002. Once the great upsurge of the social movements of *piqueteros* and the popular assemblies died down, the easy option seemed to be to work with the Kirchner government as it made its turn away from the radical version of neoliberalism of the previous decade.

91:    Fausto Bertinotti, "15 Tesi per il Congresso di Rifondazione Comunista", *Liberazione*, 12 September 2004 (my translation).

Such shifts, from radical opposition to working through parties and governments that try to manage the system for capitalism, are encouraged by the notions of a "good" "Keynesian" version of capitalism and a "bad" "neoliberal" one—or the parallel contrast between "finance capital" that does not care for workers and "productive capital" that supposedly does. The reality is that capital uses the state as much today as it did in the heyday of "Keynesianism"—indeed, even more so, insofar as it is faced with more crises needing intervention. Neoliberalism as an ideology does not guide practice when it comes to this matter. The difference with the post-war decades is that capital is anxious to cut back on many of the positive reforms it granted in a more profitable era, and states respond accordingly.

It is this which leads to the ambiguities in the use of the term "neoliberalism" by the left. The term can be used simply to designate the negative features of many governmental measures in the present phase of the system—the anti-reforms that have replaced the positive reforms it was possible to extract from capital without a great deal of struggle from the late 1940s to the mid-1970s. But the term can also be used to reinforce the illusion that minor changes in the running of parts of the system are all that is necessary to improve the situation of the mass of people. By the same token, those who see their fight as an "anti-neoliberal" one can move on to see it as "anti-capitalist", but they can also slip back into conciliation with the system. Rhetoric and slogans have a role in politics, but they are not a substitute for clarity about the enemy and how to fight it. And we will all need more clarity as the competitive pressures on national states and capitalist firms in a period of recurrent crises leads to more attacks on the wage, the social wage, working conditions and jobs.

References

Baily, Martin Neil, and Robert Z Lawrence, 2004, "What Happened to the Great US Job Machine? The Role of Trade and Offshoring", paper prepared for the Brookings Panel on Economic Activity, 9-10 September 2004, http://ksghome.harvard.edu/~RLawrence/BPEA%20Baily-Lawr%20Oct%208%20clean.pdf

Bellofiore, Riccardo, 1999, "After Fordism, What? Capitalism at the End of the Century: Beyond the Myths", in Riccardo Bellofiore (ed), *Global Money, Capital Restructuring, and the Changing Patterns of Labour* (Edward Elgar).

Bensaïd, Daniel, and Pierre Rousset, 2007, "Un Etrange Bilan", *Que Faire 6* (September/November 2007).

Bodin, Raymond-Pierre, 2001, "Wide-ranging Forms of Work and Employment in Europe", ILO report, www.ilo.org/public/english/bureau/inst/download/bodin.pdf

Bourdieu, Pierre, 1998, *Acts of Resistance: Against the New Myths of our Time* (Polity).

Bronfenbrenner, Kate, 2000, "Uneasy Terrain: The Impact of Capital Mobility on Workers, Wages, and Union Organising", The ILR Collection, http://digitalcommons.ilr.cornell.edu/cgi/viewcontent.cgi?article=1001&context=reports

Bukharin, Nikolai, 1927, *Economic Theory of the Leisure Class*, www.marxists.org/archive/bukharin/works/1927/leisure-economics/

Byres, Terry, 2005, "Neoliberalism and Primitive Accumulation in less Developed Countries", in Alfredo Saad Filho and Deborah Johnston, *Neoliberalism, A Critical Reader* (Pluto).

Callinicos, Alex, and Chris Nineham, 2007, "At an Impasse: Anti-capitalism and the Social Forums Today", *International Socialism 115* (summer 2007), www.isj.org.uk/index.php4?id=337

Campbell, Al, 2005, "The Birth of Neoliberalism in the United States", in Alfredo Saad Filho and Deborah Johnston (eds), *Neoliberalism, A Critical Reader* (Pluto).

Castells, Manuel, 2006, "The Network Society: From Knowledge to Policy", in Manuel Castells and Gustavo Cardoso (eds), *The Network Society* (Center for Transatlantic Relations).

Chang, Ha-Joon, "Breaking the Mould: An Institutionalist Political Economy Alternative to the Neoliberal Theory of the Market and the State", *Cambridge Journal of Economics 26* (2002), also available online from www.unrisd.org

Chesnais, François, 1997, *La Mondialisation du Capital* (Syros).

Duménil, Gerard and Dominique Lévy, 2004a, *Capital Resurgent: Roots of the Neoliberal Revolution* (Harvard University).

Duménil, Gerard and Dominique Lévy, 2004b, "The Economics of US Imperialism at the turn of the 21st Century", *Review of International Political Economy*, volume 11, number 4.

Duménil, Gerard, and Dominique Lévy, 2005, "The Neoliberal Counterrevolution", in Alfredo Saad Filho and Deborah Johnston (eds), *Neoliberalism, A Critical Reader* (Pluto).

Dunn, Bill, 2004, *Global Restructuring and the Power of Labour* (Palgrave).

Engels, Frederick, 1897, *Socialism: Scientific and Utopian*, (Allen and Unwin), www.marxists.org/archive/marx/works/1880/soc-utop/

Fine, Ben, 1999, "Privatisation: Theory and Lessons for the United Kingdom and South Africa", in Andriana Vlachou (ed), *Contemporary Economic Theory: Radical Critiques of Neoliberalism* (Macmillan).

Fine, Ben, 2006, "Debating the 'New' Imperialism", *Historical Materialism*, volume 14, number 4.

Garrison, Roger, 1992, "Is Milton Friedman a Keynesian?", in Mark Skousen (ed), *Dissent on Keynes* (Praeger), available online: www.auburn.edu/~garriro/fm2friedman.htm

George, Susan, 1999, *The Lugano Report: On Preserving Capitalism in the Twenty-first Century* (Pluto).

Giddens, Anthony, 1998, *The Third Way: Renewal of Social Democracy* (Polity).

Giddens, Anthony, 2002, *Runaway World* (Profile).

Hardt, Michael, and Antonio Negri, 2001, *Empire* (Harvard), www.angelfire.com/cantina/negri/HAREMI_unprintable.pdf

Harman, Chris, 1977, "Poland and the Crisis of State Capitalism", *International Socialism* (old series) 94 and 95.

Harman, Chris, 1995, *Economics of the Madhouse: Capitalism and the Market Today* (Bookmarks).

Harman, Chris, 1996a, "The Crisis of Bourgeois Economics", *International Socialism* 71 (summer 1996), http://pubs.socialistreviewindex.org.uk/isj71/harman.htm

Harman, Chris, 1996b, "Globalisation: A Critique of a New Orthadoxy", *International Socialism* 73 (winter 1996), http://pubs.socialistreviewindex.org.uk/isj73/harman.htm

Harman, Chris, 2000, "Anti-capitalism: Theory and Practice", *International Socialism* 88 (autumn 2000), http://pubs.socialistreviewindex.org.uk/isj88/harman.htm

Harman, Chris, 2002, "The Workers of the World", *International Socialism* 96 (autumn 2002), http://pubs.socialistreviewindex.org.uk/isj96/harman.htm

Harman, Chris, 2003, "Analysing Imperialism", *International Socialism* 99 (summer 2003), http://pubs.socialistreviewindex.org.uk/isj99/harman.htm

Harman, Chris, 2007a, "The Rate of Profit and the World Today", *International Socialism* 115 (summer 2007), www.isj.org.uk/index.php4?id=340

Harman, Chris, 2007b, "Snapshots of Capitalism Today and Tomorrow", *International Socialism* 113 (winter 2007), www.isj.org.uk/index.php4?id=292

Harvey, David, 1989, *The Condition of Postmodernity: An Enquiry into the Origins of Cultural Change* (Blackwell).

Harvey, David, 2003, *The New Imperialism* (Oxford University).

Harvey, David, 2005, *A Brief History of Neoliberalism* (Oxford University).

Heath, Anthony, Roger Jowell and John Curtice, 1985, *How Britain Votes* (Pergamon Press).

Hirsch, Joachim, 1987, "The State Apparatus and Social Reproduction", in John Holloway and Sol Piccioto, *State and Capital: A Marxist Debate* (Edward Arnold).

Holloway, John, 1995, "Global Capital and the National State", in Werner Bonefeld and John Holloway (eds), *Global Capital, National State and the Politics of Money* (St Martin's).

Katz, Claudio, 2007, "El Giro de la Economía Argentina (Parte I)", www.aporrea.org/internacionales/a30832.html

Koechlin, Tim, 2006, "US Multinational Corporations and the Mobility of Productive Capital: A Skeptical View", *Review of Radical Political Economics*, volume 38, number 3.

Laclau, Ernesto, and Chantal Mouffe, 1985, *Hegemony and Socialist Strategy: Towards a Radical Democratic Politics* (Verso).

Marx, Karl, 1987, The 1861-63 notebooks, in Karl Marx and Frederick Engels *Collected Works*, volumes 28-30 (Lawrence and Wishart), www.marxists.org/archive/marx/works/1861/economic/

Matthews, Robin, 1968, "Why has Britain had Full Employment since the War?", *The Economic Journal*, volume 78, number 311 (September 1968).

Rogers, Ann, 1993, "Back to the Workhouse", *International Socialism* 59 (summer 1993).

Selwyn, Ben, 2007, "Labour Process and Workers' Bargaining Power in Export Grape Production, North East Brazil", *Journal of Agrarian Change*, volume 7, number 4 (October 2007).

Shaikh, Anwar, 2003, "Who Pays for the 'Welfare' in the Welfare State?", *Social Research*, volume 70, number 2, http://homepage.newschool.edu/~AShaikh/welfare_state.pdf

Swank, Duane, and Cathie Jo Martin, 2001, "Employers and the Welfare State", *Comparative Political Studies*, volume 34, number 8.

Taylor, Robert, 2002, "Britain's World of Work: Myths and Realities", ESRC Future of Work Programme Seminar Series, www.esrc.ac.uk/ESRCInfoCentre/Images/fow_publication_3_tcm6-6057.pdf

Terrones, Marco, and Roberto Cardarelli, 2005, "Global Imbalances: A Saving and Investment Perspective", in *World Economic Outlook 2005*, International Monetary Fund, www.imf.org/external/pubs/ft/weo/2005/02/pdf/chapter2.pdf

Tomlinson, Jim, 1981, "The 'Economics of Politics' and Public Expenditure: a Critique", *Economy and Society*, volume 10, number 4 (November 1981).

Neoliberalism, happiness and wellbeing

Iain Ferguson

Visit any high street bookshop chain in Britain and before very long you are likely to encounter one or more stands devoted solely to the subject of happiness and wellbeing. Recent titles range from *Happiness: Lessons from a New Science* by Richard Layard and *The Pursuit of Happiness: a History* by Darren McMahon at the more academic end of the spectrum to *Positively Happy: Cosmic Ways to Change Your Life* by game show host Noel Edmonds at the other.[1] Interest in the subject of happiness is, of course, hardly new. As McMahon shows, happiness, and its relationship with other valued goods such as freedom and justice, have been at the heart of philosophical debate for more than 2,000 years. At a less elevated level, what makes individuals happy has long been a subject of endless popular fascination. For Karl Marx, answering a quiz set for him by his daughter, happiness meant simply "to fight", for Albert Einstein, all it required was "a table, a chair, a bowl of fruit and a violin", while for John Lennon, happiness was "a warm gun".

Three things, however, make current discussions around happiness different and worthy of consideration by socialists. First, over the past two decades a "happiness industry" has emerged,[2] a global multi-million dollar business, one element of which is the self-help book market noted above. According to Gunnell, in the UK self-help books now generate roughly

1:   Layard, 2005; McMahon 2006; Edmonds, 2006.
2:   Gunnell, 2004.

£80 million a year, while in the US they make up nearly 6 percent of the entire book market. In addition, while not the main focus of this article, counselling, therapy and, for the wealthier middle classes, life-coaching services have also expanded hugely in the UK during this period.

Second, recent years have seen the growth of serious academic interest in issues of happiness and wellbeing. The new discipline has its own peer-reviewed journal (*The Journal of Happiness Studies*, founded in 2001) and its own series of annual conferences (Happiness and its Causes, with the 2007 conference in Sydney attended by over 3,000 delegates). Here the central figure has been Martin Seligman, Fox Leadership Professor of Psychology at the University of Pennsylvania. Seligman's *Authentic Happiness*[3] is a key text of the happiness literature and his website[4] one of the most visited on this topic. While the title, style and glossy cover of *Authentic Happiness* (subtitled "Using the New Positive Psychology to Realise Your Potential for Lasting Fulfilment") are reminiscent of much other self-help literature, Seligman, a former president of the American Psychological Association, is by any criterion a substantial figure within US academic psychology, and the key theorist of "positive psychology". In the UK the main role in promoting the "science of happiness" has been played by Richard Layard, professor of economics at the London School of Economics and a Labour peer in the House of Lords. Layard is also the convenor of the Happiness Forum, a group of academics, psychologists and top civil servants which meets regularly at the LSE to consider issues of happiness and wellbeing.

The third, and most significant, development, however, is the growth of interest in happiness (or "subjective wellbeing", as it is more often called) among Western governments and policy-makers. In Britain, for example, the New Labour government has commissioned research into the influences on personal wellbeing and their application to policy-making,[5] and in 2007 undertook its first national survey into the happiness of the nation.[6] At a European level, Deutsche Bank has recently commissioned research into happiness levels within OECD countries with a view to establishing the factors which contribute to the "happy variety of capitalism".[7]

The findings both from this research and from the new psychologies of happiness and wellbeing referred to above are already having a major

---

3:   Seligman, 2002.
4:   www.authentichappiness.com
5:   Dolan, Peasgood and White, 2006.
6:   Laurance, 2007.
7:   Bergheim, 2007.

impact on public policy. Thus in the UK the "science of happiness" has been important in directly shaping both health and safety at work policies[8] and also mental health policy in England and Wales. As well as being the author of *Happiness: Lessons from a New Science*, Richard Layard is the main author of the influential *Depression Report*[9] published in June 2006, subtitled "A New Deal for Depression and Anxiety Disorders", which I consider in detail below. The language of "new deals" is not accidental. From 1997 to 2001 Layard was an adviser to New Labour and one of the key architects of its "New Deal" and "Welfare to Work" policies. Meanwhile, north of the border, this new interest in happiness and wellbeing is reflected in the Scottish government's funding of a "Centre for Confidence and Wellbeing", launched at a conference in Glasgow in December 2004 with Martin Seligman the keynote speaker. The centre, which is supported by important sections of Scottish business including Scottish Enterprise, BT Scotland and the Scottish CBI, has the aim of overcoming what its chief executive, psychologist Carol Craig, has labelled "the Scots' crisis of confidence" in her book of the same name. This crisis includes an alleged "dependency culture" which supposedly inhibits the growth of the Scottish economy.[10]

The "science of happiness"

The starting point for most of the happiness theorists is what Richard Layard refers to as the "paradox at the heart of our lives":

> Most people want more income and strive for it. Yet as Western societies have got richer, their people have become no happier... But aren't our lives infinitely more comfortable? Indeed we have more food, more clothes, more cars, bigger houses, more central heating, more foreign holidays, a shorter working week, nicer work and, above all, better health. Yet we are not happier. Despite all the efforts of governments, teachers, doctors and businessmen, human happiness has not improved.[11]

The belief that increased wealth in recent decades has not led to increased happiness is widely held by happiness theorists and appears to be supported by research evidence. According to one summary of this

---

8: DWP, 2005.
9: CEPMHPG, 2006.
10: Craig, 2003.
11: Layard, 2005, pp3-4.

evidence, cited by the health epidemiologist Richard Wilkinson, "Study after careful study shows that, beyond some point, the average happiness within a country is almost completely unaffected by increases in its average income level... Average satisfaction levels register virtually no change even when average incomes grow many-fold".[12] Why should this be so?

The most influential answer to the question is that provided by Martin Seligman. Happiness, Seligman argues, is primarily a product of two main factors. First, there is your genetic inheritance, which sets the boundaries for your happiness range and accounts for roughly half of your predisposition to be happy. Crudely, if your parents and grandparents were miserable, then you probably will be too. (In fact, given the fondness of many of these theorists for the arguments of evolutionary psychology, the happiness levels of your Stone Age ancestors are probably also relevant.) There are then a number of other factors which affect your happiness levels. Chief amongst these, he suggests, are living in a wealthy democracy, not a dictatorship ("a strong effect" on happiness levels, apparently), getting married, and acquiring a rich social network. By contrast, he argues, more money, good health and education have no impact on happiness levels. Commenting on these "findings", he notes:

> You have undoubtedly noticed that the factors that matter vary from impossible to inconvenient to change. Even if you could alter all of the external circumstances above, it would not do much for you, since together they account for no more than 8 and 15 percent of the variance in happiness. The very good news is that there are quite a number of internal circumstances that will likely work for you.[13]

A focus on these internal factors is, therefore, at the core of Seligman's "positive psychology". As the name suggests, its central message, in the title of Cole Porter's song, is the need to "accentuate the positive, eliminate the negative". Thus, whereas the "old" psychology concentrated on depression, distress and mental pain, the focus in positive psychology is on the cultivation of "positive" feelings such as satisfaction, happiness and hope.[14] By cultivating these emotions, individuals can "buffer" themselves against the factors that create mental ill health,

---

12:   Cited in Wilkinson, 2005, p294.
13:   Seligman, 2002, p61.
14:   For those unfortunate enough to suffer from more serious mental illnesses, Seligman, like Richard Layard, appears to believe that biomedical psychiatry and drug treatments have the answers, despite very considerable evidence to the contrary. See Healy, 2001.

through attitude change, for example, or the practice of meditation.[15]

A second "pillar" focuses on positive traits, strengths and virtues, such as wisdom, courage and love. Happiness, Seligman argues, is based on individuals identifying their key signature strengths (mainly inherited) and building on these. Here there are obvious similarities with Aristotelian notions of happiness as "flourishing", the realisation of one's human faculties. For Aristotle, however, and even more so for Marx, the capacity for such realisation depends largely on the type of society in which you live. As Terry Eagleton has recently put it in his short treatise on *The Meaning of Life*:

> If happiness is a state of mind, then it is arguably dependent on one's material circumstances... Happiness or wellbeing is an institutional affair: it demands the kind of social and political conditions in which you are free to exercise your creative powers.[16]

By contrast, the third pillar of Seligman's positive psychology, "positive institutions", identified as "democracy, strong families and a free press", is the one which receives least attention, mainly because, as we have seen, it is the least amenable to change.

Despite his protestations to the contrary, it is difficult not to see Seligman's positive psychology as little more than a restatement, albeit in more academic language, of earlier American self-help literature, such as Norman Vincent Peale's 1950s bestseller *The Power of Positive Thinking*. Its dominant themes are individualism and an emphasis on the necessity of changing the way you see the world. This is coupled with an almost total neglect of the impact of structural inequalities on happiness and wellbeing (the term "inequality" does not even appear, for example, in the index of *Authentic Happiness*), mainly because he seems to share Anthony Giddens's view that, beyond a very low level of income, "happiness and its opposite bear no relation to either wealth or the possession of power".[17] Instead a relentless optimism about the capacity of individuals to improve their own mental health is combined with a contempt for "pessimistic" ideas or theories which suggest that this capacity might be subject to any constraints

---

15:   As the emphasis on meditation suggests, there is considerable overlap and interchange between the ideas of the "science of happiness" and Buddhist ideas, with Buddhist speakers figuring prominently, for example, in the Happiness and Its Causes conferences. Layard similarly recommends *Happiness* by Buddhist monk Matthieu Ricard (2007), saying, "If you want to be happier and better, this is the book you should read."
16:   Eagleton, 2007, pp151-152.
17:   Cited in Levitas, 2000.

whatsoever, whether these be the effects of negative childhood experiences such as abuse or neglect (and Freud is a particular *bete noir*) or of structural oppressions, such as racism and sexism. An emphasis on such constraints is, he argues:

> the philosophical infrastructure underneath the victimology that has swept America since the glorious beginnings of the civil rights movement, and which threatens to overtake the rugged individualism and sense of individual responsibility that used to be this nation's hallmark.[18]

As opposed to such attitudes, he argues, what we need to cultivate is an individual psychology of "rising to the occasion", encapsulated in what he calls "the Harry Truman effect": "Truman, after an undistinguished life, to almost everyone's surprise rose to the occasion when FDR died and ended up becoming one of the great presidents".[19] (This view of Truman is perhaps less likely to be shared by the descendants of the victims of the atomic bombs dropped on Hiroshima and Nagasaki in 1945 on Truman's orders.)

Compared to Seligman, other theorists of happiness are more willing to acknowledge, albeit implicitly, some connection between the values and priorities of neoliberalism and the decline in levels of happiness and wellbeing. In his *Happiness: Lessons from a New Science*, for example, Layard argues that "our fundamental problem today is a lack of a common feeling between people—the notion that life is essentially a competitive struggle".[20] He identifies the growth of individualism as one of three factors (the others being changing gender roles and the impact of television) as contributing to current levels of unhappiness. In addition, unlike Seligman, he recognises a connection between inequality and levels of wellbeing, and calls for a redistribution of wealth, based on taxing the rich. In most respects, however, Layard's critique of individualism appears to owe more to communitarian rather than socialist ideas. Thus he argues, "The goal of self-realisation is not enough. No society can work unless its members feel responsibilities as well as rights." An emphasis on "responsibilities" as well as rights is, of course, at the heart of New Labour ideology, including its more authoritarian aspects. It is perhaps not surprising then to find Layard, as a key New Labour adviser on welfare to work schemes, arguing that:

18:   Seligman, 2002, p68.
19:   Seligman, 2002, p12.
20:   Layard, 2005, p163.

After a period of unemployment, benefit-recipients enter a period of grey resignation where any change can appear dangerous. Their "tastes" change. It is the role of the employment office to push people out of that state and into meaningful activity. If we could mobilise more of Europe's unemployed, those extra employees could find jobs, and at existing rates of pay.[21]

Quite how working in dead end jobs with low rates of pay and little hope of improvement increases happiness levels is not made clear.

To a greater extent than Layard, the British psychologist Oliver James explicitly locates the roots of much current unhappiness in the "selfish capitalism" that has prevailed since the 1980s. In his book, *Affluenza*,[22] much of which is a scathing critique of the values and policies of New Labour, James attacks "selfish capitalism" for giving rise to the "Affluenza Virus", which he defines as:

> A set of values which increase our vulnerability to emotional distress. It entails placing a high value on acquiring money and possessions, looking good in the eyes of others and wanting to be famous. Just as having the HIV virus places you at risk of developing the physical disease of Aids, infection with the Affluenza Virus increases your susceptibility to the commonest emotional distresses: depression, anxiety, substance abuse and personality disorder (like "me, me, me" narcissism, febrile moods or confused identity).[23]

The "vaccines" that James proposes to deal with the virus, consisting of maxims such as "Consume what you need, not what advertisers want you to want" or "Educate your children, don't brainwash them", are ones with which few socialists would disagree. Again, however, most of them involve individual lifestyle change, rather than structural change, achievable more easily by the fabulously wealthy individuals who appear to be the main victims of the Affluenza Virus in his study but more difficult for the rest of us. Thus his "vaccines" for stressed-out women are to divide the care of small children with your partner; try to find a nanny rather than using a kindergarten; and enjoy being a mother—all fairly basic and uncontentious, but still beyond the reach of many ordinary women.

Because James critiques the symptoms of neoliberal policies rather than neoliberalism itself, the valid points he makes can also easily be co-opted

---

21:   Layard, 2005, p174.
22:   James, 2007.
23:   James, 2007, pvii.

by those arguing for a return to more "traditional" values. So Tory leader David Cameron, speaking in Hertfordshire on 22 May 2006, argued:

> It's time we admitted that there's more to life than money, and it's time we focused not on GDP (gross domestic product) but on GWB—general wellbeing... It is about the beauty of our surroundings, the quality of our culture and above all the strength of our relationships. There is a deep satisfaction which comes from belonging to some one and some place. There comes a point when you can't keep on choosing and have to commit.[24]

Commenting on this, the critical social worker Bill Jordan suggests that "these themes resonate with social work's concerns about quality of life rather than material consumption or the work ethic. They also contrast with New Labour's emphasis on individual responsibility".[25] In fact, it seems more likely that Cameron's emphasis on the "strength of relationships" and the "need to commit" owes less to any critique of "selfish capitalism" than to his desire, expressed at the 2007 Conservative Party conference, to restore marriage to its place as "the central institution of our society", for example, by providing tax breaks not available to lone parent families.[26]

At their best then, it is possible to discern in the writing of some of the happiness theorists a critique of consumerism and an echo of the central slogan of the anti-capitalist movement that "the world is not a commodity". Underpinning this, however, there is an individualism that makes these theories all too compatible with the priorities and strategies of neoliberalism, whether of the New Labour or New Tory variety. Some policy examples of this will be considered in the final section of this article. Before then, however, if it is indeed the case that levels of happiness have not continued to rise in recent decades, then perhaps it is necessary to consider some alternative reasons as to why this might be so.

Neoliberalism, happiness and wellbeing
According to the theorists discussed above, as well as for researchers and governments, "average living standards" have risen in most OECD countries in recent decades, but not happiness levels. So, they conclude, income and happiness are unconnected. However, they seldom look at

---

24: Cited in Jordan, 2007, p x.
25: Jordan, 2007, p x.
26: Cameron, 2007.

what else has been going on in the lives of millions of people during the same period, which broadly coincides with the implementation of neoliberal policies.[27] In this section I shall look briefly at the British experience during this period. In this country the year in which happiness levels appear to have stalled—1975, according to Layard—is, for several reasons, rather a significant one.[28] It was the year, for example, in which the expansion of the welfare state that began soon after the Second World War, reducing insecurity and fear for millions of working class people, came abruptly to an end. The prospect of a future of huge cutbacks in health, housing and social care services was epitomised in the announcement by Anthony Crosland, minister in the Wilson-Callaghan governments and a leading Labour Party intellectual, that "the party's over" in May that year.[29]

It was also that year that saw the introduction of Labour's "Social Contract" which, over the next two years, resulted in the biggest fall in living standards since the Second World War. And it was the year which, following two decades of growing working class organisation, confidence and successful struggle, saw the beginnings of what Tony Cliff was later to label the "downturn"—a period when the balance of forces shifted decisively away from organised labour and in favour of the employers and government.[30] The next 20 years were to see workers suffer defeat after defeat, with the low point being the crushing of the miners' strike of 1984-5. The impact of that long downturn in terms of working class confidence was profound, and its effects are still evident today, in the low level of strikes, for example. Finally, the monetarist policies implemented by Labour governments during the mid to late 1970s were to be the precursor of the fully fledged neoliberal policies of Maragaret Thatcher and John Major, policies which would be continued and even intensified by New Labour governments after 1997. These policies have impacted upon the lives of working class people in three main areas.

First, there is poverty. As noted above, poverty hardly figures in the happiness literature. In part, this is because it is seen as a residual issue, affecting relatively small numbers of people. This complacent attitude is evident, for example, in the Deutsche Bank study referred to earlier: "Nearly every OECD country has achieved a high level of material

27:    One study which does look at this is *The Weight of the World*, by Pierre Bourdieu (1999), a massive study of "social suffering" in France, which has not been replicated elsewhere.
28:    Layard, 2005, p29.
29:    Cited in Timmins, 1996, p313.
30:    Cliff, 1979.

prosperity. The questions now facing individuals and societies are which priorities to set for the future".[31]

The reality is very different. A number of major studies have painted a comprehensive picture of poverty in Britain just under a decade after New Labour first came into office.[32] Thus, in 2003/4, 12 million people in Britain, about one in five, were living in income poverty. This is nearly two million fewer than in the early 1990s. It is still, however, nearly twice as many as when the Conservatives came into office in 1979. In fact, since New Labour was first elected, poverty levels have declined only among two groups: families with children (down from 32 percent to 29 percent) and pensioners (down from 27 percent to 22 percent). By contrast, the proportion of working age adults without dependent children in income poverty has actually increased by 400,000 since the late 1990s.[33]

A second reason why the literature ignores poverty is because, as we have seen, above an extremely low level income and wealth are considered to have little relationship with happiness and wellbeing. In fact, "overall, there appears to be reasonably robust evidence that individual or household income has a positive but non-linear effect on life satisfaction".[34] Similarly, the main finding of the happiness survey conducted by the Department of the Environment in 2007 was that a skilled job, good health and financial security were the keys to happiness.[35] In other words, in general people with a decent income tend to be happier, although obviously this can be affected by other factors. Conversely, the link between class, poverty and every form of mental ill heath is very well established. In their classic study of depression published in 1978, for example, Brown and Harris found that working class women were four times more likely to experience depression than middle class women. This was not simply about income, but about their whole life experience, including their employment experience, social supports and, above all, self-esteem. There is, therefore, something rather distasteful in being told by so many wealthy professors, politicians and researchers that money does not bring happiness. Ruth Levitas's reproduction of a 19th century poem seems apt:

31:   Bergheim, 2007, p1.
32:   See, for instance, Palmer, Carr and Kenway, 2005; Hills and Stewart, 2005; Pantazis, Gordon and Levitas, 2006.
33:   Palmer, Carr and Kenway, 2005.
34:   Dolan, Peasgood and White, 2006.
35:   Laurance, 2007.

Plain living may be wholesome and wondrous virtues may
Abound beneath ribs scant of flesh and pockets scant of pay,
And it may be poverty is best if rightly understood,
But we'll turn things upside down because we don't want all the good.[36]

Then there is the issue of inequality. The literature emphasises how "we are all better off". Its focus on the rise in average income obscures the extent to which some of "us" have actually become much better off than others. Inequality has increased over the past decade, not only in the US but also in the UK. In his study of *Rich Britain* Lansley found that:

Britain has been slowly moving back in time—to levels of income inequality that prevailed more than half a century ago and to levels of wealth inequality of more than 30 years ago.[37]

According to a report published in 2004 by the Office for National Statistics, the wealth of the super-rich has doubled since 1997. Nearly 600,000 individuals in the top 1 percent of the UK wealth league owned assets worth £355 billion in 1996, the last full year of Conservative rule. By 2002 that had increased to £797 billion. Part of the increase was due to rising national prosperity, but the top 1 percent also increased their share of national wealth from 20 percent to 23 percent in the first six years of the period. Meanwhile the wealth of the poorest 50 percent of the population shrank from 10 percent in 1986 to 7 percent in 1996 and 5 percent in 2002. On average, each individual in the top 1 percent was £737,000 better off than just before Tony Blair arrived in Downing Street.[38]

More than any other single theorist, the social epidemiologist Richard Wilkinson has demonstrated the ways in which such inequality impacts on every aspect of our health, wellbeing and relationships. Wilkinson cites Frank's reporting of the "consistent finding" of analyses of "how subjective wellbeing varies with income within a country...richer people are, on average, more satisfied with their lives than their poorer contemporaries".[39] In addition, as Wilkinson shows, factors such as the level of trust in fellow citizens, cited in most studies as a key determinant of a "happy society", is inversely related to the degree of inequality in any society.

36: John Bruce Glasier, cited in Levitas, 2000, p206.
37: Lansley, 2006, p29.
38: Office for National Statistics, 2004.
39: Wilkinson, 2005, p294.

"A Hard Day's Night": the transformation of work

If the impact of poverty and inequality on the happiness and wellbeing of millions is neglected within the literature, neither is there much recognition of the other ways in which the daily lives of ordinary people have been transformed by the impact of neoliberal policies over the past three decades. As Bourdieu notes:

> Using material poverty as the sole measure of all suffering keeps us from seeing and understanding a whole side of the suffering characteristic of a social order which, although it has undoubtedly reduced poverty overall (though less than often claimed), has also multiplied the social spaces…and set up the conditions for an unprecedented development of all kinds of ordinary suffering.[40]

One such form of social suffering is the insecurity arising from the increasing withdrawal of the state from areas such as housing and pensions. Another is the growing level of debt experienced by young people in particular. But perhaps the biggest change for many people has been in their experience of work. And it is also in the area of work that the real limitations of happiness and wellbeing strategies are most evident.

According to the economist Frances Green, the past two decades have been, in his words, a "hard day's night" for many of those in work.[41] Among his findings are that more people are working long hours and that hours have become concentrated in households, with the average two-adult household working an extra seven hours compared with the early 1980s. No less importantly, Green argues, there has been an intensification of work since the early 1980s. For example, in his research the proportion of workers who strongly agreed that their job required them to work very hard rose from 32 percent to 40 percent in just five years from 1992. The proportions working at very high speed all or almost all of the time rose from 17 percent to 25 percent in the five years from 1991. During this period work intensification was faster in Britain than anywhere else in Europe due, Green argues, to falling union power.

A further aspect of neoliberalism has been the application of managerial policies and priorities to the public sector. For groups such as teachers, nurses and social workers, this has often meant that the values and motivations that brought them into the job in the first place have had to take

---

40:   Bourdieu, 1999, p4.
41:   Green, 2000.

second place to the overriding demands of saving money and rationing services. Some sense of the unhappiness to which this increased bureaucracy and managerialism gives rise is evident in the following quote from a social worker interviewed as part of Chris Jones's research into front-line social work:

> I feel so deskilled because there are so many restrictions over what I can do. Yes I go out and do assessments, draw up care plans, but then we aren't allowed to do anything. I can't even go and organise meals on wheels for somebody without completing a load of paperwork, submitting a report to a load of people who would then make the decision as to whether I can go ahead and make the arrangements. I just wonder why I am doing this. It's not social work. Many of my colleagues in the adult team are looking to get out of social work altogether. They say they don't want to take this garbage any more. That's how they feel. The will to do social work is still there. They are still committed to work with people in distress. That heartfelt warmth has not gone away, but the job is so different.[42]

More generally, work is one of the major contributors to all the UK's major killers—cancer, heart disease and obstructive lung disease. The same goes for the major causes of long term sick leave, including mental illness and back pain. The UK government's own figures show that workplace sickness absence costs £12 billion a year, with 40 million days lost to occupational ill health and injury, and 2.7 million people currently claiming incapacity benefit.[43]

Rather than seeking to address the structural issues underpinning this huge pool of ill health, however, the government's 2005 strategy paper "Health, Work and Wellbeing—Caring for our Future" mirrors the individualistic assumptions of the happiness and wellbeing literature in emphasising lifestyle change and health promotion. According to a review of the strategy document in the independent *Hazards* magazine (entitled, appropriately enough, "Futile Exercise"):

> The government's health, work and well-being strategy evangelises about the personal health side of the equation, and is encouraging initiatives like Well@Work to promote exercise, smoking cessation and healthy diets. It is also pushing measures to get the sick and injured back to work, through

42: Jones, 2004.
43: Cited in *Hazards* 93, p2.

sickness absence management and vocational rehabilitation. Where it falls flat is in prevention of the poor working environments and the work pressures that drive many of us to drink, or that leave us no time or energy for exercise and neither the time nor the cash to make healthy choices about diet. Low pay is a health issue; long work hours are a health issue; hazards at work are a health issue. Telling employees to clean up their act while the workplace and the work remain unchanged is a patently suspect and potentially unhealthy recipe.[44]

Welfare reform and mental health

It is, however, in relation to issues of mental health and the drive to get people with mental health problems back into the workplace that the limitations of the analysis and prescriptions of the "science of happiness" are most evident . Nowhere is this clearer than in the *Depression Report*, written by Layard and others and published in 2006, which is already having considerable influence on government mental health policy.

The report's starting point—that "crippling depression and chronic anxiety are the biggest causes of misery in Britain today"—is one with which few could dissent. Quoting the Psychiatric Morbidity Survey, Layard and his colleagues note that one in six of us will be diagnosed as having depression or chronic anxiety disorder, which means that one family in three is currently affected. In itself, the desire to alleviate mental and emotional suffering on this scale is clearly a laudable one.

However, while similar findings about the extent of depression almost 30 years ago led George Brown and Tirill Harris to pose hard questions about the kind of society that gives rise to such levels of misery,[45] no such concerns trouble the authors of this report. Instead their second finding—the "good news" as they call it—is that most of this misery is totally unnecessary and avoidable since "we now have evidence based therapies that can lift at least half of those affected out of their depression or chronic fear".[46] Foremost among the evidence based therapies is cognitive behaviour therapy (CBT), the central notion of which is that mental ill health is the product of people holding faulty or irrational ideas about themselves (such as "I am a worthless person"). The role of therapy therefore is to help people challenge these ideas and help them develop a more

---

44: *Hazards 93*, p4.
45: Brown and Harris, 1978.
46: CEPMHPG, 2006, p1.

accurate view of themselves and their relationships.

This, they argue, is good news for two groups of people. Most obviously, it is good news for those who are currently experiencing mental distress. It is also, however, good news for a New Labour government which is currently seeking to slash spending on Incapacity Benefit. For, as the report reminds us, as well as such mental ill health being a waste of people's lives:

> It is also costing a lot of money. For depression and anxiety make it difficult or impossible to work, and drive people onto Incapacity Benefit. We now have half a million people on Incapacity Benefits because of mental illness— more than the total number of people receiving unemployment benefit.

A key objective, then, of the report is to find ways of reducing the number of people with mental health problems currently claiming Incapacity Benefit.

How are these objectives to be achieved? The solution which the report proposes is the recruitment of many more CBT therapists—10,000, to be precise—of whom 5, 000 would be clinical psychologists and another 5,000, including nurses, occupational therapists, counsellors and social workers, who, on the basis of part-time training over one or two years, would become "psychological therapists". These would be trained and recruited over the next seven years, with the aim being that by 2013 there would be some 250 teams in place in England and Wales with around 40 therapists in each.

On the all-important question of costs, by 2013 the gross costs of the service would have reached about £600 million a year, with an additional annual training cost of around £50 million. However, the report's authors suggest, these costs would be "fully offset, of course, by rapid savings to the Department for Work and Pensions and HM Revenue and Customs".

How should we respond to these proposals? On an individual level, there is clear evidence that many people find CBT, and "talking therapies" more generally, a better way of addressing their mental health problems than taking prescribed drugs. For that reason alone, the extension of talking therapies on the NHS should be welcomed. There are, however, a number of problems with the notion proposed by Layard and his colleagues that, as an "evidence-based" approach, CBT should become the primary, if not the sole, form of therapy on offer, at the expense of all other approaches including person-centred and psychoanalytic approaches.

First, there is the uncritical acceptance of positivist notions of science and of what constitutes evidence. The fact that CBT, like other behavioural approaches, lends itself more easily than other therapies to quantitative methods of evaluation is not the same as saying that it is necessarily more effective.

Second, while there is research evidence to show that CBT can be effective for people with simple, uncomplicated, mild depression, there is less evidence for its effectiveness in helping people with more complicated or prolonged depression, including depression arising from early trauma. To state the obvious, different approaches are likely to work for different people.[47] In this respect, there is a particular irony in a New Labour government, which in its promotion of a choice agenda in education and social care is continually lambasting a "one size fits all" approach, promoting precisely such an approach in the field of mental health policy.

Third, despite frequent references to evidence-based practice, there is very little discussion in any of this literature (and none whatsoever in the *Depression Report*) of what by any criterion must be considered one of the most strongly established links in any body of social science research anywhere, namely the link between poverty, inequality and mental ill health.[48]

However, the main reason for being sceptical about these ideas relates to the intellectual and political climate in which they are being proposed and the uses to which they are already being put. For, whether it be Layard's insistence that CBT can reduce the number of people with mental health problems on Incapacity Benefit by half or Carol Craig's view that the roots of Scotland's problems lie in its dependency culture, the key themes of the science of happiness fit like a glove with the dominant ideas and policies of the New Labour government in Britain and of neoliberalism more generally: notions of health as individual responsibility; rejection of poverty and inequality as explanatory frameworks; an abhorrence of dependency in any form; and of course the very specific policy, announced by the works and pensions secretary John Hutton in July 2006, to save billions of pounds by removing one million people from Incapacity Benefit.[49]

In this context, should Layard's plans be implemented (and ten pilot schemes have already been set up across England and Wales), one can only feel concern for those with mental health problems who, for whatever reason, have failed to attain good mental health after the prescribed 16 weeks of CBT.

47: Holmes, 2002; McPherson, Richardson, and Leroux, 2003; Plumb, 2005.
48: For reviews of the literature, see Rogers and Pilgrim, 2003, and Ramon, 2007.
49: The *Guardian*, 5 July 2006.

Conclusion

Thirty years ago Brown and Harris concluded their groundbreaking study of the social origins of depression by arguing that social factors shaped every aspect of depression, from the likelihood of its onset to the ways in which people interpreted their life experiences. The results as a whole, they concluded, focused attention on the importance of understanding early childhood attachments for the understanding of depressive phenomena. But they went on:

> This does not mean, of course, that they just have implications in terms of individual psychology. The social class differences have much wider implications.[50]

That approach allowed them to explicitly envisage a different kind of society in which very few people would experience depression. It is perhaps a tribute of sorts to the triumph of neoliberalism that, despite equally high levels of mental ill health today, few, and even fewer happiness theorists, are capable of envisaging such a systemic alternative. Even the best of them, such as Oliver James, who rails eloquently against the "greed is good" values of neoliberalism and the ways in which they produce mental ill health, ends up protesting that "I am not against capitalism, which does not in itself cause Affluenza".[51]

For the most part, despite nods in the direction of the need to reduce inequality, their unwillingness to address the structural factors which produce so much physical and emotional misery means in practice that achieving happiness becomes, for them, both an individual task and an individual responsibility. In that sense, Layard's vision of "mass" CBT fits perfectly with welfare to work policies. For if phase one was about equipping individuals with the practical and technical skills to survive in a globalised workplace, then arguably phase two is about providing them (and particularly those with poor mental health) with the emotional and psychological skills to do so.

Fortunately, there is both a theoretical and a political alternative. The theoretical alternative is rooted in a Marxism which argues that human happiness, wellbeing and—importantly—individuality can only be fully realised in a society free of exploitation and oppression, a genuinely socialist society where people are free to develop their unique abilities and potential. This

---

50:   Brown and Harris, 1978, p289.
51:   James, 2007, p329.

is a million miles away from Stalinist notions of prescribed "happiness from above" (where rumour has it that a favourite official slogan in the depths of the terror was "Life is better and merrier than ever before"[52]). By contrast, as Marshall Berman has argued, a core value of the young Marx was the notion of *bildung*, which Berman translates as meaning "self-development" or "becoming who you are", whereas, Marx argued in his early writings, the dominance of money meant "the overturning of all individualities".[53] More recently Terry Eagleton has argued:

> We are, by nature, sociable animals who must cooperate or die; but we are also individual beings who seek our own fulfilment To be individuated is an activity of our species-being, not a condition at odds with it. We could not achieve it, for example, were it not for language, which belongs to me only because it belongs to the species first.[54]

As an example of this interaction between group and individual, he cites the example of a jazz group with "the free musical expression of each member acting as the basis for the free expression of the others" (though presumably in a genuinely socialist society there would also be space for lovers of folk music).[55]

The political alternative is rooted in a different critique of consumerism, that provided by the anti-capitalist movement that emerged out of the demonstrations against the World Trade Organisation in Seattle in 1999.[56] In common with some happiness theorists, the starting point for that movement was a rejection of the notion that our lives, our relationships and our world are simply commodities. Unlike them, however, rather than exhorting us to change the way we see the world, movement activists argued that "another world is possible". For all its current debates and disagreements,[57] it is that movement and that critique, rather than the individualist prescriptions of the "science of happiness", which point the way out of the material and emotional misery that continues to blight the lives of millions.

52: "That's Enough Happynomics", the *Economist* Free Exchange blog.
53: Berman, 1999, pp9-10.
54: Eagleton, 2007, pp167-168.
55: Eagleton, 2007, pp171-172.
56: Harman, 2000.
57: For a discussion of these, see Callinicos and Nineham, 2007

References

Bergheim, Stefan, 2007, *The Happy Variety of Research* (Deutsche Bank).

Berman, Marshall, 1999, *Adventures in Marxism* (Verso).

Bourdieu, Pierre, 1999, *The Weight of the World: Social Suffering in Contemporary Society* (Stanford University).

Brown, George, and Tirril Harris, 1978, *Social Origins of Depression: A Study of Psychiatric Disorder in Women* (Tavistock)

Callinicos, Alex, and Chris Nineham, 2007, "At an Impasse: Anti-capitalism and the Social Forums Today", *International Socialism 115* (spring 2007), ww.isj.org.uk/index.php4?id=337

Cameron, David, 2007, Closing Speech to Conservative Party Conference, 3 October 2007.

CEPMHPG, 2006, *The Depression Report: a New Deal for Depression and Anxiety Disorders* (Centre for Economic Performance's Mental Health Policy Group, LSE).

Cliff, Tony, 1979, "The Balance of Class Forces in Britain Today", *International Socialism 6* (autumn 1979), www.marxists.org/archive/cliff/works/1979/xx/balance1.htm

Craig, Carol, 2003, *The Scots' Crisis of Confidence* (Big Thinking)

Department for Work and Pensions, Department of Health and the Health and Safety Executive, 2005, *Health, Work and Wellbeing—Caring for our Future: A Strategy for the Health and Wellbeing of Working Age People* (The Stationery Office)

Dolan, Paul, Tessa Peasgood and Matthew White, 2006, Review of Research on the Influences on Personal Wellbeing and Application to Policy Making (Defra), www.sustainable-development.gov.uk/publications/pdf/WellbeingProject2.pdf

Eagleton, Terry, 2007, *The Meaning of Life* (Oxford University).

Edmonds, Noel, 2006, *Positively Happy: Cosmic Ways to Change Your Life* (Random House) .

Green, Francis, "It's Been a Hard Day's Night but Why? An Exploration of Work Intensification in Britain", Public Lecture, 23 June 2000, University of Kent at Canterbury.

Gunnell, Barbara, 2004, "The Happiness Industry", *New Statesman*, 6 September 2004.

Harman, Chris, 2000, "Anti-capitalism: Theory and Practice", *International Socialism 88* (autumn 2000), http://pubs.socialistreviewindex.org.uk/isj88/harman.htm

Healy, David, 1998, *The Psychopharmacologists* (Hooder Arnold).

Hills, John, and Kitty Stewart (eds), 2005, *A More Equal Society? New Labour, Poverty, Inequality, and Exclusion* (Policy Press).

Holmes, Jeremy, 2002, "All You Need is Cognitive Behaviour Therapy?", *British Medical Journal 324*.

James, Oliver, 2007, *Affluenza* (Vermillion),

Jones, Chris, 2004, "The Neoliberal Assault: Voices from the Front-line of British Social Work", in Iain Ferguson, Michael Lavalette and Elizabeth Whitmore (eds), *Globalisation, Global Justice and Social Work* (Routledge).

Jordan, Bill, 2007, *Social Work and Wellbeing* (Russell House).

Lansley, Stewart, 2006, *Rich Britain: The Rise and Rise of the Super-wealthy* (Politico's).

Laurance, Jeremy, 2007, "Health, Wealth and a Skilled Job is the Way to Happiness", the *Independent*, 28 July 2007.

Layard, Richard, 2005, *Happiness: Lessons from a New Science* (Penguin).

Levitas, Ruth, 2000, "Discourses of Risk and Utopia", in Barbara Adam, Ulrich Beck and Joost Van Loon (eds), *The Risk Society and Beyond: Critical Issues for Social Theory* (Sage).

McMahon, Darren M, 2006, *Happiness: A History* (Grove).

McPherson, Susan, Phil Richardson and Penny Leroux (eds), 2003, *Clinical Effectiveness in Psychotherapy and Mental Health: Strategies and Resources for the Effective Clinical Governance* (Karnac).

Office for National Statistics, 2004, *Focus on Social Inequalities* (The Stationery Office).

Palmer, Guy, Jane Carr and Peter Kenway, 2005, *Monitoring Poverty and Social Exclusion in the UK* (Joseph Rowntree Foundation).

Pantazis, Christina, Dave Gordon and Ruth Levitas (eds), 2006, *Poverty and Social Exclusion in Britain: the Millennium Survey*, (Policy Press)

Plumb, Sally, 2005, "The Social/Trauma Model: Mapping the Mental Health Consequences of Childhood Sexual Abuse and Similar Experiences", in Jerry Tew (ed), *Social Perspectives in Mental Health* (Jessica Kingsley).

Ramon, Shulamit, 2007, "Inequality in Mental Health: The Relevance of Current Research and Understanding to Potentially Effective Social Work Responses", *Radical Psychology*, volume 6, number 1.

Ricard, Matthieu, 2007, *Happiness: a Guide to Developing Life's Most Important Skill* (Atlantic Books)

Rogers, Ann and David Pilgrim, 2003, *Mental Health and Inequality* (Palgrave Macmillan).

Seligman, Martin E P, 2002, *Authentic Happiness* (Simon and Schuster).

Timmins, Nicholas, 1996, *The Five Giants: a Biography of the Welfare State* (Fontana).

Wilkinson, Richard, 2005, *The Impact of Inequality: How to Make Sick Societies Healthier* (The New Press).

Reimagined Communities

Neil Davidson

A review of Benedict Anderson, **Imagined Communities: Reflections on the Origin and Spread of Nationalism** *(Verso, 2006), £12.99*

If there is one book on nationalism that every student is expected to read, one book that is certain to be included in any survey of the competing theories, it is *Imagined Communities*. It is, as Josep Llobera has written of the core conception, "as if people had been waiting for such an expression to be coined".[1] The appearance of the third edition therefore gives us an opportunity to reassess this original and influential work, but also to identify some of the problems to which it gives rise, problems which are, in part, the very reason for its popularity. These are not all simply the result of inevitable misunderstandings that occur when a complex concept is seized upon to fill an explanatory gap. Some are the result of Benedict Anderson's underlying theoretical assumptions. As he himself notes, "the book attempted to combine a kind of historical materialism with what later on came to be called discourse analysis. Marxist modernism married to post-modernism *avant la letter*".[2]

It is the postmodern aspects of the work which have proved the most influential, all too often at the expense of Anderson's Marxism. Nevertheless, it would be ungenerous not to begin by recognising his achievement. To understand why this book had such an impact, it is necessary first to review how nationalism had previously been dealt with in the Marxist tradition.

1: Llobera, 1994, p103.
2: That is, postmodernism before postmodernism was invented. Anderson, 2006, p227.

Strategies, definitions, explanations

Marx and Engels engaged with the issue of nationalism in the middle decades of the 19th century, in other words, during the period in which the bourgeois revolution was being completed across Western Europe, North America and Japan. They argued that the working class (and "the democracy" more generally) should support national movements and the formation of new nation-states where they would hasten the development of capitalism, and consequently the emergence of a working class, and where they would weaken the great reactionary powers of Europe, the most powerful of which was absolutist Russia.[3]

Self-determination was not necessarily the absolute priority. Marx and Engels rejected the view that every national group had the right to establish a state, the so-called "principle of nationality", as it was then known.[4] On the contrary, for them it entirely depended on whether the success of the movement was likely to lead to a progressive outcome or not. Nor was their attitude to a particular movement determined by the class nature or political attitudes of its leadership. The Hungarian rising of 1848 was dominated by the nobility, the aristocracy led the Polish insurrection of 1863 and even the Irish Fenians—in many respects one of the more politically advanced non-socialist groups of the time—were heavily influenced by the Catholic church. None of these negative characteristics was decisive, however, compared with the positive objective consequences of opening up the possibilities for capitalist development or closing down the influence of the absolutist states. By contrast, Marx and Engels refused support to the Czechs and southern Slavs during the revolutions of 1848-9 because they were backed by Russian absolutism—the "*gendarme* of Europe"—for its own purposes.[5]

The specific situations with which these socialist strategies towards nationalism were intended to deal are now largely historical, but the method employed remains of enduring value. It was, however, arrived at without any real explanation of the emergence or nature of nations, whose existence Marx and Engels essentially took for granted. Marx and Engels do have much to teach us in relation to "nation theory", but this has to be derived from their theory of ideology, and not some untheorised remarks about, for example, German tribes. They left the movement a correct strategic

---

3: Marx and Engels, 1974, p389.
4: Engels, 1974, pp381-385.
5: The claim by Engels that these nations were intrinsically "non-historic" was a piece of Hegelian baggage quite unnecessary to their critique of Pan-Slavism. For the problems with the concept of non-historicity, and the extent to which Engels later abandoned it, largely as a result of his analysis of the Irish situation, see Davidson, 2001, pp290-292 and pp297-302.

orientation on national movements together with an undeveloped theoretical position on the nature of nations, national consciousness, and so on.

The next generation of Marxists quite understandably concentrated, as a matter of practical necessity, on refining the approach of revolutionary socialists to national movements and national demands, under the changed conditions of the imperialist era. These discussions, which extended from the mid-1890s to the debates on "the national and colonial question" during the first four congresses of the Communist International (1919-1922), represent one of Marxism's greatest contributions to the question of socialist strategy.[6] But although some participants, notably Karl Kautsky and Lenin, made attempts to explain how nations emerged, these were rarely central to the argument, and usually went no further than emphasising the need for capitalism to dominate a territorial home market and the role of language in unifying the inhabitants of that territory.[7]

The Austro-Marxist tendency, represented by Karl Renner and Otto Bauer, did focus on the question of national formation, above all in Bauer's monumental *The National Question and Social Democracy* (1906). But the definition of a nation offered by Bauer was resolutely non-materialist: "The nation is the totality of human beings bound together by a community of fate into a community of character." Bauer did see capitalism as playing a role in the development of national consciousness, but only in the sense that such consciousness can only be complete when it is aware of other nations and the difference between them, which occurs most fully under capitalist development. Bauer's work has been hailed as the only serious Marxist attempt to deal with the national question, but mainly by people who welcome it precisely because of its distance from Marxism. (Indeed, even Bauer is too marked by "economism" and "class reductionism" for some of his present day admirers.[8])

Lenin claimed that Bauer's theory was "basically psychological" and endorsed instead the "historico-economic" explanation associated with Kautsky and in his own writings,[9] but failed to propose a comparably detailed alternative explanation for the emergence of nations or the nature of national consciousness. What was offered in direct opposition to Bauer was not a counter-explanation, but a counter-definition which

6:    Haupt, Lowy and Weill, 1974; Riddell, 1984, pp348-383; Riddell, 1991a, pp211-290; Riddell, 1991b, appendix 2, pp846-885; Riddell, 1993, pp137-171; Adler, 1983, pp328-331 and pp409-419.
7:    Kautsky, in Luxemburg, 1976, pp126 and 129; Lenin, 1964, p396.
8:    Nemni, 1991, p143 and pp181-184.
9:    Lenin, 1964, p308.

is unfortunately still widely accepted by many on the left today. In 1913 Joseph Stalin wrote, under Lenin's guidance, "A nation is a historically constituted, stable community of people, formed on the basis of a common language, territory, economic life, and psychological makeup manifested in a common culture".[10] Typically, he also informs us that if a single one of these factors is missing, no nation exists. The trouble with definitions of this sort is that they give a false aura of scientific objectivity, which collapses as soon as you start to think of all the nations it would exclude—the United States of America, for one. And although Stalin dismissed the demand for cultural autonomy associated with Austro-Marxism, his definition actually draws heavily on that of Bauer, by retaining the catch-all categories of "community" and "psychological makeup".[11]

With the triumph of Stalinism in the late 1920s, serious discussion of nationalism virtually ceased. The main source of discussion about the nation therefore passed to non-Marxist political and social scientists, including many who were to be the founding fathers of the academic discipline of International Relations, an orientation which suggests that their interests lay in the "state" side of the "nation-state" couplet.[12] Yet although they tended to see nationalism as a movement only emerging from the late 18th century, they also accepted that nations—at least the "old historic nations" such as Spain, England and France—long pre-existed this period.

The Andersonian moment: political and theoretical contexts

From the 1960s a "modernist" current emerged within the study of nationalism which took a much more foreshortened view of its history. Emphases varied. Of the initial "modernist texts", Kedurie's *Nationalism* (1960) privileged the Enlightenment and Gellner's essay "Nationalism" (1964), the Industrial Revolution, as the sources on nationhood. But all "modernists", as the name suggests, saw both nations and nationalism as relatively recent, "modern", creations.[13] As one survey of the field says:

> For modernists, national consciousness in the modern age has to be seen as qualitatively different from that in the Scotland of the Declaration of Arbroath or the England of Shakespeare or Elizabeth or Cromwell... It is

---

10:   Stalin, 1953, p307.
11:   Ree, 1994, p228.
12:   The classic works include Hayes, 1931; Kohn, 1944; Cobban, 1945; Carr, 1945; and Deutsch, 1953.
13:   Kedurie, 1960; Gellner, 1964.

only with modernity that a sense of national identity comes to pervade all classes, or emerges as the overriding identity.[14]

The intellectual dominance of modernism only held sway for a relatively brief period, roughly from the late 1970s to the early 1990s, but included such key works as Nairn's *The Break-Up Of Britain* (1977 and 1981), Breuilly's *Nationalism And The State* (1982 and 1992), Gellner's *Nations And Nationalism* (1983), Hobsbawm and Ranger's *The Invention Of Tradition* (1983), Hobsbawm's *Nations And Nationalism Since 1780* (1990) and Nigel Harris's *National Liberation* (1990). Of these writers, Nairn, Hobsbawm and Harris saw themselves as Marxists at the time of writing, as did Anderson.

Anderson is a specialist in East Asian politics. He went to Indonesia in 1962 to study that country's experience during the Second World War, when Japanese occupation supplanted the Dutch colonial presence. The book which resulted from these researches, *Java in a Time of Revolution* (1972), dealt only in passing with the question of nationalism, but what it does say is interesting in the light of his later preoccupations. Anderson describes how at the second congress of the youth wing of the Indonesian National Party in 1928 "the youth took the historic oath of commitment to one people, the Indonesian people, one nation, the Indonesian nation, and one language, the Indonesian language". Nationalism alone "made sense of the new life" on which young people drawn from many different places were "collectively embarked". But the nationalism was limited at the time to "politically-minded youth" who were "profoundly isolated from the rest of their contemporaries". It was not until the Japanese period that nationalism spread deeply into small-town and rural Java, and it did so then because of the new experiences encountered there, to which it gave coherent meaning.

Many of the themes rehearsed in this work—the initial growth of nationalism emerging from the collective experience of an elite group, the sense of nationalism as a means of understanding the world rather than a narrow set of political demands—were all to re-emerge in more fully developed form in *Imagined Communities*.

Anderson was expelled from Indonesia for displeasing the Suharto regime shortly after the book appeared. "Exile", he later wrote, "had the advantage of pushing my inquiries back into the nineteenth century, and from everyday politics to the transformations of consciousness that made presently existing Indonesia thinkable". There were, however, other factors which led him to write *Imagined Communities*.

14:   Spencer and Wollman, 2002, p33.

In 1978 and 1979 wars had taken place between Vietnam, Cambodia and China, but "none of the belligerents had made more than the most perfunctory attempts to justify the bloodshed in terms of a recognisable Marxist theoretical perspective". This said something about their character: "Since World War Two every successful revolution has defined itself in national terms...and, in so doing, has grounded itself firmly in a territorial and social space inherited from the revolutionary past".[15] But the idea that socialism, or even the transition to socialism, should perpetrate nation-state and nationalism was contrary to all previous Marxist positions. What implications did this have for the Marxist theory of nationalism?

There was already a perception that Marxism lacked an adequate theory of nationalism. In 1976 Tom Nairn had claimed that nationalism "represents Marxism's greatest historical failure".[16] Anderson claims that he intended *Imagined Communities* to offer critical support, but also to extend Nairn's critique from Marxism to all other political traditions, which he saw as similarly lacking.[17] What then was his alternative?

Anderson's argument

Anderson starts by arguing that nationalism is "a radically changed form of consciousness".[18] To define it, he starts with the reason why the nation has to be imagined: "It is imagined because the members of even the smallest nation will never know most of their fellow-members, meet them, or even hear of them, yet in the minds of each lives the image of their community." Anderson is insistent that "imagined" does not mean "false", because all communities beyond the original gatherer-hunter groups have to conduct a similar act of imagining: "Communities are to be distinguished, not by their falsity/genuineness, but by the style in which they are imagined." Anderson argues that there are three aspects to what is being imagined: limitation, because no nation can encompass the entire world and the boundaries of each are set by other nations; sovereignty, because nations came into existence at the time when the legitimacy once conferred by absolutist divine right was being replaced by that of the state; and community, because the horizontal solidarities of the

---

15:    Anderson, 2006, pp1-2. See also pxi, from the preface to the 1991 edition. The same conflicts are also discussed by Nairn in the second edition of *The Break-Up of Britain*. See Nairn, 1981, p371.

16:    Nairn, 1977, p329.

17:    Anderson, 2006, pp208-209.

18:    Anderson, 2006, pxiv.

nation were stronger than vertical oppositions, even those of class.[19]

Anderson identifies "the end of the 18th century" as the period which saw "the spontaneous distillation of a complex 'crossing' of discrete historical forces", and once distilled it was no longer necessary for each potential new nation to have undergone the same experiences. They could be "transplanted, with varying degrees of self-consciousness, to a great variety of social terrains".[20] But the origin of these forces goes much further back in time. Anderson argues that from the late medieval period onwards there was the collapse of three key conceptions of the world: the idea that belief systems expressed in particular script languages like those of Christianity and Islam (using respectively Latin and classical Arabic) offered privileged access to truth; the belief that society was naturally organised around and under monarchs who were persons apart from other human beings and who ruled by some form of divine dispensation; and an understanding of the past and present in terms of some creation myth. Such notions rooted human lives firmly in the very nature of things, giving certain meanings to the everyday fatalities of existence (above all death, loss and servitude) and offering, in various ways, redemption from them.

All these conceptions were subverted by economic change, discoveries, social and scientific, and the development of increasingly rapid communications: "No surprise then that the search was on, so to speak, for a new way of linking fraternity, power and time together".[21]

For Anderson, the solution was provided by the emergence of "print capitalism".[22] This created the possibility of a vast market beyond the tiny minority who could understand Latin. Print-languages "created unified fields of exchange and communication below Latin and above the spoken vernaculars". They "gave a new fixity to language, which in the long run helped to build that image of antiquity so central to the subjective idea of the nation". And they created "languages of power", with certain dialects playing a dominant part in communication through printing. These were "largely unselfconscious processes resulting from the explosive interaction between capitalism, technology and human linguistic diversity".[23]

The remainder of the book sets out how national consciousness spread

---

19:    Anderson, 2006, pp6-7.
20:    Anderson, 2006, p4.
21:    Anderson, 2006, p36. He is not making the absurd suggestion that religion had to decline in importance before nationalism could emerge, contrary to the claims of several of his critics like Ozkirilh, 2000, p153. The importance he ascribes to the Reformation proves them wrong.
22:    Anderson, 2006, p36.
23:    Anderson, 2006, pp44-45.

and was transmuted into nationalism. He argues there were three main kinds of nationalism, arising in successive waves: "creole" nationalism associated with the revolt of the American colonies ("creole" in its Spanish use means a Latin American of European ancestry); "language" nationalism associated with western Europe; and "official" nationalism associated with central and eastern Europe, and with the Asian and African anti-colonial movements.

In what is perhaps his boldest innovation, Anderson argues that the "pioneers" of nationalism were the first of these, the colonial states of the Americas. He ascribes the rise of nationalism to the attempt by Madrid to impose greater control, the influence of Enlightenment ideas and the way in which the South American continent had been divided into particular, territorially delimited, administrative units:

> In this respect they foreshadowed the new states of Africa and parts of Asia in the mid-20th century… The original shaping of the American administrative units was to an extent arbitrary and fortuitous, marking the spatial limits of particular military conquests. But over time they developed a firmer reality under the influence of geographic, political and economic factors.[24]

Two necessary internal processes translated the brute fact of territoriality into national consciousness, according to Anderson. There was the self-identification of the descendents of settlers with the colonial territory, in distinction from their European-born equivalents. And there was the emergence of a particular manifestation of print capitalism: the newspaper which "brought together, on the same page, this marriage with that ship, this price with that bishop", creating "quite naturally, and even apolitically…an imagined community among a specific assemblage of fellow-readers, to whom these ships, brides, bishops and prices belonged. In time, of course, it was only to be expected that political elements would enter in".[25]

Although vernacular language was critical to the original formation of national consciousness, once nationalism became available as a model, it was no longer necessary for new nations to have this as their basis.[26]

The emergence of nationalism was originally associated with the popular masses, but it became available for use for "conservative, not to say reactionary," ends by the state bureaucracies of societies which had not

---

24: Anderson, 2006, p52.
25: Anderson, 2006, p62.
26: Anderson, 2006, p133 and p135.

experienced successful popular movements.[27]

Anderson argues that the anti-imperialist nationalism, which began to build new states after 1945, drew on both of these aspects. "That is why so often in the 'nation-building' policies of the new states one sees both a genuine, popular nationalist enthusiasm and a systematic, even Machiavellian, instilling of nationalist ideology through the mass media, the educational system, administrative regulations and so forth".[28]

A brief exposition can only hint at the subtlety, complexity and sophistication of Anderson's arguments. More than any previous writer, Anderson established that the phenomenon of nationalism was constructed and historical, not natural and eternal. Part of the charm of the book lies in the sheer range and novelty of the examples which Anderson musters to illustrate his argument, many of them drawn from areas such as Burma, Thailand and Indonesia, which do not normally feature in discussions of nationalism. And yet *Imagined Communities* is one of those books of great individual value, but which have ultimately exerted a negative influence on socialist thought.

Postmodernist appropriation and primordialist approbation

Imagined Communities made an immediate impact on publication, but perhaps not in the way that Anderson had hoped. Although other Marxists did find his work useful, it actually provided far greater support for emerging ideologies fixated on questions of identity, above all postmodernism.

One of Anderson's more insightful critics, Anthony Smith, noted that, while Anderson's project is not itself a postmodernist reading, "it is the idea of the nation as discourse to be interrogated and deconstructed, that has proved most influential".[29] Anderson does not, of course, suggest that the nation is simply a discourse, but many of his critics have found it convenient to ascribe that view to him. The Scottish writer Murray Pittock, for example, writes, "The weakness of Anderson's notion of the 'imagined community' is that it implies that one can imagine at will, and choose an identity as the postmodern consumer chooses a lifestyle product".[30]

Smith is one of the main proponents of the 'perennialist' view of nations which sees them as rooted in much older ethnic identities. He considers it a problem that, for Anderson, "the nation possesses no reality independent of

---

27: Anderson, 2006, p110.
28: Anderson, 2006, pp113-114.
29: Smith, 1998, p142.
30: Pittock, 1999, p140.

its images and representations. But such a perspective undermines the socio-logical reality of the nation, the bonds of allegiance and belonging which so many people feel, and obscures both the institutional, political and territorial constitution of nations, and of the powerful and popular cultural resources and traditions that underpin so many nations and endow them with a sense of tangible identity".[31] Similarly Pittock wants to defend a conception of Scottish nationalism stretching back to early medieval times.

These criticisms demonstrate the revival of arguments that hold that nations are much older than "modernists" have claimed. As Pittock notes, "the idea that nations and nationalism cannot predate the French Revolution' is increasingly on the defensive".[32] The 1990s saw Greenfield's *Nationalism* (1992), Llobera's *The God of Modernity* (1994), Hutchinson's *Modern Nationalism* (1994) and Hasting's *The Construction Of Nationhood* (1997), although the final collapse into primordial essentialism was signalled by two works by Emmanuel Todd, *L'illusion Economique* (1998) and *La Diversité du Monde* (1999). Todd's key thesis has been approvingly sum-marised by Tom Nairn to claim that "nationalism is constitutive of man's social nature".[33]

Re-imagining the history of the nation

Imagined Communities can still play a role in intellectually challenging both postmodernism and primordialism, but only if its themes are integrated into a more consistently materialist framework.

The book consists of a series of impressionistic studies on particular aspects of nationalism. But the connections between them are often difficult to establish. What is missing is any central dynamic linking them together, except for the concept of print capitalism. Yet the universality of contem-porary nationalism suggests that it was originally produced and subsequently reproduced by a set of conditions wider and more fundamental than this.

The major contribution that Marxism might make here lies not in what Marx and Engels wrote about particular nations. Rather it lies in their more general observations on the historical conditions for the emergence of certain forms of consciousness, which could then be applied in the case of national consciousness, starting with their general relationship to social being:

31: Smith, 1998, p137.

32: Pittock, 1999, pp102-103.

33: Nairn, 2002, p156. Here Nairn follows Todd, 1998, but essentially as a theoretical justification for a position he had been moving towards for several years beforehand, See Davidson, 1999, pp110-111.

The mode of production of material life conditions the general process of social, political and intellectual life. It is not the consciousness of men that determines their existence, but their social existence that determines their consciousness.[34]

Certain forms of consciousness are only possible under particular conditions. The point was further developed by George Lukács, who attacked "the crudeness and conceptual nullity" of those forms of thought which obscure "the historical, transitory nature of capitalist society": "Its determinants take on the appearance of timeless, eternal categories valid for all social formations".[35] The "nation" is one of these historical categories which are only relevant to capitalist society. In making this particular error, anti-modernist writers simply follow bourgeois "normal science".

Take, for example, the work of Adrian Hastings. Hastings has argued that "nation", "the word and the idea", existed in England at least since the 16th and probably since the 14th century.[36] But, as Alasdair MacIntyre has pointed out:

To understand a concept, to grasp the meaning of the words which express it, is always…to grasp the role of the concept in language and social life… Different forms of social life will provide different roles for concepts to play.[37]

In other words, just because people used the term "nation" in, say, the 14th century, it does not follow that they meant by it what we mean by it—indeed, if we take Marxism seriously then it is extremely unlikely that they could possibly have done so. It is not simply a matter of words, but the forms of consciousness that the words express. Any Marxist account of national consciousness must therefore explain the particular "forms of social life" that could allow this form of consciousness, these modes of expression, to come into existence.

The origins of capitalism and nationalism

Anderson's argument about the coincidence of existential doubt and technological advance in print seems unconvincing as an explanation for something as all-pervasive as nationalism. A more convincing explanation

34:   Marx, 1975, p425.
35:   Lukács, 1971, p9.
36:   Hastings, 1997, p19.
37:   MacIntyre, 1967, p2 and p8.

might be the more general development of capitalism. But, like Otto Bauer, Anderson sees a purely contingent relationship between this and the rise of nationalism: "What made the new communities imaginable was a half-fortuitous, but explosive, interaction between a system of production and productive relations (capitalism), a technology of communications (print), and the fatality of human linguistic diversity".[38] The connection between national consciousness and capitalism is, however, far more all-embracing than this suggests. In fact, national consciousness took as many centuries to become the dominant form of consciousness as the capitalist mode of production did to become the dominant mode of production, and it did so as a consequence of that.[39] Four main elements combined, reflecting to a greater or lesser extent the impact of capitalism on feudal society.

The first element was the formation of externally demarcated and internally connected areas of economic activity. Europe had emerged from the first crisis of feudalism by the later 15th century as a system of states which was still dominated by the feudal mode of production. It was a system, however, increasingly adapted to elements of capitalism. In this context, the importance of capitalist development was less in the domain of production than that of circulation, for it was in the creation of trade networks that merchant capital began to link up dispersed rural communities both with each other and with the urban centres to form an extensive home market.

Linked directly to this element was a second, the adoption of a common language by the communities that were being connected to each other at the economic level. The need to communicate for the purposes of market exchange began to break down the distinctiveness of local dialects, forging a language common, or at least comprehensible, to all. Language in this way began to set the boundaries of the economic networks referred to above, boundaries that did not necessarily coincide with those of medieval kingdoms. Such economic and linguistic unification was far easier in a small centralised kingdom such as England than in a territory such as the German Empire. Indeed, establishment of state frontiers often purely determined the boundary between a dialect of a particular language and another language. And of course Anderson is right that the formation of standard forms of language was immeasurably aided by the invention of printing and the possibilities it presented for the codification of language in mass-produced works. These would not have been produced unless an audience of the literate already existed which understood their contents, but their effect was

---

38:   Anderson, 2006, pp42-43.
39:   For more on this see Harman, 1992.

to extend the size of that audience, since printers could not produce works in every local dialect, only in the one which had emerged as the standard form, or in those which were in competition to do so. The increasing standardisation of language then fed back into its original economic formation, as the merchants whose trading networks had originally defined the territorial reach of linguistic comprehensibility increasingly identified themselves with that territory, to the exclusion of rivals who spoke a different language. The rise of the vernacular was accompanied by the decline of Latin as a *lingua franca*, a process virtually complete by the mid-16th century and expressed in the new profession of interpreter, now necessary to make vernacular diplomatic exchanges mutually comprehensible.

The third element was the character of the new absolutist states. Absolutism was the form taken by the feudal state during the economic transition from feudalism to capitalism. Yet the absolutist states did not arise automatically. The replacement of the estates monarchy of the earlier feudal period by a more centralised apparatus was the political response of the feudal ruling class to the social and economic pressures—different in degree and combination throughout Europe—set in train by the first crisis of the feudal system and the greater significance of capitalist production in the economies which emerged from it. The local jurisdictions that characterised the classic epoch of military feudalism began to give way to greater concentration of state power, notably through the introduction of standing armies and, partly in order to pay for them, regular centralised taxation.

Death and taxes both involve bureaucracies that require a version of the local language, comprehensible across the state territory, thus strengthening the "linguistic" element. They also had two unintended effects. The introduction of regular taxation and the adoption of mercantilist policies reinforced the economic unity that had begun to emerge spontaneously from the activities of merchant capitalists. And the military rivalry that characterised the new system necessitated mobilising the active support of the bourgeois minority as a source of financial backing and administrative expertise. Despite these innovations it is nevertheless important not to mistake the role of absolutism in the birth of nationhood, which was that of a midwife, not that of a mother. The issue is often elided by reference to the influence of "the modern state" in the creation of nations, but this is to dissolve the difference between the absolutist state and its genuinely modern bourgeois successor. The arrival of nationhood coincided not with the establishment of the absolutist states but with their overthrow.

The fourth and final element is local manifestations of a global religious belief. The ideology of absolutism involved stressing the deeds of religious figures such as saints, who were associated with the territory of the realm, but it was the Reformation that made religion more than an ideologically pious enhancement to the image of the ruling dynasty. Wherever Protestantism became the dominant religion within a given territory after 1517 it contributed to the formation of national consciousness by allowing communities of belief to define themselves against the inter-territorial institutions of the Roman Catholic Church and the Holy Roman Empire. In part this was through the availability of the Bible in the vernacular, but this in turn depended on the existence of linguistic frameworks in which market transactions and state administration could be carried out. Protestantism acted as a stimulus to national consciousness only to the extent that the development of capitalism had provided it with the framework to do so.

Naturally the process went furthest in England, but even there it was not until after the death of Elizabeth in 1603 that Protestantism came to be separated from regnal solidarity with the monarch. It took longer for Catholicism to play the same role.

Nationalism and bourgeois revolution

There is therefore a problem with Anderson's focus as on "creole" nationalism as the major formative experience of nationalism. Apart from anything else, he contradicts himself by describing it as drawn from an earlier model: "In effect, by the second decade of the 19th century, if not earlier, a 'model' of 'the' independent national state was available for pirating." He describes this as "a complex composite of French and American elements".[40] But incredibly, this is one of the first occasions that France is mentioned. To ignore the influence of the French Revolution in establishing the "model" seems particularly perverse. The problem here is that even France and the United States are not the first nations. The United Netherlands and England all have a stronger claim to priority. To argue that nations only appeared at some stage in the later 18th century would be as absurd as arguing that capitalism only appeared at the same period. While Anderson is right to draw attention to cumulative movements, he misses something else, which is the explosive effect of the revolutionary turning points which punctuate capitalist development, and their impact in coalescing hitherto inchoate ideological elements into a national identity. His account is, so to speak, all process and no events.

The success of groups with an emergent national consciousness in the Netherlands and England in elevating this new form of consciousness into

---

40:    Anderson, 2006, p81 and note 34.

political movements led others (first in North America, Ireland and France, then generally) to aspire to national status, even if their level of social development had not previously allowed national consciousness to arise. The bourgeois revolutions effected the final transformation of the term "nation" to one which stood for "the people" as a community—although one of the most divisive issues within all bourgeois revolutionary movements was precisely how "the people" should be defined. The struggle against absolutism required the mobilisation of at least a large minority of "the people" to achieve the expulsion or destruction of the royal dynasty. This could only be done by providing some form of identity which could embrace the often very different forms of opposition to the crown, regardless of whether the ruler in question was foreign (as in the case of Spanish Habsburg dynasty in the Netherlands) or native (as in the case of the Stuart dynasty in England). Nationalism provided this identity.

National consciousness could not flourish, or even take root, unless the conditions for capitalist development were present, and for it to be consolidated across Europe, even if only among the bourgeoisie, there had to be at least one case where it made the transition to nationalism and then became embodied in a nation-state. Only when there were concrete examples of nationhood could different groups know what they were conscious of, regardless of whether they then went on to develop nationalisms of their own or not.

The capitalist nation-state became a permanent feature of the international state system only towards the end of the hundred years between the end of the English Revolution in 1688 and the beginning of the French Revolution in 1789. Thereafter new nations could be manufactured regardless of whether the original elements were present or not—although an economic infrastructure and common language would, of necessity, have to be introduced at some point for a sense of national consciousness to be consolidated. The ideological dominance of nationalism over the population depended, however, on when a particular revolution occurred in the overall cycle of bourgeois revolutions. In the two states where bourgeois revolutions were successfully completed before or during 1688, the Dutch and the English, the existence of national consciousness was directly proportional to the extent that the post-revolutionary state developed a centralised apparatus, rather than a federal or confederal structure. In this respect English nationalism was as far in advance of its Dutch predecessors as it was of its American successor, which similarly remained an alliance of semi-autonomous states down to 1865.

After 1848 all ruling classes intent on creating states on the British or

French models were forced to embrace nationalism, not because they were personally capitalists, but because all of them—Prussian Junkers, Japanese Samurai, Italian monarchists and, eventually, Stalinist bureaucrats—were engaged in building industrial societies dominated by the capitalist mode of production. The example of Italy is typical of how ruling classes were faced with the need to diffuse consciousness of being a nation down from elite level into the mass of the population, a large and growing proportion of whom were not the bourgeoisie and petty bourgeoisie who had originally formed the nation, but workers. The difficulties involved should not be underestimated: as late as the 1860s as many as a quarter of the inhabitants of the French state did not speak French.

Nationalism and the working class

Class is the great absent theme in *Imagined Communities*, yet no Marxist account can deal with the subject without exploring the role nationalism plays in class relations.[41] National consciousness begins to emerge in the social classes below the rulers of the new nation-states, partly as the result of deliberate indoctrination, but far more so as the by now inevitable pattern of life experience within societies shaped by the nation-state form. Among the working class the existence of reformist class consciousness provides the context within which national consciousness and nationalism develop. Reformist class consciousness was originally a historical product of the social conditions produced by the transition to capitalism or, more precisely, by the process of capitalist industrialisation, first in Britain and subsequently elsewhere.

Once the initial shock of industrialisation passed, workers came to accept that capitalism was not a passing aberration, but a new form of society which might have many years of vitality ahead of it. The apparent permanence of the system forced accommodation and adaptation, however grudgingly, from the new exploited class, whose horizons were anyway limited by the "dull compulsion" to work, raise families and recover from the savage exertions demanded by the factory system. Although these conditions provoked resistance, the fact that the new system generated its own defensive illusions made the possibility of a generalised revolutionary class consciousness emerging out of these resistance struggles less likely. Under early capitalism exploitation was accompanied by the economic discipline instilled by fear of the poverty which would result from being

---

41:   I focus here on the working class. The relationship between nationalism and the bourgeoisie is discussed in Davidson, forthcoming in 2008.

sacked. The actual process of exploitation, the fact that the worker produced more than that for which she or he was rewarded, was hidden from view. As a result, although workers were usually hostile to their own particular boss, this did not necessarily generalise into opposition to the system as a whole. Although trade unions grew out of worker resistance, the goal of these new organisations, whatever rhetoric was employed about the (invariably distant) overturning of the system, was improving the condition of the working class within the system itself. The resulting contradictory form of consciousness finds its most basic expression in an acceptance by workers of the wages system accompanied by a rejection of the particular level of wages which they are being offered, but it extends to all aspects of social life.

What then is the relationship of national consciousness to this reformist consciousness? National consciousness does not compete with revolutionary class consciousness directly for the allegiance of workers, but as a key element in reformist class consciousness. Indeed, one might say that workers remain nationalist to the extent that they remain reformist. And from the point of view of the capitalist class in individual nations it is absolutely necessary that they do so, or the danger is always that workers will identify, not with the "national" interest of the state in which they happen to be situated, but with that of the class to which they are condemned to belong, regardless of the accident of geographical location. Nationalism should not therefore be seen as something which only "happens" during separatist movements on the one hand, or during fascist and imperialist manifestations on the other. The capitalist system generates nationalism as a necessary everyday condition of its continued existence.

Mass nationalism was therefore initially a product of industrialisation, but not simply because it is functional for the ruling class in industrial capitalism. Industrialisation and urbanisation together produced the changes in human consciousness that made nationalism *possible* (for the subordinate classes), as well as creating societies that made nationalism *necessary* (for the dominant class). They developed new structural capacities, new modes of experience and new psychological needs in the people who had to work in the factories and live in the cities. It is the need for some collective sense of belonging with which to overcome the effects of alienation, the need for psychic compensation for the injuries sustained at the hands of capitalist society, that nationalism provides in the absence of revolutionary class consciousness, but in conjunction with reformist class consciousness.

The ideological role played by the ruling class in reinforcing nationalism is therefore only possible because nationalism already provides one possible means of meeting the psychic needs created by capitalism. Once a capitalist nation-state has been established, those who control the apparatus always seek to consolidate the hold of nationalism among the people who inhabit its territory. States need conscripts for their armies, citizens to pay taxes, workers to accept that they have more in common with those who exploit them at home than they do with their fellow-exploited abroad. This made it imperative that loyalty to a state be secured, and the nation was the means. Since the 18th century British workers have often been asked to accept rises in interest rates, cuts in wages and services, or participation in imperialist wars, but never for the benefit of British capitalism, always for the benefit of the British nation, for "the national interest".

It is not only the state that makes such appeals. The organisations of the working class themselves reinforce reformist class consciousness within a national context. At the most elementary level this is because such organisations are unwilling to challenge the nationalism within which political discourse is conducted, for fear of being labelled unpatriotic. More importantly, however, it is because they seek either to influence or to determine policy within the confines of the existing nation-state. Typically, therefore, nationalism is invested with the contradictory character of the reformist worldview.

Conclusion

If nationalism is as intertwined with capitalism as the above argument suggests, then nationalism today can only ever be progressive in certain limited circumstances, most obviously in relation to movements against national oppression. Marxists cannot be nationalists, nor can they even support nationalisms as such, although they can support particular national demands or movements. This is not Anderson's conclusion, as he hinted in *Imagined Communities* itself: "In an age when it is so common for progressive, cosmopolitan intellectuals (particularly in Europe?) to insist on the near-pathological character of nationalism, its roots in fear and hatred of the other, it is useful to remind ourselves that nations inspire love, often profoundly self-sacrificing love".[42] He made the point more clearly in a lecture given in the Indonesian capital of Jakarta shortly after the overthrow of the Suharto regime, Anderson told his audience:

42:   Anderson, 2006, p141.

No one can be a true nationalist who is incapable of feeling "ashamed" if her state or government commits crimes, including those against her fellow citizens... During the Vietnam War, a good part of the popular opposition came from just this good sense of shame among the American citizenry that "their government" was responsible for the violent deaths of three million people in Indochina, including uncounted numbers of women and children... So they went to work in protest, not merely as advocates of universal human rights, but as Americans who loved the common American project.[43]

The distinction between true and false nationalists is dangerous in the extreme. Anderson's important work, illuminating in so many ways, is ultimately a failure because he remains trapped within the ideological pre-suppositions of its subject. He has shown us that national consciousness and the nation-state are forms whose beginnings can be found in past history. But because he misunderstands the forces which brought them into being, he fails to recognise that future history may also see them brought to an end.

43: Anderson, 1999, p17. The final sentence has ominous echoes of Richard Rorty's famous declaration that white American liberals should help oppressed blacks, not because the are "fellow human beings", but because "it is much more persuasive, morally as well as politically, to describe them as our fellow Americans—to insist that it is outrageous that an American should live without hope". See Rorty, 1989, p191.

References

Adler, Alan (ed), 1983, *Theses, Resolutions and Manifestos of the First Four Congresses of the Third International*, translated by Alix Holt and Barbara Holland, introduced by Bertil Hessel (Pluto Press).

Anderson, Benedict, 1972, *Java in a Time of Revolution: Occupation and Resistance, 1944-1946* (Cornell University).

Anderson, Benedict, 1999, "Indonesian Nationalism Today and in the Future", *New Left Review* 235 (May/June 1999).

Anderson, Benedict, 2006 [1983], *Imagined Communities: Reflections on the Rise and Spread of Nationalism*, revised edition (Verso).

Bauer, Otto, 2000 [1907], *The Question of Nationalities and Social Democracy*, (University of Minnesota).

Carr, Edward, 1945, *Nationalism and After* (Macmillan).

Cobban, Alfred, 1945, *National Self-Determination*, (Oxford University).

Davidson, Neil, 1999, "In Perspective: Tom Nairn", *International Socialism* 82 (spring 1999), http://pubs.socialistreviewindex.org.uk/isj82/davidson.htm

Davidson, Neil, Neil, 2001, "Marx and Engels on the Scottish Highlands", *Science and Society*, volume 65, number 3, (autumn 2001).

Davidson, Neil, forthcoming in 2008, "Many Capitals, Many States: Logic, Contingency or Mediation?", *Cambridge Review of International Affairs*, volume 21, number 3 (September 2008).

Deutsch, Karl, 1953, *Nationalism and Social Communication* (MIT).

Engels, Frederick, 1974, "What Have the Working Classes to do with Poland?", in David Fernbach (ed), *The First International and After*, volume 3 (Harmondsworth/New Left Review), www.marxists.org/archive/marx/works/1866/03/24.htm

Gellner, Ernest, 1964, "Nationalism", in *Thought and Change* (Weidenfeld and Nicolson).

Harman, Chris, 1992, "The Return of the National Question", *International Socialism* 56 (autumn 1992), www.marxists.de/theory/harman/natquest.htm

Hastings, Adrian, 1997, *The Construction of Nationhood: Ethnicity, Religion and Nationhood* (Cambridge University).

Haupt, George, Michael Lowy and Claudie Weill, 1974, *Les Marxists et la Question Nationale, 1848-1914: Etudes et Textes* (Maspero).

Hayes, Carlton, 1931, *The Historical Evolution of Modern Nationalism* (Smith).

Kedurie, Edie, 1960, *Nationalism* (Hutchinson University Library).

Kohn, Hans, 1944, *The Idea of Nationalism* (Collier Macmillan).

Lenin, Vladimir, 1964a [1914], "The Right of Nations to Self-Determination", in *Collected Works*, volume 20, *December 1913-August 1914* (Lawrence and Wishart).

Lenin, Vladimir, 1964b [1916], "The Socialist Revolution and the Right of Nations to Self-Determination", in *Collected Works*, volume 22 (Lawrence and Wishart).

Llobera, Josep, 1994, *The God of Modernity: the Development of Nationalism in Western Europe* (Berg).

Lukács, Georg, 1971 [1923], "What is Orthodox Marxism?", in *History and Class Consciousness: Studies in Marxist Dialectics* (Merlin), www.marxists.org/archive/lukacs/works/history/orthodox.htm

Luxemburg, Rosa, 1976 [1908-1909], "The National Question and Autonomy", in *The National Question: Selected Writings by Rosa Luxemburg* (Monthly Review).

MacIntyre, Alasdair, 1967, *A Short History of Ethics* (Routledge and Kegan Paul).

Marx, Karl, 1975 [1859], "Preface to *A Contribution to the Critique of Political Economy*", in *Early Writings* (Penguin/New Left Review), www.marxists.org/archive/marx/works/1859/critique-pol-economy/preface.htm

Marx, Karl, and Frederick Engels, 1974, "For Poland", in David Fernbach (ed), *The First International and After: Political Writings*, volume 3 (Harmondsworth/New Left Review).

Nairn, Tom, 1977, "The Modern Janus", in *The Break-Up of Britain: Crisis and Neo-Nationalism* (New Left Books).

Nairn, Tom, 1981, "Into Political Emergency: a Retrospect from the 1980s", in *The Break-Up of Britain: Crisis and Neo-Nationalism*, second, revised edition (Verso).

Nairn, Tom, 2002, *Pariah: Misfortunes of the British Kingdom* (Verso).

Nemni, Ephraim, 1991, *Marxism and Nationalism: Theoretical Origins of a Political Crisis* (Pluto).

Ozkirilh, Umut, 2000, *Theories of Nationalism: a Critical Introduction* (Macmillan).

Pittock, Murray, 1999, *Celtic Identity and the British Image* (Manchester University).

Ree, Eric van, 1994, "Stalin and the National Question", *Revolutionary Russia*, volume 7, number 2 (April 1994).

Riddell, John (ed), 1984, *Lenin's Struggle for a Revolutionary International: Documents: 1907-1916, the Preparatory Years* (Monad Press).

Riddell, John, 1991a, *Workers and Oppressed Peoples of the World, Unite! Proceedings and Documents of the Second Congress, 1920*, volume 1 (Pathfinder).

Riddell, John, 1991b, *Workers and Oppressed Peoples of the World, Unite! Proceedings and Documents of the Second Congress, 1920*, volume 2 (Pathfinder).

Riddell, John, 1993, *To See the Dawn: Baku, 1920—First Congress of the Peoples of the East* (Pathfinder).

Rorty, Richard, 1989, *Contingency, Irony and Solidarity* (Cambridge University).

Smith, Anthony, 1998, *Nationalism and Modernism: A Critical Survey of Recent Theories of Nations and Nationalism* (Routledge).

Spencer, Phillip and Howard Wollman, 2002, *Nationalism: A Critical Introduction* (Sage).

Stalin, Joseph, 1953 [1913], "Marxism and the National Question", in *Works*, volume 2 (Foreign Languages Publishing House), www.marxists.org/reference/archive/stalin/works/1913/03.htm

Todd, Emmanuel, 1998, *L'illusion Economique: Essai sur la Stagnation des Sociétés Développées* (Gallimard).

Seventy Years of the Black Jacobins

A one-day conference to mark the seventieth anniversary of the publication of C L R James's classic history of the Haitian Revolution.

Saturday 2 February 2008

Keynote speakers include:
Darcus Howe, Selma James, Bill Schwarz, Marika Sherwood and Weyman Bennett

10am-4.30pm, at the Institute of Historical Research, Senate House, Malet Street, London Registration £10 (£5 unwaged). Organised by the London Socialist Historians Group

For more information go to www.londonsocialisthistorians.org or e-mail secretary@ londonsocialisthistorians.org

alternative futures and popular protest

The 13th annual Alternative Futures and Popular Protest conference will be held in Manchester from Monday 17 March to Wednesday 19 March 2008.

The conference explores the dynamics of popular movements, along with the ideas that animate their activists and supporters, and which contribute to shaping their fate.

We invite papers on matters such as:
Contemporary and historical social movements and popular protests ● Social movement theory ● Utopias and experiments ● Ideologies of collective action

Contacts: c.barker@mmu.ac.uk ● m.tyldesley@mmu.ac.uk

Shakespeare, literary history and Marxism

Joe Hartney

A review of Stephen Greenblatt, **Will in the World: How Shakespeare became Shakespeare** *(Jonathan Cape, 2004); and James Shapiro,* **1599: A year in the life of William Shakespeare** *(Faber, 2005)*

Two recent bestselling biographies of William Shakespeare have provided entertaining and accessible accounts of the famous bard in the context of 16th and early 17th century English society. These works are examples of the now dominant academic trend of literary criticism known as "new historicism". Their success in reaching a popular audience well beyond university-based specialists who teach and research literature has already generated much media comment, and will probably lead to a spate of similar "popular" works.

Books about Shakespeare are not rare. Hundreds of studies and articles on this subject appear each year, yet this is mostly work by and for academics, and seems to have very little impact on the way Shakespeare is viewed in our society in general. The suggestion that his plays might be dropped from school and college courses incites tabloid columnists to nationalistic indignation, and most schoolchildren are still forced to regard him in the same way that their parents and grandparents did: a remote icon of "English culture" and a solemn representative of "national values".

When this approach was challenged by scholars who knew better, the rarefied world of the academy and the increasingly obscure language used there excluded all but a few "professionals".

It is, then, a welcome change to see at least a couple of critics writing biographies of Shakespeare that are free of theoretical jargon, and that attempt to cut through some of the mystique and reverence surrounding this subject, presenting portraits of the writer that emphasise the world in which he grew up and lived. Many traditional approaches to Shakespeare (and literature generally) either ignore history and society altogether, focusing solely on language, or are concerned about purely "literary" matters, such as textual sources and the stylistic influences of other artists. The most common form of "history" dabbled in is the personal history of the artists, accounts of their "inner life" stressing their unique qualities as exceptional individuals. This has tended to give the impression that artists, and the art and literature they produce, are separate and distant from real life, removed and totally disconnected from the everyday world of work, human relationships and politics (an impression that reflects the position of the academy itself, hoping to maintain a comfortable distance from the grubby realities of capitalism).

One of the strengths of an approach that tries to combine an understanding of history and society with culture is that it can help bring art and literature to life for us. By stressing the connection that works of art and artists have with their own world, and the conflicts and struggles of their times, such an approach can help us grasp their significance for us today. This is why Marxist literary criticism has always stressed the historical context. This is also a professed concern of many of the "new historicist" critics, and is surely one of the reasons why these biographies have proven popular with non-specialist readers.

So there are some very positive elements in these accounts of Shakespeare's life and work, and even some advances on the usual methods adopted by new historicist critics, which I will touch on later. However, the way in which literature is placed in a historical context and these authors' attitudes to history itself raise a number of questions. In particular, many of the "new historicist" critics are influenced by various strands of postmodernism.

Some of these questions can best be answered by turning to the classical Marxist tradition.[1]

1: The most comprehensive Marxist critique of new historicism I am aware of is to be found in Holstun, 2000. Anyone interested in exploring the relationship between new historicism and postmodernism in more detail should consult this work.

What made Shakespeare?

Every potential biographer of Shakespeare has first to find a way of dealing with the simple fact that there are huge gaps in the evidence. What we actually know about Shakespeare's personal history is far too sketchy to provide enough material for a proper biography. Therefore the biographer is forced to guess and speculate to a large degree. A good knowledge of history can help make such speculation more informed, but both Greenblatt and Shapiro would accept that there is much educated guesswork involved in their accounts. Many of the more negative reviews of these biographies have focused on the "maybes", "perhapses" and "might haves" that crop up fairly regularly, but given the scant facts this is inevitable. At least a critic interested in social and political history can attempt to fill in some of the gaps in the personal record by assessing situations that would have been common for most people at the time.

Greenblatt's *Will in the World: How Shakespeare became Shakespeare* seeks to do this with digressions on the sort of society Shakespeare lived in, and attempts to reconstruct some of the perceptions and experiences that he feels would have been current in that world. So, as well as drawing on some of the more standard biographical material such as the likely curriculum of young William's grammar school in Stratford-upon-Avon (a diet of Latin classics), he also focuses on the importance of local festival days and the sorts of popular celebrations that broke up the monotony of life in Elizabethan England. These would include visits by touring troops of players putting on morality plays for the townspeople, and public spectacles created by local lords to entertain and impress the visiting queen. Many of these real life events could have had as much an influence on Shakespeare as the Latin plays he studied at school, and Greenblatt notes that aspects of "folk culture" play an important part in Shakespeare's works.

Greenblatt also gives a good account of some of the more brutal aspects of Elizabethan society, especially the sorts of punishments meted out to those who opposed the state religion. Like a number of recent biographers, Greenblatt is attracted to the notion that Shakespeare's father might have been a secret Catholic, and that Shakespeare too may have harboured some allegiance to the old religion. The evidence for this is extremely tenuous, but it does at least give Greenblatt the opportunity to recount stories about the horrific torture and executions meted out to those who were active in the service of Catholicism. Typically for a new historicist critic, the focus is on how religious ideology is enforced by the state from the top down. In contrast there is little discussion of the other side of this, where religious ideas expressed opposition to authority, which, given the context of the Reformation, makes his account a little unbalanced.[2]

Greenblatt is not a Marxist and therefore does not start from a class analysis of Tudor society. However, it is difficult to avoid the fact that this society was a very hierarchical one where class distinctions were obvious to all and maintained by force. He touches on this aspect of society when discussing his view that Shakespeare clearly aspired to become "a gentleman". He draws together some of the known facts about Shakespeare's father: that he was an artisan (a glover), who became a respected town official; he sent his son to the local grammar school, probably with the hope that he would attend university; and he applied for a family coat of arms, but then ran into financial difficulties and so did not succeed in getting one. Later his son, now a wealthy playwright, renewed the application successfully and bought himself a large house (as well as plenty of land) in the town where he was born and raised.

For Greenblatt it is important for Shakespeare, whose profession (an actor) was not well respected, to aspire to be seen as "a gentleman", a man of wealth and education. Greenblatt makes the connection between Shakespeare's father's ambitions (that seemed to end in failure), and the drive and ambition of Shakespeare himself to achieve what his father could not. This is how Greenblatt characterises Shakespeare's attitude:

I am not someone who can be treated like a hired servant or whipped like a vagabond; I am someone who does not merely pretend onstage to be a gentleman; I am a true gentleman, entitled to bear arms... And, half-concealed, another symbolic statement: I have with the fruits of my labour and my imagination returned my family to the moment before things fell apart.[3]

Although indulging a little in cod psychoanalysis,[4] this is a plausible

---

2: One omission in the account of religion is any mention of the Marprelate controversy: a pamphlet war that broke out in the 1590s sparked by some wickedly satirical puritan attacks on the bishops. This controversy prefigures some of the later debates of the English Revolution. It also indicates that religious ideas can be used to express opposition to authority and resistance to oppression. The near absence of voices of opposition and rebellion in new historicist criticism is covered well by Holstun, 2000.

3: Greenblatt, 2004, p86.

4: Those familiar with Greenblatt's criticism might be surprised at the psychological analysis implicit in this account of Shakespeare being driven by a "dream of restoring" speculation, given what we know about both Shakespeare's life and the sort of society he lived in at the time. But left at that, is this really sufficient to explain the complex treatment of class and status in the poet's work? Shakespeare was personally ambitious, but is this a significant factor in understanding his development as an artist and the plays he wrote?

Here I found myself thinking that Greenblatt's account would benefit greatly from the broader context of a Marxist approach that reaches beyond the perceptions of the day (such as an individual's aspirations to an improved status in Tudor society) to a class analysis. The distinction between class and status at this time is one that was summarised very effectively by Christopher Hill in the 1950s commenting on the debates about the role of "the gentry" in the English Civil War:

> We must surely start from the fact that "the gentry" were not an economic class. They were a social and legal class... Some yeoman were thriving to gentility; others were being submerged... It is not helpful to speak of the legal class as though it were in any sense an economic class. What we need is a far more precise analysis of the way in which the gentry was dividing.[5]

Given this distinction between status (the "legal class") and "economic class", and the strict social differentiation that existed in feudal society, we might ask how it was possible for someone to become upwardly mobile in the way that Shakespeare did. What changes were taking place in society that could allow the sons of artisans to attend grammar schools and possibly universities, and aspire to be "gentlemen"? If previously strict divisions of social status were becoming blurred and even to some degree being broken down, then what were the underlying causes of these changes, and who were the people most likely to benefit from them? Crucially, if some people can take advantage of such changes, do they not also have a clear interest in perpetuating them and pushing for further changes, and if so how does this alter their perception of the world they live in?

The answers to some of these questions, from a classical Marxist perspective, would situate Tudor society in the context of the transition

---

his father's desire to improve his status, as he is the author of what has been described as a "devastating" critique of psychoanalytic approaches to art and literature. His contention is that new historicism is superior because it does not attempt to superimpose on the past concepts and methods that arose in a different period, yet he is clearly not immune to that method here, or has found himself forced into it through his attempt to imaginatively fill in the gaps in what we know about Shakespeare's life.

5:   Hill, 1958, pp17-18.

from feudalism to capitalism. They would seek to explain how the emergence of the ideas behind the Renaissance and Reformation are intimately connected with such changes, and why it is that artists developed all sorts of new techniques and styles to give expression to these ideas. New historicist critics might complain that this "totalising" approach to history is too general to be useful when discussing individual artists or works of art. However, there is no reason why we cannot move from a broader picture to a more detailed one. In fact, placing something "in context" ought to demand precisely that method.

Even a fairly brief account can demonstrate the extent to which Shakespeare's career, along with those of other writers of the day, were shaped by the social and economic changes taking place. It is surely not an accident that many of those among Shakespeare's generation of writers came from similar backgrounds: the sons of artisans and lower middle class families that lacked strong connections to the court and nobility (in contrast to an earlier generation of Renaissance poets who were courtiers).[6] In a society where traditional forms of noble and court patronage were in decline, but where a rapidly expanding London saw the beginnings of the commercial theatre, these well educated men had an opportunity to pursue careers as professional writers, and crucially to try to live a life fulfilling the promise of Renaissance humanism—achieving success through their own excellence and endeavour.

The expression of the Renaissance vision of humanity in Elizabethan poetry and drama is clearly connected to these circumstances. Writers were reaching beyond the narrow confines of official ideas about the world to find new forms of expression, because in their own lives they were reaching beyond the traditional confines of the old society itself. Their experience may not have been typical of everyone who lived in England in the late 16th and early 17th centuries, but it was typical of an emerging class in the towns and cities seeking to capitalise on a broader transformation taking place.

A year in the life
James Shapiro looks at one year in the life of Shakespeare, where he argues that a set of historical and personal circumstances converged to transform

---

6:    In addition to Shakespeare, the son of a glover, Thomas Kyd was the son of a scrivener (a scribe); Christopher Marlowe was the son of a cobbler; Robert Greene was the son of a tradesman; George Peele was the son of a clerk; Thomas Nashe was the son of a minister; and Ben Jonson was the son of a master bricklayer.

Shakespeare from a successful dramatist to a great artist. The focus on a single year might seem restrictive, but in fact it gives Shapiro the opportunity to provide a detailed survey of social, political and artistic developments taking place at the turn of the century. Like Greenblatt he pulls together a great deal of existing scholarship and successfully incorporates it into a very readable account that works hard to transport the reader back into Shakespeare's London. Shapiro has a more intensive focus on change, because he is making an argument that this is a crucial time in Shakespeare's artistic development. He is not just telling a story, but trying to persuade at the same time, and this more polemical aspect makes for better history.

The "history at close quarters" approach of historicists and more traditional literary historians alike is used to construct a convincing case for 1599. Shakespeare is already famous and recognised as probably the best playwright on the scene, and in this year his company built and opened the new Globe theatre. As a shareholder he would directly benefit from its success. The company itself, the Lord Chamberlain's Men, now contained some of the most experienced and accomplished actors of the day. In the next few years Shakespeare would write for these players some of his most famous tragedies: *Julius Caesar, Hamlet, Othello, King Lear* and *Macbeth* (as well as a few excellent comedies). It has been clear to critics for a long time that this was a key moment for Shakespeare as an artist. It might be expected that a popular writer hoping for commercial success would "play it safe" and just give the audience what they want. But here the opposite is the case. Shakespeare starts writing plays that test both the actors and the audience like never before.

Shapiro also assesses the key political issues of the day, providing a convincing picture of a time of uncertainty, fear and conflict. One of the main areas of conflict was war: rumours that another attempted Spanish invasion was imminent (it wasn't) and the attempt to suppress rebellion in Ireland taken up with great patriotic fanfare by the ambitious Earl of Essex (an important backdrop for the patriotic play *Henry V*). Uncertainty over the succession of the old queen, now nearing the end of her reign, and the resulting increase in paranoia within the state led to intrigues at court and greater censorship. There was real fear of the state itself, of conscription into the army, of religious persecution and, of course, the devastation of the plague. This realistic picture of life in Shakespeare's London is markedly different from the conservative "golden age" image of "merry England", which crudely portrays the great art of the Renaissance as a reflection of the natural order and social peace maintained by a benevolent ruling class.

Shapiro is aware that the current affairs of 1599 are inadequate to fully explain the growing ambitions of Shakespeare's artistic endeavour. He speculates that the dramatist must have begun writing *Hamlet* at this time, which may be a tenuous assertion, but it does at least give him the excuse to engage with one of the greatest tragedies. In the best chapter in the book, "Things Dying, Things Newborn", Shapiro situates *Hamlet* in the much broader context of an old world of "chivalry" dying away and a new one of global capitalism starting to replace it.

Shapiro's method is to describe historic events as symbolising ideas, and as "forces" of history. The Earl of Essex's failure to suppress rebellion in Ireland leads him to a rash appeal to the queen, scandalously charging into her bedchamber to declare his allegiance. His actions confirm the fears of those who see him as a dangerous menace at court, and he falls from favour as a result. These failures are depicted as symbolic of the inevitable decline of the "chivalric age". In the same year, and as a consequence of the steady growth of world trade, the British East India company was founded—"a seminal moment in the history of global capitalism":

> *Hamlet,* born at the crossroads of the death of chivalry and the birth of globalisation, is marked by these forces, but unlike the caustic *Troilus and Cressida*, is not deformed by them. They cast a shadow on the play, though, and certainly inform its reflections on the possibility of heroic action. They also reinforce the play's nostalgia; there's a sense in *Hamlet*, no less than in the culture at large, of a sea change, of a world that is dead but not yet buried.[7]

It is perfectly understandable for a critic like Shapiro to want to reach beyond the immediate and everyday historical context for an explanation of a Shakespearian tragedy. *Hamlet* addresses in the most striking language what it means to be human, the individual's struggle to comprehend the world and face up to the consequences of taking action to change it. In order to understand this, more than just a knowledge of the playwright's personal life or even the current political scene is required to avoid a dreadfully reductionist account.

In order to makes sense of Shakespeare's development as an artist Shapiro identifies a conflict between an old and a new world in the play, a reflection of a similar conflict of ideas taking place in history. However, ideas cannot exist as disembodied forces, bearing the standards of "chivalry" and "global capitalism"; they arise out of attempts of different social classes to generalise and justify their experience of the world. Again I would argue

---

7:   Shapiro, 2005, pp309-310.

that the Marxist understanding of class can help to enrich the analysis and connect it more concretely to real material changes taking place at this time. In so doing it might be possible to question some of the detailed examples Shapiro gives, but nevertheless accept his overall characterisation of *Hamlet* as the work of an artist trying to come to terms with a society experiencing fundamental changes.[8]

History, context and literary criticism

The term "historical context" is widely used by literary critics, but what is meant by this? Even the strictly formalist critic, who believes that literary criticism should only ever focus on linguistic techniques, cannot escape from history. Pick up any modern edition of Shakespeare's plays and you will see that the language itself requires a certain amount of translation from the editors. This is because between the 16th century and today some words have fallen out of use and others have completely changed their meanings. A historical investigation of language itself has to be undertaken before an informed reading can even begin. This process involves taking a word and then investigating the different ways in which it was used at the time. It is an attempt to understand a particular detail by seeing it as a part of a much bigger picture.

However, the usual practice of many new historicist critics seems to approach the notion of historical context in a slightly different way. The Marxist critic Terry Eagleton has characterised new historicists as preferring "anecdote to analysis" and in practice many of these critics seem more interested in historical digressions than in understanding events or literature in the context of a bigger economic, social and political picture. Their approach typically begins with a detailed description of some sort of event contemporary with the writer or artwork under investigation. There need be no actual connection between the work of art and the event, but the critic will try and draw out some sort of ideological motif that exists in both. This, it is then argued, places the work of art in a historical context. But we have not moved from the general to the particular. Instead we have only compared coexisting particular events.

8:   In fact the Earl of Essex is not a good representative of the "age of chivalry" in the sense that Shapiro describes it. He is more typical of a new breed of aristocrat who owe their influence and power to the absolutist state. Of the factions at court there were sections of the ruling class that tended to favour pushing forward in a capitalist direction, with a more gung-ho, pro-Protestant foreign policy, and with an expansion in foreign trade. Renaissance men such as Essex, and especially Sir Walter Ralegh, were a part of this faction, and so in fact were relatively progressive elements in the ruling class.

Unfortunately this is not a very useful method if you wish to use history to provide a better understanding of art and literature, because it can only work by asserting that otherwise disconnected events are expressions of something else. This anecdotal or digressive method has been adopted under the influence of some postmodernist ideas, in a move deliberately designed to avoid the "totalising" approach of classical Marxism. Yet, for all the aversion to "grand narratives" and "meta-narratives" (stories about stories) of new historicist critics, it is difficult to see how it is possible to avoid some sort of grander narrative when putting something in context. Even in the very simple instance of the changing meanings of words through history, an individual usage (say in a play or poem) is fitted into an account of as many other usages as we can find. Hence it is an attempt to grasp the totality of possible meanings in order to derive a better understanding of the individual meaning.

In some respects, the biographical format of the stories they are telling has forced both Greenblatt and Shapiro to adopt at least a grander narrative approach to their subject. An orthodox new historicist might well be critical of this, but in my view the narrative structure of the biography is a clear advantage. A further advantage of biography is that there has to be some explanation of change, and again this brings a positive edge to new historicist criticism, which typically undertakes quite a static analysis of texts. Shapiro's emphasis on 1599 as a key year in Shakespeare's development is better here, but Greenblatt is also keen to identify some of the experiences that might have proven key formative influences on the writer. Such an approach is typical of conventional literary biography, but for the new historicists I would argue it helps to enrich the analysis.

The limits of "context"

Marxists are used to understanding things within their context in a way that allows the big picture to illuminate the detail. For example, to understand what Antonio Gramsci was really talking about in his *Prison Notebooks* we need to understand those writings in the context of his life and work as a revolutionary socialist. In the spheres of art and literature an understanding of the life of the artist and the society they lived in is also very useful. A knowledge of Milton's role in the English Revolution can throw a great deal of light on his *Paradise Lost*, and a grasp of the revolutionary ideas of poets such as Blake and Shelley can help us to better interpret some of their more opaque lyrics. Yet, despite the best efforts of scholars through the ages, our knowledge of Shakespeare's actual attitudes and opinions is extremely limited. The best we can do is try and piece together a picture of the artist from what we know of the world he lived in, and both Greenblatt and Shapiro have done a good job here.

However, if placing art and artists in context is important, is this all that needs to be done? Surely there is also a need to engage with the concerns of the work of art itself and to evaluate its success or otherwise *as art*. Even in the case of Gramsci, understanding the *Prison Notebooks* in context allows us to clarify and correctly interpret the argument he is making, but we also want to evaluate that argument and judge how relevant it is for revolutionaries today. In the case of Milton, of course we can see parallels between history and literature, but this should not stop us evaluating whether or not *Paradise Lost* is a successful *artistic* expression of the concerns, ideas and emotions of the turbulent times he lived through.

This aspect of literary criticism, as something that seeks to understand what it is that makes for a good play, poem or novel, is by far the most neglected by academics, who tend to work with a given canon of great literature. They may push the boundaries of the canon, or introduce a greater awareness of social and political issues within it, but by and large it is not challenged. The new historicists are reluctant to evaluate literature. Obviously, both Greenblatt and Shapiro believe Shakespeare is a great writer, but they assume that their readers already know that as well and they do not tell us much about what makes him great. Shapiro comes closest in his analysis of *Hamlet*, where we get the sense that he feels Shakespeare has grasped an essential human dilemma in his attempt to grapple with a transformation between the old and the new world. However, this is more implied than overtly stated.

This leads to a problem for critics who are interested in the close connection between history and literature like the new historicists. Their failure to specify the particular nature of literary art, to evaluate it as art, can lead to a form of reductionism. For many of these critics (again influenced by postmodernism), literature and history collapse into each other, and literature is reduced to history as just another set of "texts". Ironically, some new historicists reject Marxism because they argue it imposes modern concepts on the past, rather than reconstructing the past in its own terms. Yet, apart from indicating a surprising naivety regarding other non-Marxist methods of historical investigation (which certainly were not prevalent in the 16th century), the notion that everything is a "text" is a thoroughly modern concept which has been foisted upon the past in a completely indiscriminate fashion.

One thing we can be sure of is that Shakespeare knew he was writing something different to a sonnet when he was writing a play, and that when he wrote a tragedy he was aiming at something different to a comedy. Beyond these distinctions, a drama, poem or a novel is different to a history, a diary or an essay on scientific method. Writing has taken many different forms, but to regard all of these forms as "texts" with no distinct attributes of their own or intrinsic value flies in the face of the actual interests of literary critics in practice.

The unspoken assumptions about artistic value are not addressed explicitly because many of the postmodern ideas that influence literary critics simply cannot cope with any concept that implies there has to be some sort of objective criterion by which we judge art. They are caught in a dilemma, in that their actual concerns imply an objective judgement has already been made, but outwardly they deny it is possible to make that judgement. However, if we at least attempt to try and define that criterion, by regarding art, like history, as an attempt to develop a better understanding of the world but using different methods and techniques, these two different approaches to reality can complement each other.

The obvious way in which history can illuminate art is by helping us understand the circumstances of life that the artist is addressing. Left at that, however, there is a danger that we give the impression that art is just an adjunct to history, an illustration of the historian's analysis. However, because the artist is dealing with life in a different way, perhaps making it more concrete to us by addressing our emotional responses, the historical analysis can aid our understanding, but cannot be used to judge the effectiveness of that response. This problem has been addressed a number of times within the Marxist tradition. As the Russian Marxist Aleksandr Voronsky commented on Marx's own attitude to Shakespeare:

One of his favourite writers was Shakespeare who was undoubtedly a realist. The point is not that Marx "acknowledged" Shakespeare or gave him his due as an historian, or even that he received profound aesthetic pleasure from him, but that he recommended that his best contemporaries imitated him in his realism...when discussing Lassalle's play *Franz von Sickingen*, he advises him to *Shakespearise* and not to follow in the footsteps of Schiller with his transformation of individuals "into simple mouthpieces of the spirit of the times".[9]

The notion that Shakespeare is a "realist", as Voronsky puts it, may

---

9:   Voronsky, 1998, p108.

be implied by much modern criticism. After all, what would be the point of reading the works of a writer who had no relevance to our experience of the real world? Yet this idea does not really infiltrate the *methods* of literary critics, and it is absent from the literary biographical accounts of Greenblatt and Shapiro. This is unfortunate because an analysis which begins by under- standing the historical context of literature should also be uniquely suited to tease out the relationship between art and life, and in the process develop a greater appreciation of art itself.

References

Greenblatt, Stephen, 2004, *Will in the World: How Shakespeare became Shakespeare* (Jonathan Cape).

Hill, Christopher, 1958, *Puritanism and Revolution* (Secker & Warburg).

Holstun, James, 2000, *Ehud's Dagger: Class Struggle in the English Revolution* (Verso).

Shapiro, James, 2005, *1599: A Year in the Life of William Shakespeare* (Faber).

Voronsky, Aleksandr, 1998, *Art as the Cognition of Life: Selected Writings 1911–1936* (Mehring).

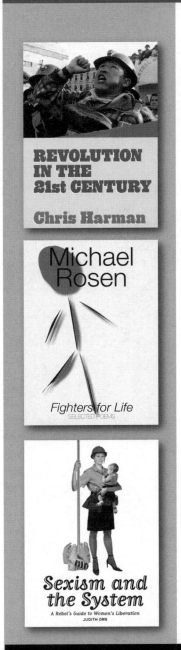

Revolution in the 21st Century
Chris Harman, £5.99

Is revolution a thing of the past? Globalisation is constantly transforming the conditions under which people make a livelihood. Yet we are told the one thing that is immune to change is capitalism itself. *Revolution in the 21st Century* answers vital questions for those who want to change the world and suggests the new millennium may have a few surprises in store.

Fighters for Life: Selected Poems
Michael Rosen, £6.99

A collection of some of the best political poems over the last 30 years, from the murder of Blair Peach to 7/7, by broadcaster and children's author Michael Rosen. All proceeds to the "Friends of Bookmarks" appeal.

Sexism and the System: A Rebel's Guide to Women's Liberation
Judith Orr, £3

A short, lively account that traces the roots of women's oppression and shows why the way society is organised continues to leave most ordinary women—and men—losing out. The fight for women's liberation isn't over, but winning this battle means changing the world.

Reviews

Pioneers of internationalism

Ian Birchall

Robert Stuart, **Marxism and National Identity** *(SUNY, 2006), $29.95*

Today Jules Guesde is remembered, if at all, for the treachery at the end of his life—he joined the French wartime government in 1914 and remained in it till the end of 1916. Leon Trotsky, on being expelled from France in 1916, addressed a letter of bitter contempt to his former comrade (www.marxists.org/archive/trotsky/1914/war/part3.htm).

But 30 years earlier Guesde was leader of a Marxist party, the POF (Parti Ouvrier Français—French Workers' Party), and was accused of being in the pay of the German government because of his anti-war line. The POF later fused with other groups to form the French Socialist Party (SFIO), in which Guesde upheld the left against the right wing of the much overrated Jean Jaurès, who would undoubtedly have backed the war in 1914 had he not been assassinated just before it started.

People like Guesde and his followers are often written off as "Second International Marxists", defined by their ultimate failure in 1914 and generally characterised by a crudely determinist version of historical materialism. But the Second International contained a rich variety of Marxisms (Lenin, Trotsky and Rosa Luxemburg were all leading members). Robert Stuart has made a thorough and detailed study of the POF, and in this book examines the internationalism of the POF, giving a picture that is a good deal more positive than one might have expected.

Guesde himself was not much of a theoretician. The real brains of the POF were Paul Lafargue and his wife Laura, Karl Marx's daughter. Lafargue was the author of the splendid *The Right to be Lazy* (www.marxists.org/archive/lafargue/1883/lazy/), an eminently relevant work today. He was a living embodiment of internationalism, combining in his own person African-Caribbean, Jewish and Indigenous American blood. He took particular pride in his black roots. He and Laura committed suicide in 1911; otherwise they might well have been at the centre of opposition to the war.

The Guesdists took as their starting point Marx's writings in the *Communist Manifesto* on the essentially international nature of capital. Capital constantly crossed national frontiers in search of profits, and in so doing it undermined the nation and created an international working class. The Guesdists can be accused of excessive optimism in believing that the nation-state and nationalist consciousness were withering away, but their analysis ensured that they made no compromise with nationalism.

The Guesdists had a clear Marxist view of the state, and therefore recognised the nation-state as embodying ruling class interests. They saw clearly that the main function of state primary education was to "poison the population with patriotism". They thus firmly distinguished themselves from the republican tradition, which, to this day, sees secular state education as a great achievement.

For the Guesdists there was nothing natural about the nation. Force alone had established "the transient unity that carries the name French nation". They had no sympathy for the desire to reconquer Alsace-Lorraine, removed from France at the end of the Franco-Prussian War (1870-1). They advocated self-determination for Alsace-Lorraine, and showed that French industrialists had greatly profited from the fact that the lost provinces were now behind a tariff wall. So hostile was the party to nationalism that one branch expelled members for celebrating Bastille Day.

Likewise they were quite perceptive as to what a future European war would mean: "slaughterhouses many kilometres square where hundreds of thousands of men will be massacred without glory and without heroism". Their only error was to believe that such a prospect would be enough to prevent the ruling class from launching a war. They condemned the arms trade and believed that capitalism was producing arms for a war that would never happen in order to counteract the falling rate of profit. They were firmly anti-militarist, pointing to the way that the army was used both for conquest abroad and to repress the working class at home.

The POF also had to face the question of immigrant labour. In the 1890s 10 percent of the French workforce was foreign. The POF took a positive attitude, pointing out that immigrants often did "the most repugnant and dangerous of jobs". The POF advocated full legal rights for immigrant workers, so that they could not be used to weaken class organisation or depress wages. The POF organised in the West Indian colonies of Guadeloupe and Martinique, so it had many black members.

The POF could perhaps be accused of complacency in the face of racism. As Stuart points out, there were often good relations between French and immigrants among skilled workers, where the POF had its main base; among the unskilled things were not always so harmonious.

Frequently the POF found itself in conflict with the anti-Semitic far right. Stuart demolishes the claims of those who, like the buffoon Bernard-Henri Lévy, have claimed that the POF was marked by anti-Semitism. The POF showed unqualified opposition to anti-Semitism, and its street fighters frequently came into conflict with the French Anti-Semitic League. When anti-Semites attacked a Jewish shop in Nantes, POF militants were among local inhabitants who defended the shopkeeper. (The police arrested the defenders—some things never change.)

The POF did set out to win over "left anti-Semites", and held public debates with the anti-Semites (as the German Communist Party were to do three decades later). But it would be quite wrong to project back the "no platform" policy of the present day onto a very different situation.

The POF could be accused of underestimating anti-Semitism, arguing that it could have no influence on workers. While it is easy with hindsight to criticise such complacency, it should be remembered that the anti-Semitic movements of the late 19th century were very different from modern fascism. Drumont, the leading anti-Semitic propagandist, was an extreme conservative, who believed that electric light was a dangerous modernising innovation. There was indeed little future for such backward looking thought. Adolf Hitler, subsidised by Henry Ford and a fervent promoter of the motor car, was a very different matter.

It is true that the Guesdists, like all the currents of the French left, failed the crucial test of the Dreyfus case, leaving it to unaligned individuals such as Emile Zola to save the honour of the left. But the POF's abstentionism (about which Lafargue had severe reservations) sprang not from anti-Semitism, but from an oversimplified notion of class. Dreyfus, it was argued, was an army officer and hence a class enemy; therefore it was not incumbent on workers to defend him against anti-Semitism.

Yet the overall balance sheet is very positive. Stuart scrupulously documents the fairly rare lapses by the POF, such as the article which expressed the fear that the French labour market would be flooded with "Chinese sodomites". He notes that some Guesdists moved to the far right, but every movement has its renegades.

Stuart claims that Guesde did not betray the left in 1914 and that he had always taken the position of defending France against German aggression. This does not adequately explain how far the rather pathetic Guesde of 1914 had moved from his earlier revolutionary principles. A full explanation of 1914 would require examination of the SFIO's development up to that year, and a study of the analyses offered by Lenin, Alfred Rosmer and others.

If 1914 is seen as the end of the story, then the POF, and the whole Second International, must be accounted a failure. But after the catastrophe of 1914 France saw a rapidly growing anti-war movement and then, in 1920, the founding of a mass Communist Party which, in its first five years at least, had a very creditable record

of internationalism. (For a fresh angle on this, see George Paizis's excellent new book *Marcel Martinet: Poet of the Revolution*.) All this undoubtedly drew on the memories and experiences of an earlier phase of internationalism.

Stuart's narrative is sometimes irritating. In his insistence to show Marxism's weakness in face of the "enduring vitality" of nationalism, he often makes parallels with 20th century history that are out of context and insufficiently developed. All too often he engages in nitpicking linguistic analysis of Guesdist texts. Nevertheless, for reviving a largely forgotten period of socialist history, he deserves our thanks.

Revolution and reaction in Spain
Chris Ealham

Andy Durgan, **The Spanish Civil War** *(Palgrave Macmillan, 2007), £14.50*

For all the thousands of books published on the Spanish Civil War, few studies of the conflict's origins, course and consequences are as valuable and welcome as this current study. The series editors' introductory notes explain that this short book aims to discuss historical debates and controversies and provide expert interpretation. All books in the series are accompanied by an annotated bibliography—in this case it is vast, and constitutes an important navigational tool for surveying the enormous literature on this subject. Also present are a chronology and a series of maps that provide a first-class introduction to the course of the war.

But this study is much more than a

starting point. Writing with enviable economy and lucidity, Andy Durgan has produced a breathtaking synthesis based on his vast knowledge of the civil war and its historiography.

This study firmly roots Spanish events within the wider social, political, economic and cultural crisis of inter-war Europe. Within this perspective, the civil war was the Spanish chapter of a more generalised European crisis: in 1936 Spain was on the verge of the fascist abyss, a situation comparable with Italy (1922) or Germany (1933). In the preceding years Spain witnessed the sharp radicalisation of the right, reflected in the growing admiration among bourgeois and petty bourgeois sectors for foreign authoritarian models.

Aware of what had been happening elsewhere in Europe, the Spanish left was not prepared to go quietly to the concentration camps. Drawing inspiration from the armed resistance of Austrian workers in 1934, the battle cry of the left became "Better Vienna than Berlin". Accordingly, the 1936 military coup met with a militant response from the working class, resulting in civil war.

It is clear then that Spain's drama was part of a wider European struggle between competing political projects for liberal democratic reform, revolution and counter-revolution. The first of these had its moment during the Republic in the years before the civil war. The social democratic PSOE, the largest left wing party before the war, was firmly identified with the reformist project and inevitably became a key player during the Republic.

The PSOE leadership was implacably hostile to revolution. Its first leader, Pablo Iglesias, described the Russian Revolution as "tragic", while the party press imposed a de facto news blackout on Russian developments, its main organ, *El Socialista*, first

mentioning the Bolshevik seizure of power in the middle of March 1918.

The PSOE failed to understand the historic significance of Spain's new regime. Longstanding divisions over issues relating to the nature of bourgeois revolution, and the relationship between democracy and socialism, came to a head within the party. While capitalism had made significant strides in the cities and in the countryside throughout the 19th century, one faction clung to the view that the Republic signified Spain's long awaited bourgeois democratic revolution and that socialists therefore had to wait patiently for the time when they could make their own revolution.

The two most important factions were centred on Indalecio Prieto and Francisco Largo Caballero, both ministers in the first Republican government, and effectively they operated as two distinct political parties by 1936. Prieto hoped to use the PSOE to stabilise the new regime by providing it with the mass base that it lacked. Largo Caballero increasingly expressed the radicalisation of the socialist masses as the Republic failed to meet its reformist promises. His rhetoric led to him being dubbed the "Spanish Lenin" by his acolytes in 1934. However, as Durgan highlights, Caballero, as prime minister during the early part of the war, gave notice of his enduring reformism by curbing the revolution and reasserting the old state power.

Durgan provides an excellent discussion of the road to civil war and the vicissitudes of the Republic, outlining the key sources of conflict—the national question, the agrarian problem, church politics, military reform and labour struggles—as well as narrating events during the final weeks of the Republic. In what is a timely corrective to revisionist historians who seek to revive Francoist fables about the Popular Front being a Communist-led Trojan horse bent on establishing a Soviet-style regime, we see here that, in programmatic terms, the electoral alliance of 1936 was a recreation of the earlier republican-socialist coalition, albeit with a different set of component parts.

The second of the competing political projects—the revolutionary one—was given greatest expression during the first months of the civil war. Durgan analyses the anatomy of the Spanish Revolution, the scope of collectivisation, its geographical unevenness, and provides a compelling analysis of its demise. Unlike in Russia, there was no clear pole of revolutionary power in Spain, where the legacy of cantonalism, anarchist federalism and opposition to centralised revolutionary structures produced a myriad of dispersed foci.

The author is especially sensitive to the gender limitations of the revolution, noting how wage inequalities remained in many of the workers' collectives. Nevertheless, he concludes that "this was a liberating experience, leading women to acquire a new self-respect and confidence, awareness of their rights, and more control over their own lives".

While attacking revisionists for their misrepresentation of Republican politics, Durgan has clearly endeavoured to challenge the analysis of the most outstanding historians of the civil war—Helen Graham and Paul Preston being the most obvious examples in the UK—who are more sympathetic to the Popular Front. He challenges the view that the only logical strategy was one based on the Popular Front. The subsequent reliance on a conventional war strategy against an enemy that was always better armed led to the abandonment of revolutionary methods, such as the workers' militias, guerrilla warfare or supporting nationalist insurrection in north Africa, on the grounds that it might upset the Western bourgeois democracies.

Durgan offers a precise discussion of the Soviet role in the war, a subject that has long been clouded by anti-Communist/Francoist distortion and revisionist historians. He locates the vertiginous rise of the Spanish Communist Party in terms of the crisis of the traditional left and the international isolation of the Republic. In the context of war, there were few demands from the Communist rank and file for clarification over its call for a "democratic revolution" rather than a socialist one.

Durgan compares this with the pre-1917 Bolshevik formula of a "democratic dictatorship of the working class and peasantry". But beneath the rhetoric the Communist Party was masterminding a counter-revolution within the Republican zone. Durgan rejects the view that the assault on the revolutionary socialist POUM was related to pre-war divisions, explaining its virulence in terms of the offensive against "Trotskyism" in the Soviet Union, which intensified after April 1936.

While Durgan accepts the view that the civil war comprised a mosaic of conflicts, he nonetheless argues for the primacy of class. Accordingly, when, following the Popular Front election victory in February 1936, the oligarchy no longer felt itself capable of defending its interests within the structures of the democratic Republic, it embraced a new authoritarian counter-revolutionary project that would introduce a more savage exploitation of the working class, as well as offering a more felicitous structure for foreign capital.

This presupposed the slaughter of working class militants and a systematic purge of society, graphic in the rural south, where the social order was most challenged during the Republic. As the Francoist forces marched on Madrid during the first months of the civil war, a vicious repression was unleashed against real, potential and imagined supporters of social justice. Only the impact of labour shortages prompted a diminution of the slaughter, the scale of which actually shocked some Nazi observers.

As a corrective to revisionist claims that Francoism was not "genocidal" and did not seek to eliminate the left, Durgan argues that, in addition to the wartime carnage of around 100,000 executions, and the post-war repression that claimed the lives of tens of thousands more, a further 200,000 died of hunger and disease during the first years of "Franco's peace". That the overwhelming majority of these deaths were among the social constituencies of the pro-Republican groups revealed a "determination to obliterate a whole generation of political activists". As in Hitler's Germany, biological racist theories were invoked to stress the "alien" nature of the "defeated", whose "foreign organic material" was a threat to Spanish racial purity.

The book concludes with a survey of the formation and evolution of the Franco dictatorship. Durgan depicts the regime as a compromise between the financial oligarchy and key conservative institutions, such as the church and the army, that combined contemporary fascism with the militant Catholicism of the Inquisition.

That all this is achieved in 140 or so pages is an impressive achievement, not least because each page is overflowing with penetrating analysis and insightful commentary.

The economics of barbarism
Donny Gluckstein

Gotz Aly, **Hitler's Beneficiaries: Plunder, Racial War and the Nazi Welfare State** *(Verso, 2007), £19.99*

Hitler's Beneficiaries is an important milestone in the study of Nazism and the Holocaust. At first glance, a book on German government financial policy and taxation is not likely to set the heart racing. However, a detailed study of these aspects yields some extraordinary results.

Aly begins with the pre-war Nazi period, 1933-9. When Hitler's chancellorship began, unemployment was around 40 percent or six million. By 1937 it had fallen to 1.6 million. At the outbreak of the Second World War there was a severe labour shortage, which partly motivated the Nazi policy of blitzkrieg and foreign conquest. The economic turnaround was the result of a huge rearmament programme which would inevitably lead to war and devastation. But until 1939 that fact would not have been evident to those who were formerly unemployed. Furthermore, the resources needed to fund the war drive did not come from the German working class. The Nazis were mortgaging the economy to speculative profits to be obtained in the future through European conquest.

In the meantime, however, a short-term financial boost could be obtained through "Aryanisation" of Jewish assets both in Germany and, with the annexation of Austria and conquest of Czechoslovakia, further afield. Though Aly barely touches upon it, there was of course an ideological motivation here. The Jewish minority was not singled out arbitrarily. However, the drive was also financial. Göring, head of the Four Year Plan that was designed to prepare Germany for war, insisted that proceeds from the requisition and subsequent sale of Jewish businesses, warehouse stocks, furnishings and works of art "whether in Munich or Nuremberg, in Stuttgart, Karlsruhe or Hamburg", belonged "exclusively to the reich central government". This was necessary because: "I know no other way to keep my Four Year Plan and the German economy going."

Once the war began, the Reich aimed to avoid the economic burden falling upon ordinary German people and so sought to "shift responsibility for funding the Nazi war machine to the citizens of foreign lands". In 1943, after Mussolini was strung up by his own population, Goebbels would write that "the people must be convinced that we are their fair and generous administrators."

The methods the Nazis employed to "shift responsibility for funding" were as varied as they were outrageous. Aly relentlessly exposes every one in all its nauseating detail. From a stylistic point of view, several of the chapters are so dense and technical that they border on the unreadable. But ultimately the effort of wading through it is worthwhile because the weight of the evidence becomes overwhelming.

Conquered lands were forced to pay Germany for having the Wehrmacht occupy their soil. Poland, for example paid 100 million zlotys per month for the "services" of 400,000 soldiers, even though a mere 80,000 were stationed there. The same method of extortion was extended across Europe as the reich expanded. And it was not only foes who were caught in the net. Romania was bled dry in order to satisfy the financial appetite of its Nazi ally.

When the German army marched into a country it would issue its troops with its own currency—Reich Credit Bank certificates. The exchange rate for these against local notes was artificially fixed to make it easy for German soldiers to buy foreign produce at bargain basement rates. This kept ordinary soldiers happy, and they brought mountains of food and manufactures home in their bulging kit bags, or sent them home through the postal service. Shelves were emptied around Europe, leading eventually to mass starvation in places like Greece (where 300,000 perished in less than two months).

Aly reminds us of the Brecht quote, that it is easier to rob people by setting up a bank than by raiding it. Through these bank certificates the "benefits" of foreign occupation filtered through to broad sections of the German population. The government was keen to keep it that way. Restrictions on the amounts of contraband soldiers could shift were lifted, with Göring telling the finance minister, "Mr Reinhardt, desist with your customs checks... I'd rather have unlimited amounts of goods smuggled in."

Allied bombing shook the home population out of a sense of complacency. To cushion the blow it was decided "to have the Jews evacuated so that at least some of those who had been hit by the bombs could be given new apartments". This was an explicit item at the Wannsee Conference in January 1942, which planned the Holocaust in detail.

As problems on the Russian front mounted in 1943, so did the scale of the larceny. For example, the Belgian state spent 83 billion marks domestically during the war, while the German occupiers extracted 134 billion. The same picture was repeated, with minor variations, across Western Europe. In the East, Nazi treatment of the people was still more savage. The reich commissioner for the Ukraine put it in these terms: "Ukraine is required to provide everything Germany lacks.

This requirement is to be fulfilled without regard to casualties… The grain we lack must be extracted from Ukraine. In light of this task, feeding the civilian population there is utterly insignificant."

At the same time millions of Soviet POWs were being starved to death. The destination of the food was clear. Göring declared, "We are feeding our entire army from the occupied territories," and announced an increase in food rations at home. This was "guns and butter", with the Reich's grain supplies growing by 10 percent and meat supplies by 12 percent.

Aly's findings have wide significance. Simply compare *Hitler's Beneficiaries* with the infamous bestseller by Daniel Goldhagen, *Hitler's Willing Executioners*, whose title Aly almost seems to echo. Goldhagen makes two central claims in his book. First, he makes the Holocaust a unique and privileged feature that can be treated independently from wider Nazi policy. Second, he insists on the centrality of Nazi ideology in the genesis of the Holocaust. This is held to have penetrated so deeply into the German psyche that all sections of the population became active accomplices of the greatest crime in history.

By contrast, Aly sees the Holocaust as one element of a much broader picture, in which the gas chambers, the military occupation of Europe, and the German domestic economic and political situation are all intimately linked. This approach is essential. If the Holocaust is wrenched out of its historical setting, it cannot be adequately explained. One is forced to depend on ahistorical or psychological categories such as irrationality. Unfortunately Goldhagen is not alone in doing this. There is a trend among some very good historians (such as Michael Burleigh and Wolfgang Wippermann in *The Racial State: Germany 1933-1945*) to overemphasise the

element of racial ideology in Nazism at the expense of an overall understanding.

From a Marxist point of view this is to turn the relationship between base and super-structure upside down, privileging the latter over the former for one special event that is held to be so exceptional it stands above all others. The 55 million who died in the war become extras in a backdrop for the Holocaust, while fundamental features such as politics, class and capitalism disappear from view.

Unlike Goldhagen, Aly locates the Nazis' primary drive in the history and politics of Germany rather than pathology. The key background was the outcome of First World War. In November 1918 a revolution occurred in Germany that culminated in the overthrow of the Kaiser. Hitler remembered very well how, just two days later, the army admitted defeat in the First World War. Germany had lost the war not so much through defeat on the battlefield as on the "home front". Even worse, from the Nazis' point of view, the German Revolution unleashed a movement that came within an inch of winning the country over to Bolshevism. As Hitler revealed in *Mein Kampf*, it was his life's work to undo the effects of defeat and revolution.

The shadow of November 1918 hung over Nazism throughout its history. But the ghosts that Hitler hoped had been exorcised by crushing of the Communists and Socialists could easily revive. He was shocked on 3 September 1939 when the masses, who had been fed on a diet of Nazi militarism for six years, greeted the outbreak of war with a sullen resentment. This reaction steeled his determination to bolster the "home front" at any cost, and he declared on that day, "A November 1918 shall never repeat itself in German history."

Aly argues, against Goldhagen, that the dictatorship's ideological hold on the German masses was much weaker than was the case in the Western democracies. He points out that Winston Churchill made "blood, toil, tears and sweat" speeches and, like Franklin Roosevelt, was far more open about the perils and costs of all-out warfare than Hitler. Both Western leaders were able to raise billions in war bonds to finance the conflict because their populations were convinced of the need to destroy the evils of Nazism. Hitler did not dare to make an equivalent appeal to the pockets of ordinary Germans to fight the Allies. As Aly says, "The much celebrated, seemingly omnipotent Führer never saw himself in a position to demand openly that his people entrust him with their savings."

Instead of asking for self-sacrifice (and risking refusal), the Nazis sought to pacify the German masses. It is important here to reiterate that there is a distinction between Aly and Goldhagen, though both see the German people as tainted by Nazism. For Aly the large scale apathy shown for the fate of the Jews was not the result of ideology but of material corruption.

There is continuing doubt about how much ordinary Germans actually knew about the Holocaust itself. For Goldhagen's thesis to work they had to be fully aware, and therefore conscious accomplices. For Aly this is not essential and he ignores the question. His argument does imply that many Germans knew about the exploitation of conquered territories. Of this there can be no doubt, because anything up to 12 million foreign slave labourers were to be found scattered across Germany. Indifference towards them was due, says Aly, to many Germans having been bribed by the loot extracted through conquest.

Hopefully it is clear by now how original Aly's approach to the issue of the Holocaust is. In this horrific picture of general pillage right across Europe, it was the weakest sections of the population who paid the highest price and, given the anti-Semitism of the Nazis, this was bound to be the Jews. So politics and economics became entwined in a deadly race towards extermination. Aly does not pose this relationship in abstract terms, but in meticulous detail.

One example is the transport to Auschwitz of the 1,767 Jews of Rhodes. It occurred late in the war when the Wehrmacht was preparing to pull back towards its German heartland to ward off the Red Army. The diversion of a cargo ship and trains for this seemingly pointless murderous operation has been said to expose the "whole insanity of the Nazis".

Aly argues that at this particular stage the occupying forces in Greece needed a quick injection of finance, especially gold, because their depredations had destroyed the value of the local money. As one Nazi official put it, "The delivery of fresh supplies...was endangered and [this] called, in the interest of the islands' defence, for the ruthless impounding of gold and currency." The Jews of Rhodes were doomed to provide this quick monetary fix.

This argument can be taken too far. In his article "Plumbing the Depths" (www.isj.org.uk/index.php4?s=resources) Alex Callinicos rightly warns that "however instrumentally rational the bureaucratic organisation of the Holocaust may have become, this crime was dictated by considerations neither of profitability nor of military strategy". The seizure of wealth from the Jews of Rhodes did not require their removal to Auschwitz, nor their extermination in gas chambers. An ideological obsession is a necessary part of the picture here.

In his defence, Aly's purpose in *Hitler's Beneficiaries* is not to explain the Holocaust alone, and so he virtually ignores the specific role of anti-Semitic ideology. Nonetheless, the book provides important new information that helps explain how many interlocking motivations and drives combined to produce political stability inside Germany, tumbling living standards in France, mass starvation in Russia and extermination in the death camps of Poland.

If the evidence contained in the book is riveting and worthy of the closest attention, the same cannot be said of the analytical framework that accompanies it. Aly is leagues ahead of people such as Goldhagen. However, as the title of Aly's book suggests, his intention is to show that the ordinary German people, and the working class in particular, benefited from Nazism and by implication were accomplices to the crimes of Nazism.

It is one thing to argue that the Nazis feared revolutionary upheaval during wartime and so bought off discontent. It is another to say the people were incriminated in the plundering and murderous activities of their government. The distinction might seem rather too subtle or semantic to be of importance, but the contrary is true.

If the German working class had a material interest in the slaughter of Jews and ransacking of Europe, then they were the enemy of all non-Germans and Jews, along with Hitler and his gang. They could not, therefore, have been the victims (albeit paying a lesser price than many) of Nazi tyranny. The logic of the position is to see the Nazi government and German people as united in the very *Volksgemeinschaft* (racial community) that Hitler claimed he stood for. Aly comes close to arguing this, and along the way makes some extraordinary statements. We are told that under Nazism "greater equality…was achieved" and that National Socialism took "an anti-elitist stance" which aimed at "levelling out class distinctions". The concentration camps seem almost benevolent institutions where at the end of 1936 "only 4,761 people—some of whom were chronic alcoholics and career criminals—were incarcerated".

There is no space here to expose the deeply elitist thinking that infused Hitler's *Mein Kampf*, but some practical examples are worth citing. In Hitler's "anti-elitist" Germany 200,000 people had been compulsorily sterilised even before the war. The target was the 20 percent deemed "unfit to reproduce". Some 35,000 forced abortions occurred after the policy was introduced in 1935. Between 1939 and 1941 70,000 Germans (mainly disabled children) were eliminated in gas chambers through Action T4. And so it went on. In the year before the war began the number of political prisoners in concentration camps stood at 163,000. This regime was not based on equality or benevolence, but was thoroughly elitist not only in relation to the different "races", but within the "race" itself.

The fundamental problem with Aly's approach is that it suggests the German working class were not exploited, but were in effect exploiters, because they were relatively better off than the victims of Nazism elsewhere in Europe. Aly himself gives evidence to show this was not the case. In 1928, before Hitler's accession, the total wages paid in Germany were 42.6 billion marks. In 1935 the figure stood at 31.8 billion. Perhaps the first transports of Jews away from Germany to Poland (and eventual extermination) were in order to free up homes for other Germans. However, the latter were homeless because of the war Hitler started and the resultant RAF bombing raids—hardly a benefit for ordinary Germans. By the end of the war 25 percent of housing was uninhabitable.

Aly spends a long time showing how "the upper classes forked over the lion's share" of increased wartime taxation, as compared to the workers who basked in "Nazi socialism" (not given in parentheses in the book). His proof is that "middle-income" Germans shouldered only 10 percent of the additional wartime tax burden (compared to 20 percent for the rich and 70 percent for Jews and forced labourers). If this is evidence of socialism then the introduction of income tax in Britain during the Napoleonic Wars, by which the rich paid more, ushered in a socialist society 200 years ago. We just didn't notice it!

In wars the resources of society are thrown into supporting the fight and so it is often the case that those with the most wealth—the exploiters—are required to cough up relatively more than those with the least. Food rationing and state control did not make Churchill a socialist or an "anti-elitist". Even if Aly's tax figures are correct, it is still the case that the burden on the poorest increased as a result of Hitler's criminal war.

In fact, the whole thesis that workers benefited from Nazism is unsound. Every year before the war saw a decline in the portion of the national income going to wages. Soldiers abroad might have sent home loot, but it is not true that their living standards doubled or tripled, as the profits of firms such as IG Farben, AEG and Krupps did. For socialists there is a fundamental distinction between benefiting from the system and merely suffering a lighter burden of exploitation. During the industrial revolution the income of British textile workers may have been higher than slaves on the US plantations, but both were exploited and could, during the American Civil War, unite, with British unions backing a blockade of the Confederates. This is not to deny the impact of differentials on working class attitudes and activities.

Divide and rule is the oldest trick in the bosses' book. But it is the role of socialists to argue that divisions are superficial compared to the fundamental unity of all those exploited by capitalism.

So there are deep flaws in some of Aly's analysis. Nevertheless, this book is a brilliant piece of research. It brings a surprisingly fresh new perspective to an aspect of 21st century history that has been pored over for decades. *Hitler's Beneficiaries* deserves careful consideration.

Tales from the land of the Basques
Joe Linehan

*Paddy Woodworth, **The Basque Country—A Cultural History** (Signal Books, 2007), £12*

> "Yet many Basques today feel no identity with either Spain or France, and want independence, or something close to it"—from the preface.

Bernardo Atxaga, "like many of his generation", is an erstwhile ETA sympathiser who, "since democracy, has never supported violence". So Paddy Woodworth describes probably the best known Basque language novelist. Woodworth, who does not miss a twist or a turn in the imbroglio that is Basque politics, also points out that Atxaga is opposed to "the tide of 'anti-terrorist' rhetoric which has swept many Basque intellectuals and artists".

Woodworth writes in lovely language when telling us of all the icons of *Euskal Herria*—the land of the Basques—not just those of the political conflict, but also the literary, architectural, gastronomic and artistic ones. The author also offers lesser known, but equally fascinating, insights into ecology, gender politics, traditional music, Basque sports and mountains, all garnished with a little Basque magic. He sees, for example, that things bucolic and Basque are in danger of being lost: the native holm oakwoods along the Urdabai estuary nature reserve being encroached upon by eucalyptus and acacia, the mad speculative building boom or the decline of the traditional fishing industry

The author describes the class struggle in the emerging capitalism that was 19th century Bilbao, with its coal, iron, steel mills, shipyards and tenements on the left bank of the city's River Nervion. "Directly opposite, new palaces loudly proclaimed the power of the industrial oligarchy, as if wealth had drained from one side of the river to the other and, magically transmuted, flourished on the other side." And with equally rich and succinct language he explains the Carlist Wars (between traditionalists and smallholders on the one hand, and budding capitalists and "liberals" on the other) in the same century.

Today there is another fracture in Basque society—not religious or ethnic, but "primarily ideological"—looking either to Madrid/Paris or otherwise to some form of independent Basque Country. The author draws on the three distinct nationalist versions of events (Basque, Spanish and French), providing hitherto unnoticed or unreported insights—for example, the fact that the most famous of Basque women, Dolores Ibárurri, *La Pasionaria*, has been greatly ignored by Basque institutions, nationalists and mainstream socialists.

He argues that the Franco "dictatorship made a grim reality out of" the founder of Basque nationalism "Sabino Arana's

fantasy that the Basque Country was an occupied and subjugated nation" and the author's conclusion on the role of the state in the current political/armed conflict is crushing: "the Spanish state has made its own criminal contribution to the cycle of killing" (a reference to state terrorism of the 1980s). "ETA can be considered... as the offspring of Francosim's systematic rape of Basque culture," he adds.

This is a book for all who have been to the land of the Basques, for anyone who is thinking of going there and for everyone who dreams of a place of much magic.

Religious persuasion?
John Rose

*Nur Masalha, **The Bible and Zionism: Invented Traditions, Archaeology and Post-colonialism in Israel-Palestine** (Zed, 2007), £19.99*

As I wrote this review in mid-November 2007, the Bush administration was claiming to be rebooting the Middle East "peace" process with its conference in the US city of Annapolis. Even the Saudi and the Egyptian governments were highly sceptical, let alone the Palestinians. The Israeli side was not even prepared to commit in advance to freeze its construction of West Bank settlements, let alone make any promises to dismantle them.

Nur Masalha provides an ideological explanation for this depressingly familiar saga. It is a variation of the "Israel lobby" argument. An ideological fanaticism binds the US to Israel. At its root lies US acceptance of the Zionist state's claim to Palestinian land based on the Bible's mandate. God promised this land to the Jews. Good Christians should support them.

Nur Masalha is one of all too few Palestinian scholars contesting Zionism within academia. His earlier pioneering books on the Palestinian refugee crisis anticipated the work of the much better known Israeli "new" historians by several years. While I disagree with Nur (and he has been a great fan of my own book, which he references here), his argument should be read and taken deadly seriously.

As well as providing detailed documentation of the Israelis' manipulation of Bible stories, Nur makes a fascinating comparison between US backing for Israel today and British Christian backing for the Zionist project over a hundred years ago. Both represent a complete reworking of traditional Christian anti-semitism. Having often made life hell for the original "people of the book" for nearly two millennia, in the modern age of empire and imperialism, many Christians came to recognise that the Jews have, after all, a mandate from heaven.

In the 19th century an impressive array of British aristocrats, led by the seventh earl of Shaftesbury, rallied to the cause of the "Restoration of God's Ancient People". The immense impact of Christian Zionism on Victorian Britain was reflected in books such as Byron's *Hebrew Melodies*, Disraeli's novel *Tancred* and George Eliot's novel *Daniel Deronda*.

It was that peculiar mix of obsession with biblical prophecy and imperial interest that helped land the Jews in Palestine. The Balfour Declaration secured this process both for the Jews and the British Empire as the Lloyd George government embarked on its land grab in the Middle East as the finale to the First World War.

"Baffy" Blanche Dugdale, Balfour's niece, wrote that her uncle's fascination with the Jews originated "in the Old Testament training of his mother, and his Scottish upbringing". Much the same was said of Lloyd George, his pious Welsh non-conformism replacing Balfour's no doubt equally pious Scottish Calvinism. But Herbert Asquith, British premier immediately prior to LG, would have none of it: "LG didn't give a damn for the Jews, their past or the future." But he did give a damn about securing Palestine for the British Empire. And herein lies my quarrel with Nur. He doesn't fully see that this crass Christianity is an ideological outrider subordinate to the more sordid concerns of empire, rather than its ideological soulmate.

Comparing British Empire attitudes to Zionism with US attitudes today, he writes, "In both, as the international power brokers of their day, religion and politics became inextricably entwined." There was a "convergence of British strategic colonial interests and Christian Zionism... Likewise current American foreign policy in the Middle East largely coincides with that of the powerful Christian Zionist lobby."

By giving the impression of equal partnership, Nur artificially elevates the religious influence. Not that we should ignore it. On the contrary it is pernicious and, to put it bluntly, dangerously bonkers. The Christian peddlers of "Armageddon theology" have indeed been at the door of the White House. There was a special excitement in the build up to the year 2000. According to one writer you could feel the "PMT"—premillennial tension. Hal Lindsey, prophesising the destruction of the Muslim "Dome of the Rock" in Jerusalem and its replacement by the "Third Temple" as a precondition for the return of Jesus Christ, counts his book sales in tens of millions.

Nur highlights the, by now infamous, "Israel lobby" thesis of two American scholars, Meirsheimer and Walt. Now this argument has been maliciously attacked for alleged covert anti-Semitism: Israel lobby equals Jewish lobby equals "Jewish conspiracy". But, as Nur points out, building upon the two authors' own arguments, the "Israel lobby" has far more Christian than Jewish supporters.

In 2000 George Bush received 50 million votes, 30 million from evangelical Christians. Of these about 15 million were "dispensationalists", who believe that Israel's rebirth and, crucially, its expansionist agenda are part of God's will. Evangelical neocons such as John Bolton embedded themselves at pivotal points in the US power structure. Yet, following the Iraq debacle, Bolton is largely a discredited figure and the neocons are in disarray. The Christian right is unable to agree on a candidate to replace Bush in the next presidential election and there are repeated reports of deep demoralisation among its ranks.

But at the same time the Democrats are posturing, just as aggressively as the Republicans ever did, over the perceived "threat" posed by Iran. Surely this is about something far more mundane than the following of providential will. It is about the threat posed to perceived US economic and political influence, pure and simple.

Nur's book takes a number of detours. There is a chapter on the rise of Hamas and impressive tributes to Edward Said and the Christian liberation theologist Michael Prior who, before he died recently, co-edited with Nur the academic journal *Holy Land Studies*. But the chapter that interested me most in this book is the all too brief one, "Reinventing Maimonides".

Maimonides is the greatest Jewish theologian of the medieval period and the recognised link in Judaism between biblical history and modernity. But he is also Musa Ibn Maymun, a highly respected Arab physician and philosopher from one of the high points of Islamic civilisation, 1,000 years ago. Because of the character of Nur's book, he is mainly preoccupied with the way the Zionists have tried to recruit Maimonides to their cause, stripping him of his Arab Islamic identity. This leaves the reader unintentionally tantalised about the real historical Maimonides. Nur, this has to be your next book and the best one yet...

Chartism in one town
Keith Flett

*Robert G Hall, **Voices of the People** (Merlin, 2007), £15.95*

Since the turn of the century the number of studies of Chartism—the world's first working class party, formed around the six points of the People's Charter in 1837—has burgeoned. The work of the Merlin Press Chartist series, of which this work is the eighth volume, and its indefatigable editor Owen Ashton deserve special praise. The series has demonstrated that there are many new sources and issues to explore in the study of Chartism. With the availability, shortly, of the Chartist paper, the *Northern Star*, as an online resource, the possibility for further studies seems considerable.

North west England was a centre of Chartism, and several major studies have been published in the past 35 years, in particular John Foster on Oldham and Neville Kirk's study of the rise of mid-Victorian reformism in the working class. Hall's book is not an argument with either of these authorities, but instead provides new and detailed research on the town of Ashton-under-Lyne.

Ashton in the first half of the 19th century might be likened to an American frontier town of the same period. It was overwhelmingly working class, based on cotton mills, with a rapidly growing population. The infrastructure of the local state was largely absent—the forces of authority and law and order, and a wider ruling class presence, could be numbered in handfuls. That allowed the Chartists considerable room for manoeuvre. However, it also meant that action to challenge the existing order would need to be coordinated across a wider area than just Ashton.

Hall starts the book with an examination of the workplace and the impact of changing technology in the mill on the working class. That marks the book out as unusual in the range of Chartist studies, with the work of Kirk and Mick Jenkins on the 1842 General Strike being among a small number of other studies to focus on this crucial area. Hall's conclusion is interesting too. He argues that the introduction of new technology did not go all that smoothly, took much longer than had been thought and therefore did not have such a dramatic impact in terms of deskilling existing workers, spinners for example, as historians had supposed.

Hall goes on to focus on who the Chartists were in Ashton, the impact of defeat in 1839, when a proposed general strike in August and armed uprising in November both failed, and the relationship between Chartist leaders and supporters. He also makes useful general points about Chartist historiography, showing a grasp of the work of revisionists such as Gareth Stedman Jones and Patrick Joyce, but judging it against his research about Ashton.

For example, Stedman Jones in *Rethinking Chartism* (1983) argued that the language of the Chartists should be taken entirely at face value; Hall demonstrates that in fact, both in Ashton and nationally, they were careful about the political platform that they constructed. So on the decision to exclude the vote for women from the six points of the People's Charter Hall notes that there was considerable structural discrimination against women in the labour market, and this was also echoed in divisions in Chartism about a "women's place". However, he suggests that the Chartists decided to focus on the vote for men because they realised that taking on prejudice against women would reduce support for the Charter. The point of the Charter was to construct a political programme that would find widespread support, and therefore actually change the political landscape.

Focusing on local Chartists, Hall suggests that the leadership of the movement was a sharply politically conscious group of individuals very much focused on learning and education. He also argues that the Ashton leadership were disappointed with the lack of politically advanced ideas held by their followers. He uses the example of the London costermongers, who Henry Mayhew found to be instinctive Chartists, particularly when it came to a fight with the police, but with little real idea of what Chartism stood for. A valid point, but of course a concept of "them and us" where the working class in the main was supporting "us" was still a better starting point than otherwise.

The two concluding chapters look at the demise of Chartism in the ten years after 1848, and how Chartism was remembered by those who had been active in it. Hall takes on board Patrick Joyce's point in his book *Work, Society and Politics* (1980) about factory culture in the mid-Victorian period—that relations between workers and mill owners in towns such as Ashton did improve in the 1850s as the owners tried to pursue a policy of conciliation. But Hall suggests that this policy only worked up to a point.

It is argued that the reasons for the decline of Chartism were partly to do with its success. In some areas Chartists did get elected to local councils and then worked with radical middle class elements to pursue practical changes such as better sanitation and street lighting. Hall also suggests that this desire to actually achieve positive change found an outlet in single-issue causes that Chartists occupied themselves with, finding that the overarching push for political reform was foundering. There were a vast range of these causes in the 1850s, from building societies and cooperatives to temperance groups.

Finally, Hall reviews the memoirs of William Aitken, written in 1869. Hall points out that, although Aitken writes as if the Chartists were simply one precursor to the new Liberal Party, in fact Aitken was only able to make this argument by leaving out all the bits of his own past—physical confrontations with the authorities, for example—that did not fit with the newly constructed Liberal "traditions".

For those seeking an introduction to Chartism, *Voices of the People* is not the place to start. However, for those with some familiarity with the debates within Chartist studies over the past 35 years Hall's book provides both some stimulating new research and approaches and a useful but not overstated riposte to some of the revisionist approaches that have claimed that Chartism never amounted to anything much anyway.

How humans make themselves
Paul Blackledge

Sean Sayers, **Marxism and Human Nature** (Routledge, 2007), £20.00

Is there a human nature, and is it a barrier to socialism? For generations of reactionaries, the existence of class based societies generally, and capitalism specifically, has been evidence enough to answer yes to both of these questions. Some Marxists have responded with the argument that the myriad of different cultures in which people have lived over the past few millennia actually suggests that there is no human nature.

While this approach is a useful counter to those who can't see beyond the narrow horizons of their own time and place, denying the existence of human nature not only flies in the face of modern science—Stephen Jay Gould once pointedly countered this claim with the suggestion that human history would have been rather different if we had the ability to photosynthesise—it also leads to irresolvable relativism, whereby no two ways of life can be judged more or less in tune with our needs.

Another response to the claim that we are by nature capitalistic has been to argue that human nature, forged over millions of years as our ancestors evolved to live in communal foraging groups, is essentially socialist. Unfortunately, while this approach might offer a powerful basis from which to condemn capitalism, it is less clear how it is able to explain the horrors of the 20th century, let alone the rest of the history of civilisation.

In *Marxism and Human Nature* Sean Sayers attempts to provide a sophisticated Marxist answer to the problem of human nature which avoids the pitfalls associated with assuming either that it is fixed or that it does not exist at all.

The starting point for Sayers' book, as it is with most Marxist examinations of human nature, is Marx's sixth thesis on Feuerbach. Here Marx argued that "the essence of man is no abstraction inherent in each individual. In reality it is the ensemble of the social relations." This statement has often been read as proof that Marx dismissed the concept of human nature. But Norman Geras's *Marx and Human Nature: Refutation of a Legend* (written long before Geras joined the B52 liberals) convincingly showed that Marx was in fact rejecting Feuerbach's confusion of human nature with its modern historical form.

Marx argued that, because Feuerbach abstracted "man" from real history, he assumed exactly that which must be proved: that the contemporary form of behaviour is universal. Marx repeated a similar argument two decades later when he criticised the English utilitarian Jeremy Bentham for his "naivety" in assuming "that the modern petty bourgeois, especially the English petty bourgeois, is the normal man".

Against this approach, Marx argued that any analysis of human nature "would first have to deal with human nature in general, and then with human nature as historically modified in each epoch". Developing this point, Geras suggested a distinction be drawn between "human nature" as a relatively constant entity which exists across history, and "the nature of man" as the historical aspect of our make-up including the "all-round character of human beings in some given context". The plausibility of this argument stems from the way that our needs for food and water, etc, are more basic and less historical than the culturally constructed ways in which we produce to

meet those needs. However, according to Sayers, Geras pushes this division too far, suggesting a too clear cut division between nature and nurture.

Sayers argues that Marx is best understood as embracing what Sayers calls "a historical form of humanism". He basis this interpretation of Marx on the latter's claim that, by working purposefully together on nature to meet their needs, people not only change the world around them, but also change themselves. As Marx wrote in *Capital*, "Through this movement he acts upon nature and changes it, and in this way he simultaneously changes his own nature."

Following this suggestion, while Sayers agrees with Geras's claim that there exist "certain needs and characteristics which are common to all human beings", he insists that Geras makes the mistake of believing that these can usefully be understood as being separate and distinct in practice from our "socially and historically developed desires and preferences". By contrast, Sayers claims that even something as basic as "hunger always takes a social form". Moreover, any social theory that roots itself in a static model of universal human nature will be both unable to explain the complexity of human history and too abstract to underpin an adequate ethical critique of capitalism.

This failing is perhaps most obvious in Geras's attempt to reinterpret Marx as a moral philosopher. According to Geras, in his essay "The Controvery about Marx and Justice", Marx's morality is evident in his claim that communist society would subscribe to a form of distributive justice based upon the needs principle: "From each according to ability, to each according to need." Geras suggested that Marx's great contribution to moral theory was to recognise that as the forces of production developed through history so did human needs and capacities.

Consequently, for Marx, the standard of human need is a historical standard of reasonable need dependent upon the productivity of labour within society, where what is reasonable under communism would be decided upon by some democratic procedure. While there is not much to criticise in this argument as far as it goes, Sayers points out that it does not go nearly far enough in conceptualising human nature historically.

Marx, Sayers argues, was not interested in judging capitalist society against some absolute standard of human wellbeing, whereby the development of the forces of production allow for the increasing possibility that we might be freed from labour to realise our potential. Quite the reverse, Marx was interested in how we remake ourselves through work, and how the future potentialities of humanity emerge from this remaking of our nature. Sayers suggests that Marx condemned capitalism, for instance, "not solely in terms of universal human needs, but also of needs and capacities which have been made possible and developed by the gigantic growth of productive power under capitalism itself".

Superficially, this argument might read as a variation of the point already made by Geras. However, it differs in an important way. For, according to Sayers, the development of the productive forces creates not merely new needs and capacities for individuals; it also reshapes our individuality itself. For instance, it was the development of the forces of production under feudalism that underpinned the emergence of capitalist relations of production, and which in turn gave rise to the development of modern individualism and concomitant notions of freedom, equality and human rights.

The problem with capitalism, of course, is that these notions of equality and human rights tend to be defined such that our freedoms only reach as far as our wallets allow: we're all equal before the law, but the aim of the law, as the classic English liberal philosopher John Locke argued, is the preservation of property, and our rights are the rights of property owners. In practice this means that the less property you have, the less rights and freedoms you have.

While this difference is evident every time we go shopping, it is most apparent at work where the "freedom" most of us have from the ownership of the means of production entails, in the first instance, that we are compelled to work for someone else to make ends meet. This real loss of freedom is then compounded in the workplace, where competition and "a manager's right to manage" translate into a process whereby we are put under constant pressure to increase our productivity, both by the introduction of new technology and by working harder.

Socialism, according to Marx, is rooted in the struggle entailed by this situation. The idea of freedom, which was the rallying cry of the classic bourgeois revolutions, becomes in the context of capitalist exploitation a site of conflict. On the one hand, capitalists and their apologists use it to legitimise the right of capital to dominate labour; on the other hand, when workers take up the demand for freedom they tend to challenge this right.

This is evident on a daily basis, from the recent dispute in Royal Mail to the struggles against Nicolas Sarkozy's reforms in France. In both cases the freedom of capital and the freedom of workers are in conflict. These examples illuminate the way in which, when workers pick up the concept of freedom, the unfreedoms of bourgeois society begin to become apparent.

Moreover, in making the existing concept of freedom their own, workers also transform its very nature. If the only way to defend their freedom is through collective action, then workers develop a need for solidarity against management.

It is this new need which transforms both the idea of freedom and (potentially) the workers' own natures. Because the victory of their interpretation of freedom can only be guaranteed by their collective success in the struggle for control over the production process, it must be won not just against the political power of the state, but also against the economic power of capitalists. Because the victory of the workers in this struggle can only be won collectively, their individuality can cease to be competitive in nature. As Marx argued in the *Communist Manifesto*, in this new context "the free development of each is the condition for the free development of all".

This emergent need for solidarity was, for Marx, the basis for socialism. He believed that the modern working class developed at a specific point in history, and became conscious of itself as a distinct group within society through its struggles over the working day, etc. These struggles not only exposed the sham freedoms of capitalist society, but also showed the existence of an alternative way of life through which a deeper freedom might be realised. For Marx, the core of the socialist project was the movement from below which began to realise, in a limited form, the negation of capital. "In order to supersede the idea of private property", he wrote, "the idea of communism is enough. In order to supersede private property as it actually exists, real communist activity is necessary."

Marx suggested that workers not only feel compelled to struggle against the power of capital, but that in so doing they also begin to create modes of existence which offer a virtuous alternative to the egoism characteristic of capitalist society generally—and more particularly, working class life within that society.

As Marx wrote, "When communist workmen gather together, their immediate aim is instruction, propaganda, etc. But at the same time, they acquire a new need—the need for society—and what appears as a means has become an end. This practical development can be most strikingly observed in the gatherings of French socialist workers. Smoking, eating, and drinking, etc are no longer means of creating links between people. Company, association, conversation, which in turn has society as its goal, is enough for them. The brotherhood of man is not a hollow phrase, it is a reality, and the nobility of man shines forth upon us from their work-worn figures."

As Sayers points out, it is on the basis of this movement from below rather than from some abstract concept of right that Marx condemns capitalist society. Marxism, therefore, "does not involve a moral approach to history; but rather a historical approach to morality".

It is this historical method which makes it almost impossible to fit Marx into the categories of either traditional social science or modern moral theory. Because both of these approaches tend to reduce human nature to its dominant modern selfish form, they can only understand morality as an imposition against our desires. Indeed, according to Marx, for all its power modern moral theory is best understood not as part of the cure for the ills of capitalism but as a symptom of our alienated existence. Modern moral philosophers, writing from the standpoint of a world in which production is for profit in the marketplace, tend to naturalise the historically specific alienated way that capitalism splits our productive activity from the satisfaction of human needs.

As result they are unable to agree upon an account of the meaning of life by which they might resolve apparently intractable ethical dilemmas.

By contrast, because Marx recognised the historical nature of capitalism, he was able to look to a process whereby capitalist alienation might be overcome. The struggle against alienated labour, by aiming to take production back into the hands of the producers, offers the possibility of restoring meaning to our lives. This possibility is, moreover, a product of history. Because Marx understood humans to be social and historical creatures, he recognised not only that our nature is in a constant process of evolution, but also that there can consequently be no absolute universal moral standards by which society and individuals might be judged. Indeed, this would be a pointless task, for the only ideals that matter are those that are fought for by interested groups within society, and these emerge through history.

This is not to say that Marxism does not include a deep ethical dimension. If in England in 1649 and in France in 1789 the ways of life which competed for hegemony within society were represented by royal absolutism on the one hand and egoistic bourgeois individualism on the other, it was the bourgeois individualism that embodied a progressive expansion of the realm of freedom.

However, from the beginning, bourgeois individualism was contradicted by spontaneous acts of solidarity whose social basis is in the collective struggles of workers at the point of production. If the low level of the development of the forces of production meant that this movement existed initially only in embryonic form, the expansion of industry strengthened its basis. The importance of the development of the productive forces to the socialist project is thus less about reaching some mythical point of abundance than it is about creating a class of people whose freedom is dependent upon building forms of solidarity which contradict the egoism of capitalist society.

And if the extent of the resistance through which this solidarity is realised may ebb and flow, it is from this historical perspective that Marxists base their critique of capitalism, and it is on the wager that the resistance might generalise into a movement that possibly will triumph against capitalism that we base our political work and our hope for an alternative to the present system. This is the historical and ethical basis for Marx's claim that socialism can only come through "the self-emancipation of the working class".

Lenin's Petrograd
Ken Olende

*Alexander Rabinowitch, **The Bolsheviks in Power** (Indiana University, 2007), £17.99*

Alexander Rabinowitch details the October Revolution of 1917 in Petrograd, and how power was won and held over the period until the celebrations of the revolution's first anniversary. The narrow focus on Petrograd is both a strength and a weakness. It allows a detailed examination of all aspects of organisation in the soviet, the Bolshevik Party and other organisations. However, about halfway through the period the government moved to Moscow, which means the latter part of the book is less taken up with decisions of national importance.

Rabinowitch has previously written about

the Bolshevik Party in the run-up to insurrection in *Prelude to Revolution* (1968) and earlier events following the February Revolution in *The Bolsheviks Come to Power* (1976). In the preface to this volume he explains that the third book was drafted in the 1980s, but the collapse of the Soviet Union and access to the archives which that allowed led to a complete rewrite and a long delay.

He adds that where the first volumes showed how the Bolshevik Party was "open, relatively democratic and decentralised", he felt this volume must explain how the party and the state became centralised and oppressive. This frequently makes the book infuriating. For the most part he sides with the cautious line of Lev Kamenev in arguments on the Bolshevik central committee—against the "recklessness" of Lenin (and occasionally Leon Trotsky).

Rabinowitch is a good enough writer not to let this distort other people's ability to make their own minds up about the documents to which he refers. There is nothing here likely to significantly change the opinion of anyone who had previously supported Lenin.

For people who already know something of how the events unfolded, what makes the book valuable is the wealth of detail about discussions and debates on issues vital or trivial. It is worth quoting an example at some length to get a flavour. This is a report of a crucial meeting of the Petrograd trade union council in early November 1917:

"Close to 200 Petrograd trade unionists participated. Lenin gave the main address, 'On the Current Moment', after which members of the council jumped on him for focusing the brunt of his attack on the Mensheviks and SRs [the

social revolutonaries] rather than on the Kadets. An unidentified Menshevik-Internationalist insisted that the repressive politics of Lenin and Trotsky were a sign of weakness rather than strength, and of obsequiousness toward the masses, and that 'a party which placed impossible challenges before the proletariat was not its friend'. Judging from the protocol of this meeting, nobody spoke out in Lenin's defence. Yet at its close, a Leninist resolution endorsing the existing government as 'a true reflection of the interests of the vast majority of the population' was adopted by a vote of 112 to 33."

The author's narrative tends to present Lenin as a driven, impractical figure putting his personal vision ahead of day to day compromises, though this is not a necessary interpretation of the documents presented.

An example from the discussion on food requisitioning gives a flavour. Lenin said in March 1919 that Bolsheviks had made "terrible errors" in relating to the peasantry, "because of the inexperience of our workers, [and] the complexity of the problem." Rabinowitch asks, "But why was the problem so complex, one wonders? And who more than Lenin was responsible for the terrible errors?" This is typical of comments that make it hard to recommend the book to a general reader who does not already know something about the events.

Rabinowitch's gloss is that the October insurrection was unnecessary as a broad coalition of socialists was forming around the Petrograd Soviet, which was coming to undermine the Provisional Government. The soviet could have expanded into a new government around the newly called Constituent Assembly. By forcing through the insurrection the Bolsheviks (or more specifically Lenin and Trotsky) jeopardised the future of the revolution and isolated themselves from what would have been a broader multi-party socialist government.

As with many arguments Rabinowitch puts forward, this follows the detail of minutes and documents, but leaves out the dynamic of events. Lenin, however, was analysing and acting on events as they occurred when he insisted that the need to take power was urgent and that the opportunity would not last indefinitely.

Because of arguments like this, I would recommend reading *The Bolsheviks in Power* in conjunction with other works. One of the most useful is Victor Serge's *Year One of the Russian Revolution*, written by a participant and originally published in 1930 during high Stalinism. Serge's work is much stronger on both the external threats and the excitement, as well as celebrating the level of democracy and participation in Russia just after the revolution.

Also invaluable is Marcel Liebman's *Leninism Under Lenin*, which takes a far more sympathetic look at Lenin's political decisions throughout his political life, including the specific arguments in the period covered by *The Bolsheviks in Power*. Particularly relevant here is the section "The Coming of the Monolithic State", which goes over much of the same ground.

With the same provisos about political conclusions, the book goes on to fascinating discussions on how the soviets came to run local government institutions, how the policy of getting out of the war was pursued, the Bolsheviks' split with the Left Social Revolutionaries (who had initially taken part in the revolutionary government) and the "red terror" against feared counter-revolutionaries.

There is an in-depth analysis of the negotiations with the German high command at Brest Litovsk to end Russia's participation in the First World War. Ironically Lenin was seen as being on the right of the party now, as he insisted on signing a peace treaty at a time when most Bolsheviks demanded no compromise with imperialism. Rabinowitch reports of the Petrograd Bolsheviks' conference in early 1918, "Discarding as irrelevant Lenin's warning that 'the cream of the Petrograd proletariat would be sacrificed in a struggle against the Germans', the conference adopted a sharply worded resolution censuring the central committee."

All this detail makes the volume extremely useful for a specialist audience. Arguably it complements Trotsky's definitive *History of the Russian Revolution*, which emphasises the role of the masses, while sometimes lacking in detail on the role of the party. For readers who don't know the story already, John Reed's journalistic eye-witness account, *Ten Days that Shook the World*, is also well worth reading and comparing to the presentation of various incidents in this book.

Marx misconstrued
Dan Swain

Etienne Balibar, **The Philosophy of Marx** *(Verso, 2007), £9.99*

Etienne Balibar is one of the most prominent of the former students of the anti-humanist Marxist Louis Althusser. Today he is a leading figure in French Marxism, and involved with campaigns around migrants' rights. This book, first written in 1995, attempts to fulfil two different roles. First, it is an attempt at an introduction to Marx's philosophy; second, it presents a specific philosophical argument.

The book is at its best when it is explaining aspects of Marx's thought, especially when rescuing them from the cruder characterisations in mainstream introductions. For example, the section on ideology is particularly strong in explaining how Marx attempted to account for the limits and basis of human thought.

But Balibar's second aim is to present Marx as a conflicted, contradictory thinker. Marx formulated "a plurality of doctrines which has left his readers and successors in something of a quandary". For instance, the notions of ideology and commodity fetishism are presented as competing, mutually exclusive, solutions to one specific problem. This is unconvincing. Balibar rightly identifies the differences between these notions, and their different origins, but does not show why we should choose between the two.

He points to several other key strands in Marx's thought and tries to show that these represent important shifts within Marx's work. Among these strands, Balibar argues, there is a rich theoretical universe for philosophers to draw on. He writes, "There is no Marxist philosophy and there never will be; on the other hand, Marx is more important for philosophy than ever before."

In fact, for Balibar, the major importance of Marx's work is as an object of study for academic philosophers. But he denies that there is a unified "Marxist philosophy" that can act as a guide for socialists. Rather Marx sometimes "goes beyond" philosophy in attempting to explain it in its social context, and sometimes "falls short" of it by making dogmatic claims. Balibar cites as an example of Marx's dogmatic

claims the famous line that "men make their own history, but not of their own free will; not under circumstances they themselves have chosen". It is true that this is not clearly derived philosophically from any other aspect of Marx. Nonetheless it seems like a claim worthy of philosophical treatment.

Another weakness is Balibar's style and language, which occasionally render the claim that this is an introductory text laughable. After five years in socialist politics and three studying philosophy I still found some sections opaque.

Finally, for Balibar, the period of 1890 to 1990 added nothing to a better understanding of Marx, and in fact inhibited it. The end of this period has "swept away the interests which opposed its being opened up... Freed from illusion and imposture, we gain a theoretical universe."

But surely any attempt to understand Marx's writings benefits from an examination of a century of attempts to put them into practice? The Russian Revolutions of February and October 1917, the support of the German Social Democrats for the First World War and the rise of state capitalism in Russia (to name but three) must hold important lessons to remember when studying Marx's work in the modern world.

Of course we should debate, study and interpret aspects of Marx. But there is a core to Marxism that it is important to retain. Crucially, it is a philosophy that benefits from application to actual struggle. To examine Marx as a philosopher is a fascinating exercise, but it cannot be the overriding priority for Marxists.

Rescuing history

Matt Perry

Mike Haynes and Jim Wolfreys (eds),
**History and Revolution: Refuting
Revisionism** *(Verso, 2007), £17.99*

Chris Wickham (ed), **Marxist History
Writing for the 21st Century** *(Oxford
University, 2007), £14.99*

These two volumes are timely and complement one another. Both stand as testimony
to the continued vitality of Marxist historical writing and formulate an illuminating
critique of some of the dominant trends
within the writing of history. Having said
that, they approach the same problem
from different angles. While the volume
edited by Chris Wickham is concerned
with Marxist history as an evolving body
of work, the challenges it faces and the
current state of play, *History and Revolution:
Refuting Revisionism* focuses upon the turn
in historical debates against social explanation of historical change.

Based on a conference assessing Marxism's
contribution to the writing of history,
Marxist History Writing draws together both
Marxist and non-Marxist scholars and their
views vary from those such as Wickham
and Alex Callinicos, who work from an
avowedly Marxist framework, to those, like
W G Runciman, who wish to maintain a
dialogue with Marx, who they recognise
as a rich and suggestive theorist, though
one they ultimately reject. In one way or
another, all the participants addressed why
Marxism, which had such profound influence on the writing of history during the
1960s and 1970s, has subsequently been in
apparent decline.

A preliminary point offered by both
Wickham and Eric Hobsbawm is that the
idea of decline can mislead. Marxism—

alongside other socially-orientated schools
of history such as the French Annales
school—modernised history in the 20th
century. They dragged it away from its
traditional obsessions: high political history
(kings, queens, politicians and generals),
the objective unquestionable nature of
the evidence (usually provided by state
archives), and the need to avoid the adulteration of history with other intellectual
disciplines.

Historians, especially in the 1960s and
1970s, deployed Marx's "fundamental
questions" about human history and its
great transformations. Many still draw on
this framework in an unacknowledged
way. Despite this, Marxism has been on
the defensive within history since that
time. This results from a trend by some
historians to deny any sense of an objective
past reality, and substitute explorations of
identity and discourse, as well as the connected rise of relativism and the rejection
of the Enlightenment principles of universal rights and emancipation.

These tendencies dissolve the very possibility, to paraphrase Hobsbawm, of
locating patterns and regularities in the
past that historians can meaningfully
explain. The upshot is an identity-based
history wherein "the past 30 years has
been a golden age for the mass invention
of emotionally skewed historical untruths
and myths" which constitute a "public
danger", for example in the historical
writing of the US, Hinduist India and
Berlusconi's Italy.

If "defensive" is more accurate a portrayal of Marxist history than "moribund",
explanations of its current malaise take
two forms: conjunctural and internal.
For Gareth Steadman Jones the reason is
internal: Marx's inability to provide a convincingly alternative to capitalism, which
Jones speculates was what Marx was trying

to elaborate in *Capital*. Jones, however, fails to provide any convincing evidence that this was indeed Marx's intention. His argument is circular and has neoliberalism in its genetic code. Jones assumes that there is no alternative to the market and, therefore, that Marx intended to but failed to find one.

Conjunctural explanations stress the historical context. But it is too simplistic to point to the fall of the Berlin Wall and the fate of Stalinist regimes. As Chris Wickham observes, the process was well under way before 1989. By 1980 the political situation was turning against the post-1968 new left in each of those countries where Marxism had become academically influential; an intellectual rival in the shape of post-structuralism also appeared on the scene.

Several of the contributions provide very useful summaries of the contribution of Marxism to particular historical periods. Andrea Giardina surveys Marxist studies of Roman history. From the 1960s undogmatic Marxist historians and archaeologists opened up new horizons in this field. Marx's own writings provided a useful starting point, using theory to pose new questions, especially about the political dimension of Roman culture.

Marxists aimed to raise archaeology from a technical to a historical discipline, allowing cross-fertilisations from other disciplines, with a particular affinity with Maurice Godelier's anthropology. Marxist Roman historians of the Gramsci Institute also used interdisciplinarity and the key Marxist concepts of mode of production, socio-economic formation, class, crisis and transition to provide new insights into their field. Giardina then considers Geoffrey de Ste Croix's magisterial work on class and class struggle in the ancient world.

Wickham considers the impact of Marxist historians on the study of the medieval period, setting it within the wider comparative study of feudalism. Catherine Hall tries to incorporate Marxist categories into a reading of the crisis moment of 1829-32 for British rule on three continents which is sensitive to race and gender. Her argument is that while Marx did not emphasise these latter elements, this should not be taken as a reason to abandon Marxism in favour of these forms of identity.

Wickham, Giardina, Robert Brenner and Hall all observe that the drift away from engagement with Marxism has impoverished the level of debate in each of their respective fields. Callinicos examines the utility of Marxist historical writing in understanding how the dynamics of capitalism shaped the 20th century through a discussion of Brenner, Harvey, Giovanni Arrighi, Hobsbawm and Perry Anderson. Brenner recasts his views on the transition from feudalism to capitalism.

Mike Haynes and Jim Wolfreys's collection, *History and Revolution: Refuting Revisionism*, considers the seemingly ubiquitous revisionist trends within the history of revolutions. While historians usually lock themselves into their own period, this volume is based on the observation that common elements can be found in the writing of history of the English, French and Russian revolutions. Just as Wickham's volume identified the spirit of the times that rendered Marxism unfashionable, so *History and Revolution* tracks the modish return of totalitarianism as an explanation of revolution and its connection to a complacent liberal acceptance of global capitalism.

In an intellectual climate where the politicians of the political mainstream, left or right, were declaring there was no alternative to the market, and political philosophers that history had ended because capitalism had won the Cold War, revisionist historians have denied the impact of great revolutions upon history, defining them in narrowly political terms and emphasising their irrationality, violence and terror.

Thus François Furet could declare that the French Revolution was over at its bicentenary, meaning that the revolutionary ideals of liberty, equality and fraternity no longer had a place in the world. Haynes and Wolfreys astutely observe the symmetry between the political myopia of the present and the limited horizons of historians: In late 1980s France Furet's "revolution without revolution went hand in glove with Mitterrand's socialism without socialism and prime minister Rocard's reformism without reform."

Two connected elements are common to the revisionist historiography: first, a displacement of the causes, dynamics and consequences away from long-run and social dimensions, to the short-term, accidental and political; second, the resurgence of totalitarianism as a theoretical framework to understand mass movements, ideologies and revolutions. However, such a project must avoid exaggerating the influence of such revisionist writers or of according them a greater coherence than they in fact possess.

Geoff Kennedy scrutinises the English Revolution of the mid-17th century and assesses the rejection by revisionist historians of its social interpretation. The way that the history of the revolution has been rewritten since the 1970s is to reject the social reductionism ascribing political radicalism to a straightforward rationalisation of material grievances. Yet in its place, we are asked to believe that social power relations play no role in shaping events and political ideas. The revisionists were able to justify this because of the deficiencies of the model of bourgeois revolution, which formed the centrepiece of the social

interpretation. He calls for a return to the social interpretation of these events based on a more nuanced understanding of the transition of feudalism to capitalism.

The French Revolution, which began in 1789, is reconsidered in two essays. Jim Wolfreys unpicks François Furet's polemical reinterpretation of the revolution, which sought to demolish the social interpretation in favour of a political one that identified Jacobinism, a political ideology, with a totalitarian drive to terror. Wolfreys argues for a modified view of bourgeois revolution, seeing it as a great social eruption that creates new legal and constitutional frameworks facilitating the development of capitalism. Florence Gauthier also scrutinises the new political history of the French Revolution through the question of rights of man and the abolition of slavery which took place during the most radical phase of the revolution.

Two chapters consider the Russian Revolution of 1917. Mike Haynes demonstrates that the revisionist histories of Orlando Figes and Richard Pipes present 1917 in a simplistic black and white. Far from simply manipulating events, the Bolsheviks operated within a matrix of rival political parties and forces, each making choices and conditioning the outcome of events. Indeed, the Bolsheviks were more successful than their rivals because they were more democratic and more closely reflected popular radicalisation than their competitors.

Haynes shows that the other left parties' abandonment after October of the network of councils (soviets) that formed the infrastructure of the Russian revolutionary movement contributed more to the formation of a one-party state than a conscious decision of the Bolsheviks to create one. Lars Lih re-examines Trotsky's misunderstood policy of the "militarisation of labour" during the civil war. Rather than an ideologically driven flight into communist fantasy, as is asserted by historians, close scrutiny of Trotsky's speeches shows it to be a sober assessment and pragmatic response to national emergency.

The book also addresses the concept of totalitarianism. These models derived from totalitarianism neglect the questions of class and social structures, providing static rather than dynamic accounts. As Marc Ferro observes in his essay, the totalitarian model establishes a simplistic equation between Stalinism and Nazism, and passes over the latter's continuities with the practices of European imperialism.

Enzo Traverso details how the resurgence of totalitarian theory has contributed to a new anti-communism. A new pitch in hysteria has been reached in works such as Furet's *Passing of an Illusion* or the collection *The Black Book of Communism*. Geoff Eley's contribution to *History and Revolution* argues that, rather than mass movements automatically leading to totalitarianism, they provided the vital pulse of democratisation of Europe in the 20th century.

Daniel Bensaïd's final chapter and Wolfreys and Haynes's introduction both observe that revolutions did not just make the world we live in today, but also point beyond it. Many who are drawn into the mass movements against capitalism and war today are rediscovering revolution through great revolutionaries of the past— Gerard Winstanley, Thomas Paine, Karl Marx, Lenin and Che Guevara. Together these two books provide a manifesto for the renewal of Marxist historical writing, an agenda for challenging the commonplace distortions of much of mainstream history, and a guide for writing history that is engaged with the attempt to understand and transform the world we live in.

Catalonian conflicts
Andy Durgan

Angel Smith, **Anarchism, Revolution and Reaction: Catalan Labour and the Crisis of the Spanish State, 1898–1923** (Berghahn, 2007), £42.68

Following the publication of Chris Ealham's *Class, Culture and Conflict in Barcelona* (reviewed in *International Socialism 106*), Angel Smith's equally outstanding study enriches further our understanding of Catalan anarchism and syndicalism.

While Ealham centred on the relationship between working class community, anarchism and the struggle for the control of urban space, Smith's approach is set within the parameters of more orthodox labour history. He traces the development of the Catalan workers' movement from the end of the 19th century, the emergence of anarcho-syndicalism and the foundation of the CNT union federation, through to the culminating years of mass struggle and defeat following the First World War.

Smith details the specific economic and social conditions that gave rise to one of the most militant working class milieux in early 20th century Europe. Rather than describing it as a millennarian movement of essentially rural origin, as has often been claimed, the author demonstrates the industrial proletarian roots of anarchist-syndicalism (preferring this term to "anarcho-syndicalism").

Likewise, he disproves the widely accepted view that the influx of politically inexperienced and radicalised peasant migrants into Barcelona in these years provided the human material for the subsequent radicalisation of labour relations. Yet while centring on the organised working class at the point of production, Smith does not lose sight of the rich tapestry that made up the anarchist and syndicalist movement in its broadest sense: its presence outside the workplace, the pivotal role of education and culture in the formation of its activists and the influence of rationalism and anti-clericalism.

The emergence of an anarchist-syndicalist labour movement, Smith shows, was due to a combination of employer intransigence, a corrupt political system, state repression and the specific conditions produced by rapid economic growth. "Apoliticism" provided the ideological backdrop to this movement. Hostility to "politics", or at least to its institutional form, had been one of the defining features of the Catalan labour movement since its beginnings in the first half of the 19th century. This was reinforced by the nature of the Restoration system (1876-1923) which followed the brief federal and libertarian experiment of the First Republic. Under the corrupt bi-party system, participation in quasi-democratic institutions was blocked for working class representatives. Thus the reformist gradualism and legalism of the Spanish Socialist movement contributed to undermining its attempts to influence Catalonia's increasingly combative labour movement.

A strategy that emphasised direct action and mass mobilisation, as advocated by the different strands of anarchism and revolutionary syndicalism, fitted most workers' experience far better. From the 1890s on, through to the great metal workers' strike of 1902 and the insurrection of 1909 (the so-called Tragic Week), the Catalan working class repeatedly pitched itself against a deeply reactionary ruling class, backed by a state that more often than not was prepared to use outright repression, and was loath to make even the most limited concessions. The victories of the workers' movement were generally shortlived, followed by the sacking or imprisonment, or even murder, of activists and union members.

What would really change the fortunes of the CNT, which was founded in 1910, was the boom in the Catalan economy during the First World War. As a result of Spain's neutrality, Catalan industry could supply both sides with uniforms and other equipment. Thus an expanding working class suddenly found itself in a far stronger position than previously. By 1918 the CNT, which had now developed into a state-wide organisation, was on the verge of conquering Catalonia's industrial working class.

Its peculiar organisational structure—the *Sindicat Unic* (One Union)—which united workers in any particular trade in each locality, gave it a great advantage over the craft based socialist and "professional" unions. The lack of any bureaucratic structure also contributed to sustaining the CNT's radicalism. Disputes in one factory could swiftly lead to stoppages in others. The CNT's control of transport would prove particularly damaging for the employers.

With the end of the First World War, and a contracting market, the Russian Revolution would provide the backdrop to the new upsurge in class conflict in Catalonia, as elsewhere. In Spain it was the anarchist-syndicalists, rather than the socialists, who would initially be most inspired by the Bolshevik example. The CNT even joined the new Communist International. By late 1919 the CNT claimed more than 700,000 members, half of them in Catalonia.

The wave of struggle reached its high point with the general strike in support of the workers of the hydroelectrical company, La Canadeca. This would prove a turning point not only for union organisation, but also for the hopes of many workers for social revolution.

Victory was turned into defeat, both as a result of a new strike in defence of victimised workers that seriously overstretched the union's organisational capacity and what would become an ongoing offensive by the bosses against the workers' movement, which culminated in the dictatorship of General Miguel Primo de Rivera in 1923. Smith argues that the chances of this movement challenging the state were undermined by the fact that, unlike in Russia, the army was not divided. However, this does not take into account the effect of workers' radicalism on the conscripts who made up the army's ranks. As would be seen in 1936, military authority disintegrated when the rank and file refused to fight an insurgent mass.

By 1919 two apparently contradictory tendencies had emerged in Catalan anarchist-syndicalism: reformist pragmatism and violent direct action. As Smith shows, the dividing line between the two was never clear. Both strategies, in fact, meant a turn away from mass mobilisation and would be a recurring characteristic of the CNT's politics, or lack of them, throughout its traumatic history.

Collaboration with "political" forces and even with state institutions, rather than representing the antithesis of direct action, also sprang from anarchist apoliticism. Of course, for militant trade unionism, collaboration with "political" forces can prove essential to achieving working class unity. However, the anarchist-syndicalists' sectarianism towards their socialist and Marxist rivals, added to the common ground they often shared with liberal individualists, led them more often than not to collaborate with petty bourgeois reformism.

This tendency towards collaboration had reached a climax with the aborted civil-military movement of mid-1917, aimed at overthrowing the Restoration regime. Had this movement been successful, Smith argues, a more pragmatic trade unionism could have taken hold in the Catalan workers' movement. But fear of the unions, which had been provoked into a premature general strike on the eve of the planned uprising (depicted in Victor Serge's classic *The Birth of Our Power*), led both the military opposition and middle class politicians to back away from their erstwhile anarchist-syndicalist allies. After 1917 even the vague possibility of some form of democratic transition evaporated.

With the decline of the mass movement after 1919, and in response to growing repression, the more radical elements of the CNT stepped up armed attacks on employers and scabs. By 1920 there was a veritable war on the streets of Barcelona. As Smith shows, the anarchist action groups, despite initial success, were condemned to failure in this unequal struggle with the state. The advocates of direct action were equally unable to transform the revolutionary potential of the Catalan and Spanish working class into a sustained assault on the system. Caught in a spiral of revenge and the need to counter state and employer terror, the anarchist action groups provided the perfect justification for ever increasing repression and the physical elimination of worker activists.

The employers, aligned with the upper echelons of the military, financed death squads to eliminate union leaders and activists, and eventually forced the government to establish, effectively, a local military dictatorship in Catalonia. This was combined with lockouts and mass sackings. An exhausted workers' movement found itself undermined organisationally and isolated from an increasingly disorientated and demoralised working class when the military took over completely in September 1923.

Although outside the scope of Smith's study, the CNT's counterposing of pragmatic political collaboration to minority violence would return to undermine Catalan and Spanish anarchist-syndicalism in the 1930s. Sectarian armed actions led the CNT, under the influence of the radical anarchist action groups, to launch three separate armed insurrections during the run-up to the civil war years, with disastrous consequences. The apparently opposing tendency of collaboration would, in 1936, mean the CNT helping to rebuild the very state machine it so resolutely opposed in theory. As a result, not only was the revolution defeated, but the anarchist and syndicalist movement in Spain would never recover.

Culture purged of revolution

Mike Haynes

Katerina Clark, Evgeny Dobrenko, Andrei Artizov and Oleg Naumov (eds), **Soviet Culture and Power: A History in Documents, 1917–1953** *(Yale University, 2007), £35*

Big books are fashionable these days. *Soviet Culture and Power: A History in Documents, 1917-1953* comes at around 500 pages but it is only a selection of documents in English from a much larger three-volume Russian collection edited by Andrei Artiozov and Oleg Naumov. Together the three Russian volumes contain a huge mass of material, primarily from the Soviet archives. The Western editors, Katerina Clark and Evgeny Dobrenko, have then made their own selection from the Artizov and Naumov selection. In terms of producing a large number of documents in English they have made us all grateful. Sadly, however, this is as much as can be said, for they have produced this collection in such a tendentious way that it needs a severe health warning.

First, Clark and Dobrenko have selected documents that reflect arguments about the fate of major figures well known in the West. They have therefore missed the opportunity to broaden our understanding of the USSR by looking at some of the less obvious issues.

Second, these documents allegedly deal with the period 1917 to 1953, but the first significant document dates from 1921, after four years of bitter civil war and unbelievable destruction and immiseration. We therefore see nothing of the inspiration of the revolution in the area of culture. We see nothing either of the painful way in which the hopes for a world in which the "cultural front" would be the first front were crushed by military necessity and economic dislocation.

It is, rather, as if we were to create a documentary history of the French Revolution which began in 1794, treating what came before as a minor prologue. In this revolution there would be no Wordsworth to be inspired, no bliss to be alive. And there could be no Shelley to rebuke his inconstancy in the face of difficulties driven from the outside and not least from his own country. On the contrary, English counter-revolution would be presented as doing all artists and writers in France a great favour by seeking to release them from the impending rise of the Napoleon-Stalin figure.

The peculiar lack of a reference point in 1917 is part of a wider strategy, which is to create the idea that there was no revolution to degenerate. What there was instead was incipient totalitarianism. The editors disdain the word, but the concept walks like a ghost through these pages, the commentary and the selection.

The editors (not least Katerina Clark) have written well on Russia before, but here there are unpleasant echoes of the way documentary collections were put together under Stalin to reinforce one particular view. We are invited to accept that Soviet Russia would inevitably become a top-down society, driven by a maniacal leader who strove to keep his finger in every pie.

The crudity of the implicit argument is mitigated only by the occasional gesture towards more trendy postmodernist comments, such as the editors telling us that Stalin's Russia was marked by "textual anxiety". This focus is then reinforced by the additional selection principle of keeping every document written by or to Stalin or in which his "vote or participation is recorded". This is not to deny the centrality of repression or the fact that on many occasions Stalin (and lesser leaders) played a "hands on" role. But this is hardly new. The problem is that we need a proper explanation of how this developed, and here the commentary and selection militate against it.

Chapter one, for example, starts with the prohibition on travel for intellectuals and others at the end of the civil war. For the editors this is part of a deliberate attack on "the intelligentsia". No attempt is made to reflect the context and the painful choices that had to be made when ordinary Russians were dying of hunger and diseases in their millions in a blockaded country. This is not to say that the documents that follow are not interesting and important but they are framed in such a way as to guide the reader to the interpretation that the editors want. This is history more akin to Fox News. Readers should therefore be invited not so much to ignore the book but, as with Fox News, to read it with the sound turned down, interpreting the pictures themselves and wondering what other pictures there are that they cannot see.

In chapter two the Fox News approach to history becomes even more apparent in documents relating to the debate over the status of the Bolshoi Ballet in 1922 (context not discussed—a wrecked country and a famine in which perhaps five million or more die). Here Lenin argues that subsidising the Bolshoi when money was needed to wipe out illiteracy was "an entirely indecent proposal" made by the commissar of education, Anatoly Lunarcharsky.

In fact Lunarcharsky won the argument, but for the authors it was a sign of things to come that the issue was even posed. They do not explain how the Bolshoi then became the privileged core of the Soviet theatre. Or perhaps they do? In true Fox News style there is an explanation, and it is related to wanting to have sex with ballerinas. Readers will excuse the crudity but the framing is not mine: "It was no secret to anyone...that those involved in its destiny—Lunarcharsky, Kalinin, Yenukidze, and later Voroshilov—were great admirers of the Bolshoi Theatre ballerinas. Stalin took full advantage of this circumstance blackmailing his comrades in arms with the threat of publicity and of being compromised."

It will then hardly come as a surprise to learn that Leon Trotsky was part of the problem rather than the solution. When he wrote that "the sphere of art is not one where the party is called upon to command. It can and must safeguard, assist and only indirectly guide", our editors know authoritatively that there is no ambiguity here—textual or otherwise. Trotsky's words seemingly mean their exact opposite: "This is a revealing statement, since 'indirectly guide' meant to define the political course in the cultural sphere."

This logic inevitably flows into later sections on the periods 1932-41 and 1941-53. We are presented with a partial selection and a partial commentary, which makes it difficult to understand what, other than fear and gestures to nationalism, held the USSR together. Early on the editors ask when Stalin became a Stalinist, but the documents offer fewer clues than we might hope for.

During the Stalin era people lived and loved, watched sport and played it. They sang and danced, listened to the radio, went to the cinema, read books and enjoyed a developing culture in both a narrow and wider sense, even as the gulag was built and a significant minority of the Soviet population were sent there. What is needed is surely some attempt to provide evidence through which this amalgam can be understood.

Clark and Dobrenko stress the repression of those who stepped out of line and the huge material rewards for those who stayed loyal. Both are important, but something more was happening. In terms of mass culture, for example, dream factories were developed in the 1930s in the advanced world but these needed positive nurturing. We see little of this in the documents translated here from Stalin's Russia. Censorship was only one aspect of this. Another was the privileging of the favoured figures and themes, and yet again the documents chosen throw little light on this. When they do, as in the 1946 instructions of how to remake the film *Admiral Nakhimov*, Clark and Dobrenko treat this simply as a positive case of "creative censorship".

Despite these criticisms, in a book of this length there cannot fail to be much of importance. It is safe to say that the documents here will be widely quoted. The plight of many writers and artists is already well known and some documents do little more than pile on the agony. Occasionally we get significantly more. A shorthand report of Stalin's speech to Ukrainian writers in January 1929, for example, throws considerable light on the emerging logic of "socialism in one country" and how it interacted with nationalism and culture.

Likewise, the comments around the 1934 writers' congress are invaluable and illuminating. With careful reading much can be teased out about Soviet culture and ideology. The famous phrase from the time is that Soviet intellectuals were expected to be "engineers of the human soul". To see this simply in terms of manipulation from on high, however, is to miss the extent to which the Soviet leadership themselves both made this world and were trapped within it.

Pick of the quarter

The 2008 *Socialist Register* is the best buy of the quarter. In previous years reviewers in *International Socialism* have often balked at recommending something of book length which might contain one or two good articles and a dozen poor or mediocre ones. This issue is different.

It begins with an excellent piece, "Islam, Islamism and the West" by Aijaz Ahmed, which begins by challenging the notion held by both Islamophobes and Islamists that there is a single Islamic culture and identity. It goes on to analyse how this notion has been encouraged by the machinations of imperialism over the past three decades, and then infected not only liberals but also sections of the left. Its only weakness is that it misses how the rise of Islamism was in part a product of the failures of official Communism (particularly its support for the foundation of Israel in 1947-8) and the secular nationalist regimes in the 1960s and early 1970s.

Other excellent pieces (by William Robinson, Margerita Lopez Maya and Wes Enzinna) solidarise with the struggles in Venezuela and Bolivia without falling into the trap of so much of the international left of ascribing them to "saviours from on high" who are immune to any criticism. Even the much less critical piece on Venezuela by Marta Harnecker recognises the problems of corruption and bureaucratisation which have to be fought.

If that is not enough, the account of the peaceful uprising in the city of Oaxaca in Mexico—the "Oaxaca Commune"—by Richard Roman and Edur Velasco Arregui

deserves to be on everyone's bookshelf. The article by Emilia Castorina on Argentina six years after its uprising, while not in the same league, is very useful. So too are GM Tamás on Eastern Europe, Kim Moody on US immigrant workers' struggles and Sabah Alnasseri on Iraq.

For more than a decade Chile has been the toast of those who claim letting the market loose can create economic growth and prosperity in Latin America. The September-October issue of *New Left Review* (which did not arrive until November) contains a valuable piece by Manuel Riesco, "Is Pinochet Dead?", which takes a serious look at economic and political developments in the country, including the school students' protests and workers' strikes of the past 18 months www.newleftreview.org/?page=article&view=2685

The most interesting article in last summer's issue of *New Politics* was an analysis by Sam Farber of current developments in Cuba, including an unpublicised protest by some of its leading intellectuals www.wpunj.edu/newpol/issue43/Farber43.htm (also in Spanish: www.wpunj.edu/newpol/issue43/FarberSp43.htm.

Two issues ago we tried to unpick New Labour's economic record over the past ten years and point to likely problems ahead. If the November issue of the *Cambridge Journal of Economics* had come out a few months earlier it would have saved us a lot of research. It contains in-depth analyses of the record by a range of Keynesian and left economists, including Ken Coates, Andrew Glyn, Bob Rowthorn, Malcolm Sawyer and Frank Wilkinson. Themes covered include not only general economic policy, but also the patterns of unemployment, the real reasons so many people are on invalidity benefits and the scale of poverty. Unfortunately, most of our readers won't get a chance to see this journal, since online access is restricted to subscribers, but it should be available in most university libraries.

Work, Organisation, Labour and Globalisation is a new journal edited by Ursula Huws and published by Merlin Press at £14.95. The second issue contains more than a dozen articles analysing the degree to which firms and the workforces they employ have been fragmented or concentrated by international economic and technological changes in recent years. It is a valuable resource for anyone interested in what is really happening to the working class.

The Marxist Internet Archive now contains a growing number of pieces from the first series of *International Socialism*, starting nearly half a century ago. Five full issues from the early 1960s (issues 4, 10, 12, 13 and 19) are now online (www.marxists.org/history/etol/newspape/isj/). Apart from the major articles, there is an amazing array of book reviewers (Michael Kidron, Nigel Harris, Tony Cliff, Alasdair MacIntyre, Ken Coates, Sam Farber, Ray Challinor, Hilary Rose, Barry Hindness, John Palmer and Peter Sedgwick, as well as people such as Ian Birchall and Colin Barker who still write for us)—and they all managed to do their reviews in about a fifth of the word count that our present reviewers do!

Another treat in the archive is the classic Marxist study of the 1930s slump, *The Decline of American Capitalism*, by Lewis Corey (aka Fraina): www.marxists.org/archive/corey/1934/decline/index.html